The
New Rules
of Marriage

The
New Rules
of Marriage

What You Need to Know
to Make Love Work

Terrence Real

BALLANTINE BOOKS

New York

2008 Ballantine Books Trade Paperback Edition

Published in the United States by Ballantine Books, an imprint of
The Random House Publishing Group, a division of Random House, Inc., New York.

BALLANTINE and colophon are registered trademarks of Random House, Inc.

Originally published in hardcover in the United States by Ballantine Books,
an imprint of The Random House Publishing Group,
a division of Random House, Inc., in 2007.

LIBRARY OF CONGRESS CATALOGING-IN-PUBLICATION DATA
Real, Terrence.
The new rules of marriage : what you need to know
to make love work / by Terry Real.
p. cm.
ISBN 978-0-345-48086-6
1. Marriage.   2. Man-woman relationships.   3. Married people—
Psychology.   4. Intimacy (Psychology).   I. Title.
HQ734.R28 2007
646.7'8—dc22   2006047666

Printed in the United States of America

www.ballantinebooks.com

9

Book design by Mary A. Wirth

To the gleeful, enduring spirit of
Michela Harriman.

And to her family, who have cherished and
who are cherished so profoundly.

Contents

Introduction

The New Rules of Marriage provides operating instructions for twenty-first century relationships. It walks you, step by step, through the fundamental skills of *getting, giving,* and *having,* teaching you how to *get* what you're after in your relationship, how to *give* your partner what he needs from you, and how to *sustain and enjoy* the closeness that healthy getting and giving brings.

Why do today's relationships need a new rule book? Because we are in a time of great change. The roles of men and women have dramatically shifted, and so have our expectations about relationships. We have never wanted more from one another—more passion, more support, more connection. But our new desires have not been matched by a corresponding new set of skills, and for most of us, whatever we learned growing up about relationships is simply not sophisticated enough to deliver all that we hope for. Am I saying that we now need to be actively schooled if we want to have a satisfying relationship? Yes. That is exactly what I'm saying.

As children, most of us were taught how to read and write, but precious little about how to conduct ourselves in the one area that means the most. We don't expect someone to step into a car for the first time and drive without training. And yet this is precisely what we expect of ourselves interpersonally—as if handling an automobile were a more complicated task than keeping your relationship on course. Relationships might have been that simple back in simpler times, but they're certainly not that simple now. And the unfortunate results of our naïve inattention clog our roadways with wreckage. Bad wrecks—in the form of rampant divorce. Limping wrecks—in the form of marriages that survive, but not very happily. And functional heaps—in the form of banged-up relationships that run well enough but that could be a lot more satisfying.

Fortunately, you can do better than this—much better. You can assert your wants and needs in ways that maximize the possibility of getting what you're after; you can bring your relationship back on track when it lurches off course; and, most of all, you can cherish and enjoy each other, building on each other's strengths just as you did at the start. You can do all of these things. You can do them consistently. And you can do them well.

But you must learn how.

How This Book Came to Be

While I have had the privilege of practicing and teaching couples and family therapy for close to three decades, the evolution of *The New Rules of Marriage* began in 1997 with the publication of my first book, *I Don't Want to Talk About It: Overcoming the Secret Legacy of Male Depression*. At that time depression was widely considered a "woman's disease," so much so that *I Don't Want to Talk About It* was the first book ever written about the condition of male depression, even though it affects millions of men and their families. The book struck a chord, and I began getting calls from around the country. Some of the calls were from men but most were from women—desperate women who'd already dragged their husbands to two, four, or even six couple's therapies, all to no avail. Reading about the highly unusual therapy techniques described in *I Don't Want to Talk About It* sparked a last glimmer of hope. Did I know someone in their area, these callers asked, who worked in the manner shown in the book? In 2002 I followed *I Don't Want to Talk About It* with my first book on couples, *How Can I Get Through to You?: Closing the Intimacy Gap Between Men and Women,* and the number of calls increased.

At first, with regret, my answer to these urgent inquiries was no. I could not recommend someone in their area who'd been trained in this model. I directed the callers, as best I could, to local resources. But after a year or so of such frustrating nos, it occurred to me one day to ask if the couples might be willing to come to Boston to work with me. Many were, and what quickly evolved was a couple's intensive in which the partners and I agreed to work for two solid days, at the end of which time a determination would be made that they were either back on track or else filing for a divorce.

The success rate of these intensives was surprising. Easily nine out of ten couples renewed their relationships. I don't claim that these interventions "fixed" those relationships, but they did succeed in pulling the couples back from the edge of marital self-destruction. The therapeutic techniques that evolved from the challenge of these encounters were unusually quick, powerful, and very different from common practice.

Wanting to make this unconventional way of working with couples more widely available, I formed, with the help of wonderful colleagues, The Relationship Empowerment Institute for the purpose of training therapists in the new model. And I'm delighted to say that, so far, hundreds of clinicians from around the country have come to Boston to train with us. At the same time, public media were getting wind of my couple's intensives and began covering them. Most dramatically, the television show *20/20* came to my office one crisp New England spring morning with a couple I had never met who were on the verge of divorce. The cameras rolled and the couple and I had five hours to save their marriage. We did.

The professional training we offered at the Institute made it clear that the techniques I had been using could be articulated and taught to other clinicians. The next question was whether we could devise a curriculum, a process, that would enable a group of ordinary men and women to stimulate in one another something akin to the accelerated learning that occurred in the two-day intensives. With help and encouragement from my colleagues at the Institute, I created a three-day Relationship Skills Workshop in an attempt to answer that question. And the answer has been a resounding yes. Although the Workshop was not designed exclusively for couples in dire straits, many such couples claim to have found unexpected new hope, while couples along the whole spectrum—from those in crisis to basically healthy couples hoping to become better—claim that the experience of the workshop changed their lives.

The next question seemed clear. Could a manual be created that would walk a reader through a process akin to the three-day Skills Workshop? Could someone without professional coaching, either singly or with a partner, take in the information and begin the practices we taught in our groups? And the answer to that, as well, is a resounding *yes*.

That manual is in your hands.

How to Use This Book

Becoming relationally fit is just like becoming physically fit. Understanding how to achieve the goal is essential, but the best results come from the doing. You will find exercises throughout this book, some in the body of a chapter, others in separate practice sections following the chapters. These exercises are designed to guide you through three steps:

1. Assessing some aspect of yourself or your relationship
2. Envisioning with clarity the changes you'd like to see
3. Beginning your practice of a new technique

I encourage you to do the exercises and to practice the skills presented in this book. I'd like you to use the book as a guide through a process—the process of beginning to master the art of having a great relationship. Think of it as your own private tutorial.

And what about your partner? Wouldn't it be best if he were to read the book, and even do the exercises, along with you? Yes, that would be ideal. And those partners who participate together are well on their way toward improving their relationship. But with or without your partner's participation, *you* can develop a level of skill and mastery that will astound you (and, by the way, surprise your partner as well). *The New Rules of Marriage* gives you everything you need to step out of your well-worn rut. And while there are no guarantees, powerful and unexpected things do happen—with or without your partner's deliberate participation—when you move beyond your habitual role. Along the way, *The New Rules of Marriage* will also equip you to evaluate your relationship, to determine realistically what the balance is between how much you get from it and how much you pay. You will learn when and where to turn for professional help and how to help your therapist help you.

At the end of the book you will find a list of additional resources. And finally, you will find a Quick Reference Guide that offers pared-down versions of the most important ideas and techniques covered in the book.

While I have described what you are about to read as a new rule book, an owner's guide to today's relationships, its real goal goes beyond introducing you to the ideas and tools of an effective relationship technology. Its deepest ambition is to introduce you to a whole new way of life I call *full-respect living,* an artful way of handling yourself that allows you to assert your truth and your needs while at the same time honoring the truth and needs of each person with whom you interact—especially those you love.

I have called this book a new rule book in order to stress its practicality. But, at its core, *The New Rules of Marriage* is meant to be more than either an informative good read—as wonderful as that may be—or a manual of instructions, as useful as that may be.

It is an invitation . . .

The
New Rules
of Marriage

Chapter One

Are You Getting What You Want?

OUTGROWING THE OLD RULES

Are you happy with the relationship you're in today? Or are you frustrated, knowing that no matter how hard you try, the openheartedness that first drew you and your partner together seems awfully hard to win back? Perhaps you're in a difficult relationship that needs substantial change, or perhaps you are in a good-enough relationship that could be made better. Maybe you're looking for a new relationship that doesn't repeat the mistakes of the past. In any case, if you are reading these words, chances are, you feel that something has been missing. It may be tempting to avoid acknowledging that feeling, but I'd like to ask you to trust your instinct. Twenty-five years of helping couples change and grow has taught me that if you feel that things could be better, you're probably right. A lot better, in fact.

People may tell you that what you're looking for is unrealistic. I don't think so. Well-meaning friends and family may focus on your need to compromise. I don't want you to. Your relationship is too important for compromise. Your work may be rewarding, your kids great, and your friends wonderful, but in the end, your bond with the person you live out your life with—the one you grow up and grow old with—is the single most important connection you will ever have. I want you to go after what it is that you want—with skill and with love—and get it.

Both in counseling couples and in workshops I've led around the country, I have taught people from all walks of life how to turn bad relationships into good ones, and good relationships into great ones. Because great is what you're really after. Great is what you deserve. Not merely a relationship you can live with, but one that is truly alive—passionately, tenderly, maddeningly filled to the brim with unexpected twists and turns, with comfort and solidity, with the sense of knowing and being known, and loving each other anyway. How do you get such a relationship? You don't get it, you build it, thoughtfully and skillfully, brick by brick.

Do you have the skills to do this? Have you been taught the craft of creating and sustaining a truly great relationship? If you're like most of us, your upbringing—that curious mixture of what you've picked up about how to be close from society in general and from your family in particular—has not only failed to give you the tools you need, but has actively filled your head with a bunch of unhelpful nonsense. Nonsense like "You'd better not make him too angry." Or, "If she really loved me, she'd . . ." Or, "I could be happy if only you'd . . ."

Like a tennis player who's performed well enough with rotten technique, in order to master relationships you don't just have to learn how to do it; first you have to unlearn all your bad habits. Think of me as your intimacy coach. Together, we're going to strip down your usual relationship routines and redo them, from the very basics. Will it be comfortable? Probably not. If it is, it means I'm not doing my job. Imagine going out on a tennis court with a totally new grip after years of holding your racket in one familiar way. Comfortable? No. But does the new, proper grip give you a more effective stroke? Once you get used to it, there's no comparison.

Reading this, a part of you may be wondering, "Has the game of love really grown so technical that I need an intimacy coach just to have a decent relationship? Whatever happened to falling in love and, well . . . just getting along?" That kind of spontaneity is fine—if it's working for you. Ask yourself: Is it? If you're like most people, the honest answer is somewhere between a definite no and "Not as well as I wish it would." If that's the case, don't be embarrassed; you're in an awfully big boat. The truth is that navigating your relationship by simply doing what "comes naturally" actually stacks the odds against achieving lasting happiness. Roughly half of all marriages fail altogether, and of those marriages left standing, how many are really fulfilling? How many truly great relationships do you see around you? Everywhere you turn, it seems that people who can be terrific parents, friends, workers, and neighbors fall short in the one arena that matters the most. As if that weren't sobering enough, consider this: The grim picture of relationships I'm describing has been relatively stable for the last forty years. The emergence of couple's therapy in the 1950s has done nothing to change it. Self-help and psychology haven't put a dent in it. Multimillion-dollar government programs and church initiatives have been helpless in the face of our current intimacy crisis. What is going on?

Twenty-first-century Love

Try as they might, most "experts" aren't helping much because they fail to address the fundamental issue. What's robbing your relationship of the closeness and passion you deserve is history; or, more precisely, your particular moment in history. If you are like the millions of men and women who feel dissatisfied, *you have been trying to negotiate a twenty-first-century relationship using twentieth-century skills.* Your expectations of what an intimate relationship is—emotional sharing, mutual support, responsibility, vitality—belong to a new kind of marriage, one very different from your parents' or grandparents'. But your old rule book, and your bag of relationship tools—your game plan and ways of coping—are not nearly as fresh as your vision is.

The Big Picture: Where Are We Now?

One of the reasons men and women are so frustrated and confused with one another is that the nature of marriage itself is undergoing a sea of change.

In the beginning of the twentieth century, with the coming of the industrial revolution, men left their farms in droves and moved into the city to work. Before urbanization everyone pitched in together in all sorts of ways, but from then on men began working away from their families while women and children stayed home. The great roles for men and women of the twentieth century were forged: Man-the-Breadwinner and Woman-the-Caretaker. Both at home and in school, children were raised to have character traits that suited these roles. Boys learned to be strong, goal oriented, and competitive; girls learned to be caring, emotional, and cooperative. For at least fifty years, this arrangement, if not always equally rewarding for both partners, was nevertheless largely stable. Through the 1950s and well into the 1960s, divorce was exceptional, and in all but the most extreme cases, if marital unhappiness existed, it was kept discreetly behind closed doors.

In the second half of the twentieth century, the sleeping giant of half the population began to wake up. Starting in the 1970s and moving with accelerating pace, women became the largest addition to the workforce. Women gained economic freedom, political power, a new psychology, and a collective drive to support feminine strength and independence. The women's movement changed our society forever.

Newly empowered, women across America turned to men and began insisting on levels of emotional intimacy that most men— raised under the old regime—were not readily able to meet.

The reason things have been so difficult between men and women in the last several decades can be pared down to this: *In the last generation women have radically changed and men, by and large, have not.* This is not a criticism of men. It is a simple fact.

If Woman the Caretaker was compliant and repressed, the new Liberated Woman was armed and angry, leaving many men feeling unappreciated and bewildered. "What do they *want* from us?" men asked. "Why can't they accept us for who we are?" On the women's side, finding a "good man," a man who "got it," seemed to grow more and more difficult. If the ancient Greeks identified with heroic Odysseus setting sail for adventure, we moderns cheer on Carrie, Samantha, Charlotte, and Miranda of *Sex and the City*, as they quest for a satisfying heterosexual relationship, or as Charlotte once put it, "to dream the impossible dream!"

What most of the men I work with don't "get" is that their relationship job description has changed. According to the unspoken rules governing traditional twentieth-century marriage if a man was a reliable provider, a steady hand, and didn't drink a lot or beat anyone, he was a good husband. A generation ago, if a woman went to her mother and complained of such a spouse that "He never takes my feelings seriously," or "He puts me down in public," or "He's so shut down I feel like I live with a stranger," what do you imagine she would have been told? Stop whining, suck it up, and go home—of course! But we have outgrown those rules, and now it is just such quality-of-relationship issues that break up modern couples—or, perhaps worse, render a once-loving union chronically miserable. Just as women's roles have radically changed, so, too, have their expectations of long-term relationships. While many men would be delighted if women retained more of their traditional caretaker role, most women need men to be more than providers. The refrain I hear over and over again from dissatisfied women is "I don't feel like I have a real partner." A partner who shares in the details of domestic life and in her concerns about the kids. An intellectual partner who cares about what she thinks and supports her development. And most of all, an emotional partner who shows interest in and appreciation for her feelings and who has a few feelings of his own to bring to the table. As women join their husbands as workers, as they step beyond the confines of their caretaker role, they redefine the rules of marriage and of relationship itself. The breadwinner/caretaker paradigm of marriage that came into existence at the beginning of the twentieth century ended at the century's close.

The twentieth-century marriage was traditional in the sense that, like marriage for centuries before, happiness meant, above all, being *good companions*. Husband and wife pulled in harness together. Shoulder to shoulder, they faced life's challenges, raised their kids, paid their taxes, and faced war and deprivation, good times and bad. No one seriously expected marriage to be passionate, or thought about long, complicated, exquisite communication. That was the stuff of romance. And romance was for kids, for the start of relationships, before things settled down, or, in some instances, for love affairs. But, as we faced a new millennium, women began to want more.

The new marriage takes the stability, the building of a life together, that was the whole of marriage a generation ago, and grafts onto it the expectations of a lifelong romance—deep talks, exciting times, and great sex.

Contemporary women want to be more than companions with their spouses; they want to remain friends and lovers. If the twentieth-century marriage was *companionable*, the new marriage is *intimate*—physically, sexually, intellectually, and, above all, emotionally.

The fly in the ointment is that while some men might be thrilled if their wives remained as sexually provocative and generous as a mistress, the rest of the new package—particularly emotional closeness— leaves them feeling inadequate and mystified, if not downright put-upon. And while women's new empowerment may well equip them to stand up for themselves, it does a terrible job of teaching them how to stand up for the relationship.

From Disempowerment to Personal Empowerment

If most of the last century kept women corralled in a disempowered position, the final decades extolled the virtues of personal empowerment.

In consciousness-raising groups, assertiveness trainings, and codependency meetings, women adopted a new attitude of strength a male client once described as "I was weak. Now I'm strong. Go screw yourself!" As liberated women raided men's domains many appropriated, among other things, the privilege to act as obnoxiously as men had. As Gloria Steinem famously quipped, "A woman needs a man like a fish needs a bicycle." Ask yourself this question: What is the one value shared by mainstream culture and virtually all of the so-called countercultural or human potential movements? Answer: The sacred value of the individual. Whether the movement is traditional psychotherapy, twelve-step groups, feminism, or most forms of spirituality, personal growth means *personal* growth, not relational growth. The clarion call of personal empowerment is "I'm mad as hell and I'm not gonna take it anymore!" This attitude will inevitably get your supporters to climb up on their chairs and shout, "Go, girl!" But while this kind of self-righteous anger may be a step up from disempowerment, it is by no means a step closer toward a healthy relationship. And, despite all the good they have done, many of these growth movements have lost steam precisely because women understand this. Women recognize that they, in fact, do need men, just as men need them.

Contemporary women have two "sets" of relationship strategies: the traditional set handed down from the beginning of the twentieth century, and the "liberated" set handed down from the end of the twentieth century. Neither gets you the love you want and deserve.

If the traditional role leaves you silenced and unhappy, if the new empowered role leaves you shrill and unloving, and if doing nothing guarantees that your needs won't be met, then what, exactly, are you supposed to do? Along with a new vision of relationships, we need a road map showing how to get there, a new set of rules that can help men become more responsible and more emotionally available while helping women become less resentful and more effective.

Georgina and Dan: A Charming Couple

Georgina smooths out her skirt and twists tight the blond hair of her ponytail. She looks older than her thirty-six years. Though she is still pretty, time has thickened and worn her. "Baby weight," she offers, smiling. Catching my glance, she pats her tummy. "Just can't get it off." She and her forty-three-year-old husband, Dan, have flown in from Dallas to see me as a last-ditch attempt to salvage their marriage. Looking at them in our first moments together, I am reminded of how much I like Texans. Dan's forthright manner and Georgina's sexiness are a refreshing change from politically correct Cambridge, Massachusetts. Over the years, I'd worked with enough couples from the South and Southwest not to be lulled into assuming that a woman who appears more traditionally feminine is necessarily content in a traditional marriage. Whether it was in Dallas, Texas, Baton Rouge, Louisiana, or Mason City, Iowa, farmer's daughters or debutantes, the times they've been a-changing.

Dan fidgets on the couch across from Georgina. Swiveling her head to take him in, Georgina's bright smile morphs into something dark and disappointed. "Dan's a great guy," she tells me. "Everybody likes him. They love him. He's funny and smart, a great businessman. We have two kids together, a wonderful life, really . . ."

"It's just that . . ." I prompt.

"I can't actually say that I'm all that happy," Georgina explains. More fidgeting from the couch. "My life," she sighs. "If it were a sitcom, it'd be called *My Three Sons*."

"Including Dan?" I guess, not remembering for a moment how many kids they have.

"Dan's the oldest," she replies, radiant smile, distant eyes. "Most of the time, anyway."

I turn to her husband. Tall and lanky, with short hair and a nice build, he was a handsome man, and he knew it.

"She thinks you're a boy," I tell him.

"I *am* a boy," he concurs. His voice is surprisingly deep and sonorous, like a radio announcer's. He sounds frustrated.

"You're not arguing with that?" I ask.

"Nope," he answers. "I wish I could, but . . ." His words trail off, amiably. His face is wide open, full of goodwill. With his Texas tan and Texas good manners, he seems born for the golf course and the clubhouse. I feel like I could just hang out with him, pleasantly, all day.

"Charming, isn't he?" Georgina says, as if reading my thoughts.

"A hard guy to stay mad at, I'd guess," I answer.

"Well now," she responds, sighing again, "that just depends on how much practice you get at it, doesn't it?"

Georgina had had it. Over the course of several years, she had watched her husband finesse his way around two therapists and a trusted pastor. She had little hope left for their marriage. And she was right about at least one thing: Dan was a charmer. He'd gone into his father's real-estate development business and had grown it fivefold, with hard work, to be sure, and a good head for business. But, more than anything else, Dan had succeeded because people just liked doing business with him. Good-looking, funny, and smart, everyone wondered what Georgina could possibly have against him. What they didn't know was that, as Georgina described it, while Dan made a first-rate pal, as a responsible husband and father he left a lot to be desired.

Dan did nothing outrageous. Rather, he left a trail of small mishaps that were constant, cumulative, and corrosive. Georgina ticks off a mental list of them: Forgetting he'd promised to help a kid with his homework and falling asleep on the couch. Saying he'd be home by five and then showing up at six or seven without calling. Leaving his nine-year-old waiting on the steps of his school for over an hour. Parking tickets, dented fenders, kids put to bed without brushing their teeth, forgotten medicines, fights with his staff, fights with *her*. She becomes exhausted just describing it all, while over on his side of the couch Dan seems equal parts dejected and irate. "Okay, Okay!" he finally blurts out, his head bent down by the cascade of her words.

"And *that's* why we're here!" Georgina intones, pointing at Dan, like a prosecutor who'd just tripped up a key witness. "That kind of *response!*" She pauses, observing our reaction. "Look," she says, softening, "I don't *need* my husband to be perfect. I am not a shrew, although I feel like I've become one. All I need, what I really need, is: so okay, you made a mistake, so *deal* with it. Between Dan and me it just escalates. It's not about what *he* might have done or what he might need to do different. Somehow it always turns back on me and how I say it, and, basically, what a bitch I am. Right?" she questions Dan, as if prodding his slouched body with her toe. "Wouldn't you say that?" she presses on. "Dan?"

"So you two fight?" I ask, hoping to dazzle them with my perceptiveness. But I don't even get that right.

"Oh, Dan doesn't fight," she quickly replies. "He never—well, rarely, *rarely* ever fights. In some ways, I might like that better. No, Dan is ever reasonable, ever good-natured. Good old soft-spoken Dan. *Reasonable* Dan. *I'm* the one who goes nuts, wouldn't you say that, honey?" Dan seems to squish even farther down on the couch. He examines the material of the cushions supporting his long frame as if scanning for a possible trapdoor. "Wouldn't you agree?" she tries again. "Dan?"

"That's fine," I tell them both. "It's okay. I think I get it."

Like most of the couples I see, Georgina and Dan did a terrific job of showing me the "ouch" within their first minutes of meeting me, and I thanked them for it. Their dynamic wasn't hard to discern. Georgina and Dan were caught in what I call a Controlling Mother/Resistant Son Deal. The more Georgina tried to "get him to be responsible," the more Dan "yes'd" her, only to blow off his commitment later. And the more Dan refused to act like a grown-up, the harder Georgina tried to get him to become one. It was an endless dance between them. A vicious circle. Like a windup toy that, once set in motion, went on and on— until it ran down. Running down was where it was now. Georgina had gone from *trying* to *complaining* to, most recently, *fatigue*. If I believed her, and watching the two of them interact, I did, there wasn't much left in the tank. Dan's family was a hairbreadth away from coming unglued.

Despite Georgina's flirty charm, her belief in the sanctity of marriage, and, as she later told me, her strong ties to church and community, when it came to accepting those aspects of the traditional male role that rendered her husband less than ideal, this demure-seeming gal was having none of it. She was gutsy.

DOES GIVING IN WORK?

Many women would have just put up with Dan's behavior, sliding quietly into ever-greater resentment, "compromising"—which really means settling—for an ever-more-distant marriage. Giving in is one common way women handle the collision of twenty-first-century expectations with a twentieth-century mate. They back off and shut up. The problem with this strategy is that, unlike their mothers or grandmothers, who did not have such high expectations, when today's women back off, they do it resentfully.

No matter how hard you may try to take the high road, the discrepancy between the marriage you want and the one you've got gnaws away at you like a slow-growing cancer. When you back away from your real needs, when you stop telling the truth—to your partner and to yourself—you shut down. We humans are not clever enough to surgically clamp down on our feelings, denying *this* one but keeping *these others* open. When you shut down the truth, you shut down yourself—your generosity, your sexuality, your vitality.

This was the great lesson learned by that generation of women who realized that depriving themselves of their true voices amounted to depriving them of their very selves. As women recover their voices, they deliver to men the same message that Georgina delivered to Dan that day in my office: "We need more!" More sensitivity, more "showing up," more closeness. But in order to help Dan give her what she wants, Georgina first needs to appreciate how big the change is that she's requesting. *The shift from seeing marriage as companionship to seeing marriage as a sustained form of intimacy is a transformation of historical proportions.*

The expectation of true intimacy in marriage has never been seen before—at least not anywhere I know of in the West. In the patriarchal world we all live in, intimacy itself is deemed feminine, a real-life "chick flick." As a society, we regard intimacy the way we see most things considered feminine—we idealize it in principle and devalue it in fact. So falling in love, the wedding, and the honeymoon are all portrayed in airbrushed delight. But what about the real relationship after the honeymoon? A thunderous silence. I challenge you to come up, in the whole of western literature, with three portraits of hot, scintillating, wonderful marriages. Good luck! Stretching all the way back to Lancelot and Guinevere, lovers were lovers and spouses were spouses and, evidently, never the twain should meet. Until now. Until this very moment when women, for the first time ever, have won the resources to ask for more.

WILL BACKING OFF WORK?

The most organized response to this shake-up in relations between men and women has been a backlash, a wish for women to disown their new uppity demands and restore a nostalgic sense of order. Whether it's the far Christian right, the Million Man Marchers, or authors telling us that since men hail from a different planet, we shouldn't expect too much of them, women are being told that their wishes for increased intimacy must be leavened. If we could all just go back to the old rules of the 'fifties, marriage would restabilize.

Don't hold your breath.

The genie of women's empowerment will not be stuffed back into the bottle. We cannot deal with the collision of women's new demands and men's lack of change by going backward. *Instead of asking women to back down from their relationship demands, I want to empower men to step up and meet them.* But in order to help men do that, women need a new understanding and a new set of skills themselves. Like most of the women I meet, Georgina desperately wants her mate to be more available. While Georgina's vision for the relationship is new, faced with her husband's lack of change, she thinks she must choose between two all-too-familiar twentieth-century reactions: accommodating or speaking out. Her problem is that neither of these gets her a responsive husband. Here is a breakdown of her plight:

Georgina is not happy with the way Dan acts.

Because we don't raise boys to be intimate, when they grow up and become men, like Dan, they aren't very intimate. Dan is chronically irresponsible, and he's charmingly dismissive whenever his wife tries to hold him accountable.

Unlike Georgina, Dan is not unhappy with the way Dan acts.

This is my biggest problem with most couple's therapy and self-help literature. Because men haven't changed much, the status quo of marriage works reasonably well for them. Women, by contrast, want radical transformation in their marriages. When therapists and other experts act as if both partners were equally dissatisfied and equally motivated to change, they are living in a fairy tale. *Men are not all that unhappy in their marriages. They are unhappy that their women are so unhappy with them.* Like Dan, what most men really think is that if their partners would just simmer down (i.e., get off their backs), things would be fine.

Georgina's dilemma:

If Georgina doesn't confront Dan about his behavior, he will not change on his own and she will not get what she wants and needs.

If Georgina does confront Dan about his behavior, he still won't change, but now it will be her fault because she's "controlling" and "witchy."

Poor Dan. In truth, after three, four, five thousand attempts to talk to him about his lack of responsibility—after trying to be lighthearted, forthright, playful, rewarding, teasing, serious, instructive, punishing, positive, and giving him space—by now Georgina *has* grown witchy. And it isn't as if Dan isn't trying. I've never met a man who wasn't willing to make some accommodations. The problem, as I hear it from women like Georgina all over the country, is that their men just don't try hard *enough*. After some blowout, Dan will make a real effort to be more thoughtful and will perform in all sorts of considerate acts for a few weeks, maybe even a month or two. But as Georgina gets happier with him, as the gun is removed from his head and Dan gets comfortable, his old selfishness starts showing up again, a little at first but growing quickly. Some "liberated" women wouldn't stand for it; they would throw themselves into a blistering fit at the first signs of backsliding. More "traditional" women would accommodate, concentrating on the good things, thinking that they couldn't win. Like most of the women I meet, Georgina bounced back and forth between these responses, the traditional and the personally empowered. Neither worked. Faced with an unresponsive partner, her mother's acquiescence hadn't helped Georgina, and, to be frank, her "sisters' " indignation hadn't helped much either.

Carol Gilligan, a pioneer in gender research, once said, "There can be no relationship without voice, and there can be no voice without relationship." The mores of the first half of the twentieth century taught Georgina how to love Dan with all her heart. The breakthroughs of the latter part of the century taught her how to stand up to him.

Now, she needs to learn how to do both at the same time.

Relationship Empowerment: Operating Instructions for the Twenty-first Century

The final decades of the last century helped millions of women move from disempowerment to personal empowerment. Now it's time to take the next step to what I call *relationship empowerment*. Relationship empowerment is this: "I was weak. Now I'm strong. I'm going to bring my full self and full strength into this relationship. I'm going to stand toe-to-toe with you and do my very best to insist on healthy intimacy between us *because I love you*. Because I love us, our relationship. And because we both deserve it."

Relationship empowerment has a very different feel to it than personal empowerment. It's not about being right, or about self-expression or control. It asks these questions:

1. How are we going to be together in a way that works for both of us?
2. How are we going to negotiate our needs?
3. When there is conflict or hurt, how are we going to move back into loving connection?

Relationship empowerment asks both partners to verbalize:

1. This is what I'd like.
2. Tell me what you'd like.
3. And tell me what you need from me to help you deliver.

RULE: THE GOLDEN RULE OF RELATIONSHIP EMPOWERMENT IS:
    "WHAT CAN I GIVE YOU TO HELP YOU GIVE ME WHAT I WANT?"

This new approach empowers you, the individual, to take risks, tell the truth, and go after your needs. And it also helps you empower your partner, doing your best *to help him succeed.*

Traditional femininity taught women to shut up and eat it. Feminism taught women to speak out and leave it. Relationship empowerment asks women to stand firm and mean it.

And what about men? Relationship empowerment helps men meet their partner's new demands while insisting, no less than women, on appreciation and love. Ironically, one of the few things held equally by both men and women is a false belief that straightforward negotiation with the other sex is doomed. Women believe that their partners will be too insensitive and feel too entitled to care about their deepest needs. And men believe that women will be too irrational and too critical to ever be satisfied.

The skepticism with which each sex views the other is not paranoid or stupid. The negotiation of emotional needs in most relationships does fail, or at best succeeds only marginally. But not for want of goodwill, only for want of good skills.

There is a technology to working a relationship, a new set of rules that succeeds. In this book I will teach you to:

- Identify and articulate your wants and needs
- Listen well and respond generously
- Set limits, and stand up for yourself
- Know when to back off
- Know when to get help
- Know when to embrace what you do have with appreciation and gratitude
- Share yourself and receive your partner
- Actively cherish each other

Georgina and Dan

After a few sessions, and some preparatory coaching, Georgina sits on the couch beside her husband. Turning toward him, she draws close, holds his hands in hers, and looks into his eyes. "Dan," she begins softly. "I have never loved anyone as much as I love you. I can't imagine not loving you and I don't want to even try. No one means more to me than you do. And what I'm about to say doesn't change that. So," she takes a deep breath, obviously nervous, "so, here's the thing, honey. As we both know, I grew up with this kind of irresponsible behavior."

"Spell it out for him," I say quietly, coaching her.

"You know," she says, "looking on it now, Daddy had a drinking problem. I know you've said that yourself about him. I wasn't ready to see it then." She draws in another breath, holding back tears so she can speak. "I know Daddy loved me. He loved all of us; he really did. But, I can't really say he was there for me. I mean he literally wasn't around that much and his feelings for me were . . . I don't know, kind of . . .

generic." She laughs a bit at her own phrasing. Dan laughs with her, his eyes warm, a little sad. She searches for some tissues and blows her nose. "Dan," she says, taking his hands in hers again. "Sweetheart, you just have to come through for us, now. You know what I mean? You're a wonderful, wonderful man. There is so much to love about you. You're just shooting yourself in the foot with this stuff you do. Now look, I watched my mom put up with Dad's stuff—the drinking, other women, probably . . ." Dan moves to interrupt, but she stops him. "I'm not saying, Dan. I'm not saying that. I'm just . . . I am saying that you have to stop acting like a *boy*. You have to start being *responsible* around me and the boys." Again, Dan starts to interrupt and again, she stops him. "I know you're going to say you've been trying and I know you have been trying, some. But your expectations for yourself have got to change. We need a whole different level, Dan. A whole different you." And now her tears come. "Dan," she says, no longer able to look at him. "Much as I love you, I will *not* let you do to the kids what my parents did to me. I will not shrivel up like Mom and I won't turn into the bitch I've been turning into. I won't do it. I just *won't*." She cries in earnest now.

"Aw, honey," Dan coos, drawing her into his arms, but she resists.

"Listen to me, Dan. Don't *dismiss* me! You've been dismissing me for five years now. I am not making too much of this, and it will *not* just blow over."

"Okay, okay honey," Dan says as she cries.

"You'd better take this seriously."

"I do," he assures her. "I do." After a pause, Dan looks up at me. "Can I speak?" he asks.

"Sure," I reply, "talk to your wife."

He takes her hands. "Georgie, honey," he begins, "I'd do anything for you three, you know that . . ."

"But, I *don't* know that," she cries.

"Okay," he soothes. "Okay. I understand. But you *should* know that because it's true. And Georgie, everything I have done these past few years, every wrong turn I've taken that made you doubt that, I'm sorry. Really. I take responsibility for it."

"So the question is," I interject, "what do you plan to do about it?"

"Well," Dan says, taking his time to continue. "I think the message is pretty clear. It's time for me to grow up." He pauses, looking at me. "To be honest, I'm not sure I know what that means all the time, but . . ."

"Well, you have a wonderful teacher," I say, smiling at him.

"You mean you?" he more says than asks.

I laugh. "No, I mean Georgina," I reply. "Georgina has a set of operating instructions. She'll tell you. She's been telling you. You just need to listen. Right, Georgina?" I ask. "You'll help him?"

"Why do I have to help him?" she asks through her sniffles. "I've helped him enough."

"It's not fair," I tell her.

"Why can't he help himself for a change?" she asks. We sit together in silence for a minute or so.

"So, you'll help him?" I ask again. She looks up at her husband, his big, handsome face scrunched up with concern, and she laughs.

"You don't have to look *that* bad," she tells him. "It's not cancer."

"Don't even say that," Dan tells her, his face scrunching up even more. He looks pathetic.

"You want to give her a hug?" I ask him. He nods and opens his arms, and she lets herself lean into them. He hugs her tight, his eyes closed, full of emotion. Another time, I might have gone after everything he wasn't expressing, but this moment felt good enough as it was.

"Moron," she says, holding tight. "*Boy!*"

"Wonder boy," Dan suggests.

"Yeah right," she snorts. "Boy wonder." They take their time and then disengage slowly.

"So, now what?" Georgina asks me, gathering up her many used tissues.

"Now what?" I echo, handing the trash basket to Dan, who hands it to her. "Now we begin."

Get the Intimacy You Want

If the model of relationships has moved from being companionable to being intimate, how should we define intimacy? And how can you get an accurate read on how intimate you are? As we proceed I'll offer a few different definitions of intimacy, but the most important one is this:

RULE: INTIMACY OCCURS WHEN TWO OR MORE MATURE INDIVIDUALS CHOOSE TO SHARE THEMSELVES WITH ONE ANOTHER.

Healthy sharing is like breathing—inhaling and exhaling, receiving and transmitting. The partners must be open enough to receive each other, while at the same time not so open that they lose themselves in the relationship. Sharing is a process of *connection* that occurs in the five areas of human experience: *intellectual, emotional, physical, sexual,* and *spiritual.* If you have optimal intimacy in a particular domain, you feel satisfied that your partner fully receives who you are and fully expresses who he is. In the intellectual domain you would enjoy sharing your thoughts with your partner, your ambitions, concerns, questions, and insights. You would feel stimulated by his response and also by what he shared of his own thoughts and reflections. You would respect each other's thinking whether you agreed or not, feeling curious rather than judgmental.

You will become dissatisfied if your partner dismisses your thoughts (a problem with receiving) or if he has trouble sharing his own (a problem with transmitting). We've all seen couples with low levels of intellectual intimacy. They're the ones who sit across from each other at a restaurant with little or nothing to say.

I once coached a brilliant scientist who was so focused on his work that he had no room in his brain for much of anything else. He didn't watch television, read books, or even read the newspaper. While he took a lively interest in what other people wanted to share, when it was his time to talk, he either fulminated against academic politics, mumbled about some arcane piece of the scientific problem he was trying to solve, or, most commonly, went stone silent. His wife, especially once their children left home, felt lonely—and understimulated. My therapeutic intervention was simply to help this man commit to start reading the papers, take an interest in current events, lift his head from the petri dish long enough to look at some art, take in a movie, or hear some music. Then he needed to share his thoughts, insights, and curiosity with his wife.

As with the intellectual domain, so too with the other four; intimacy means that the channel is open, that giving of yourself and taking in what your partner offers—spiritually, physically, sexually, and emotionally—is valued and happens easily.

When a couple shares spiritually, they share ideals, values, and a sense of purpose. They share dedication to some higher good beyond their personal concerns. Such a shared value could be spiritual in the religious sense, but it could also be dedication to art, a political belief, charity, mentoring, or raising children. Relationship empowerment helps us understand that if I win and you lose, we both lose in the long run. Healthy intimacy always demands dedication to the higher good of the relationship itself. In this sense, *every form of real intimacy is spiritual.* I believe that you can actually feel the spirituality of authentic connection if you're attuned to it. In a workshop, for example, when a participant in a state of angry indignation reaches beyond himself to experience—perhaps for the first time in years—real empathy and compassion for his partner, everyone looking on can sense a palpable change. We are moved by such moments when a new force, love, seems to enter the room.

Physical sharing means hugs and holding each other in nonsexual ways, but it also extends to all sorts of physical care, such as exercise, shared health concerns, and sharing physical space—building a house together, or even bringing flowers into a room. Sexual sharing simply means giving and receiving erotic pleasure, teaching each other how to be good lovers, which requires each partner to be neither overly selfish (and ungiving) nor overly selfless (and unreceptive).

Of all the domains of intimacy, the one that most couples find most difficult is emotional sharing. And nothing better illustrates the conundrum for both sexes than when women try to have twenty-first-century relationships with twentieth-century guys. Why is this issue so fraught? Because *a central aspect of traditional, twentieth-century masculinity is the denial of emotions.* Traditional masculinity commands: Thou shalt not be vulnerable. As boys "learn" to be men, they are taught to disown their own vulnerability and to deride vulnerability in others. This is most obvious when men are contemptuous of "weakness" in other men. But it's also why men have such a hard time listening empathetically to their partners. Most men, even if they try to "be good," really just want women to "stop being emotional and *do* something about it!"

How can you tenderly respond to vulnerable feelings in your partner, let alone openly share your own, if you view vulnerability as nothing but a flaw? The answer is that you can't. And while the code is changing, it is far from changed. And while younger men may find this issue less difficult than those born earlier in the twentieth century, men of all ages still struggle, still see strength and emotional vulnerability as being mutually exclusive. And, by the way, so do many women! I can't tell you the number of men who complain that when they finally do "open up" and show vulnerability to their partners, they are suddenly viewed as wimps! *Both* sexes need to step into a new, twenty-first-century understanding that in order to be healthy, all of us need to be whole.

When feminists started claiming power and teaching their daughters to be strong, a hue and cry went up that the women's movement was "masculinizing" girls. Looking back, those fears seem hysterical now. We're going through a similar transition with men. Helping boys and men learn how to be both tender and tough, strong and bighearted, is a new ideal that will take some time to digest. But, having worked with men day in and day out for decades, I know from experience that they can reclaim the language of emotion—once they see the sense of it. And what is the sense of it? Why should we men engage in the very hard work of learning to identify and share our emotional lives, or, for many, learning to have an emotional life to begin with?

Because our families need us to.

Never mind that it's good for us, that it will make us happier and healthier, and probably add years to our lives. The truth is that many men, left on their own, would be perfectly content to remain just as we are. But we are not on our own. Once we choose to have a family, the old ways no longer suffice. The bar has been raised by women. And, as most of the men I work with readily understand, the bar has also been raised by our children. Virtually every man I talk to wishes to be a better dad to his kids than his own dad was to him—more involved, more understanding, more connected. We can't do that from behind a wall. The people we love want more from us, both as husbands and as fathers, than our paychecks. They need our open hearts.

Chapter One
Practice Section

Your Relationship Notebook

Find a notebook that's small enough to carry with you, but big enough to be easy to write in. This will be your Relationship Notebook. In addition to noting the answers to various quizzes, exercises, and evaluations in this book, use it to journal your feelings about your relationship, about relationships in general, and your observations about other people's relationships—even those in books and movies, and on TV. Also, the purpose of this book is to provide you with an experience of significant change. Keep a record of this important time by journaling about your thoughts, feelings, and reactions as you absorb and begin using the tools that will be presented.

Here is your first assignment. In order to know what work lies ahead for you and your partner, you need to have an idea what areas of intimacy are strong or weak in your relationship and how you really feel about that. Become *conscious* of what you want!

YOUR INTIMACY INVENTORY

After doing the following exercise, you will be able to focus on areas that need improvement.

Five Areas of Intimacy

Assess how well you transmit (share yourself) and how well you receive (take in what your partner shares) in the five domains of intimacy. Then assess your partner. Give an overall grade for the relationship in general.

SCALE: **1** poor   **2** infrequent and/or difficult   **3** fair   **4** consistently good   **5** excellent

INTELLECTUAL:
The mutual sharing of ideas in respectful, nonjudgmental ways.

YOU

Transmission	1	2	3	4	5
Reception	1	2	3	4	5

YOUR PARTNER

Transmission	1	2	3	4	5
Reception	1	2	3	4	5

YOUR RELATIONSHIP

Transmission	1	2	3	4	5
Reception	1	2	3	4	5

EMOTIONAL:

The expression of one's fears, joys, sadness, anger, etc., and the receiving of each other's feelings with respect and compassion—without disqualifying, attacking, or withdrawing.

YOU

Transmission	1	2	3	4	5
Reception	1	2	3	4	5

YOUR PARTNER

Transmission	1	2	3	4	5
Reception	1	2	3	4	5

YOUR RELATIONSHIP

Transmission	1	2	3	4	5
Reception	1	2	3	4	5

PHYSICAL:

The active participation in mutual activities. Support in each other's physical care. Physical nurture and affection.

YOU

Transmission	1	2	3	4	5
Reception	1	2	3	4	5

YOUR PARTNER

Transmission	1	2	3	4	5
Reception	1	2	3	4	5

YOUR RELATIONSHIP

Transmission	1	2	3	4	5
Reception	1	2	3	4	5

SEXUAL:

Honoring the mutuality of sex. Being open to your partner's desires without doing something you don't want to do. Being open to your own desires and expressing them.

YOU

Transmission	1	2	3	4	5
Reception	1	2	3	4	5

YOUR PARTNER

Transmission	1	2	3	4	5
Reception	1	2	3	4	5

YOUR RELATIONSHIP

Transmission	1	2	3	4	5
Reception	1	2	3	4	5

SPIRITUAL:

The sharing of a spiritual life, however defined. Support for each other's sense of purpose and meaning. Support for each other's devotion to a larger force (religious, artistic, social) beyond oneself.

YOU

Transmission	1	2	3	4	5
Reception	1	2	3	4	5

YOUR PARTNER

Transmission	1	2	3	4	5
Reception	1	2	3	4	5

YOUR RELATIONSHIP

Transmission	1	2	3	4	5
Reception	1	2	3	4	5

EXPERIMENT: THE MAGIC WAND

This is a journaling exercise. Get out your relationship notebook and go somewhere quiet. Imagine that you now possess a magic wand that can instantly and permanently transform both you and your partner so that you can enjoy the satisfying level of connection—intellectual, emotional, physical, sexual, and spiritual—that you both deserve. Imagine a scene that captures your relationship as you would ideally like it to be, with all areas of intimacy unblocked and open. The scene you envision could be as simple as the two of you strolling down a beach, holding hands and talking, or one in which you share some deep concern with your partner and he responds with kindness and understanding. Don't try conjuring up something grand and extravagant. Instead, picture an interaction that embodies you and your partner being happy with each other.

Write the answers to these questions:

- What is the scene you've envisioned?
- In the scene, what qualities are present in each of you that are lacking now?
- In the scene, what is it like to get from your partner what you've been wishing for? What is it like for you to express qualities you may not be currently expressing?
- With the scene as your guide, make a list of the five most important changes you want to see in your relationship.

Learning the Language of Emotions

The following exercises are for men (and women) who have difficulty "coming to the table" with much to say about their emotions because they are not used to paying attention to them. Don't despair! The great news is that while you may have been missing out on your emotions, they have never deserted you. They've always been with you and still are. You must learn to turn your radar dish inward and listen. Here are some ways to do that:

FEELINGS CHECK-IN

Seven Primary Emotions

Joy
Pain
Anger
Fear
Shame
Guilt
Love

As you go through your day, take three to six feelings checks. Simply freeze whatever you're thinking or doing for a moment and ask yourself, "What am I feeling right now, this second?" Choose from the list of basic emotions, as in, "Right now, on my way to catch a plane in order to do a presentation in Chicago, I feel:

- some fear that I'll be late for the plane.
- some joy (excitement) about the trip and hanging out with my colleagues.
- some pain and guilt about leaving my kids.
- a little anger at Bill for not finishing all of the graphics till the last minute.

Here are some tips:

• Your emotions don't have to be big.
You can feel a little of this and a little of that.

• **Your emotions don't have to be consistent.**

We handle this by saying "a part of me," as in, "A part of me feels excited about being with the guys and hanging out someplace nice. And another part of me already misses the kids."

• **Use "and," never "but."**

"But" cancels out whatever came before it. "And" is roomy enough for all of your many feelings.

FEELINGS JOURNAL

At the end of each day, take no more than fifteen minutes to journal. Sit down somewhere quiet and simply ask yourself, "What am I feeling right now as I sit here?" You can start by identifying physical sensations, such as tightness in your throat. But then see if there are any thoughts or emotions attached to the sensation and if not, move on.

Don't judge yourself. Chances are, you are priming a pump that's been dry a long time.

Feelings check-ins will make this exercise easier.

DREAM LOG

Keep a pen and a pad of paper right by your bed. The *instant* you wake up, jot down notes, as best you can, of your dream. Don't talk, don't go to the bathroom—just take a few seconds to write. You'll find that even if you think you don't dream or that you never remember your dreams, more will stay in your mind if you do this each day. Within a couple of weeks you'll be amazed at the detail and vividness of your recall.

Once your dreams begin to stay with you, jot down not just the facts of your dream but also the emotions that were attached—for example, not just that you'd lost your wife and were calling to her, but that you were frightened.

Here's the trick to this exercise. In your waking state you may have learned to suppress your feelings, but no one can do that in his dreams. Try some armchair psychology on yourself. Ask yourself, "What did that dream mean?" Talk it over with your partner. Engage her help. If she's rarely experienced you as introspective or emotionally articulate, she will be delighted.

Chapter Two

The Crunch and Why You're Still In It

BAD RULES IN A LOSING GAME

Summary

In the last chapter, we mapped out the big picture: where long-term relationships are now; why there's so much friction between women with twenty-first-century ideals and their twentieth-century partners; why neither of the relationship strategies of the previous century—*acquiescence* or *personal empowerment*—gets the results women want; and what a new model—*relationship empowerment*—might look like. The practice section offered exercises designed to clarify your relationship wants and needs, as well as an exercise to help those who have been cut off from their feelings.

Why Don't We Get What We Want?

If life were simple, your good use of the previous exercises would be all that was required to improve things. A clear understanding of what you'd like to see changed would be matched by a partner as willing to make those changes as you are. In a perfect world, you would be nearing the end of your journey of relationship improvement. But relationships are complicated. Armed with the knowledge of changes you'd like to make, both you and your partner might start off with nothing but goodwill and the best of intentions. However, the odds are that neither of you would maintain those intentions for very long. What happens to us? Why is it so excruciatingly difficult for good people who love one another to give their partners what they're asking for and get their own needs met in return? What relationship saboteur derails us? Actually, there is not just one element we can blame for all our relationship troubles, there are five. Here are *five losing strategies* that trip us up:

1. Needing to be right
2. Controlling your partner
3. Unbridled self-expression
4. Retaliation
5. Withdrawal

Whenever one or some combination of these losing strategies takes hold, *you will never get what you want.* You have been seduced away from your real agenda of getting your needs met and instead you've been waylaid by other goals that almost always seem perfectly understandable at the moment. But, as common and accepted as they might be, they are *completely unnecessary and utterly dysfunctional.* Before moving toward an understanding of how to avoid these traps, you will need to know what they look, feel, and sound like. Let's take a hard look at what you and your partner may already be doing that guarantees failure—the behaviors you need to stop.

Vickie and Bob: "You cannot *talk to me that way!*"

Visibly angry, Bob and Vickie stride into my office for a two-day, last-ditch, intensive session as if they both wish they were anywhere else. Even though they moved to Florida a few years ago, in their appearance and manner they are pure New York City: brassy and tough. They remind me of the families I grew up with in New Jersey, and I feel right at home. In his mid-fifties, Bob is short, bald, and muscled up, with a thick neck and huge biceps and thighs. Vickie, also middle-aged, is barely Bob's height, with a carefully done-up mop of blond hair, a Florida tan, and bright eyes. People might describe her as "feisty," or perhaps "adorable."

"How was the flight up?" I ask.

"Yeah, fine," Bob answers. Vickie won't even look at him.

"Well, you two look happy." I try breaking the ice.

"We have our ups and downs," Bob allows. We all sit in silence for a minute.

Vickie can't stand it. "Are you telling him or am I?" she asks Bob.

"Well, Vickie, it's your problem," he says.

"*My* problem?" Vickie snorts. "You think this is *my* problem?"

"I just mean," Bob explains, "you know. Your *issue.*"

"Forget it. I'll do it," she says. Fed up with him, Vickie turns her attention to me. "Bob's out of the house," she begins, "traveling. What is it, seven days, eight days?" she asks her husband.

"Whatever," he concedes.

"It's Elizabeth's recital later that morning. Sunday. Her piano recital. Elizabeth is really quite talented." Bob nods, showing an enthusiastic agreement that doesn't seem to cut much slack with his wife, who continues. "You might think Bob, traveling like he's been, you might think he could manage to spend a few minutes with his daughter on the day of her recital. She was nervous." She turns back to Bob. "Un-der-stand-a-bly," she says, enunciating each syllable as if the word were serrated. "But, unbeknownst to us, my husband has arranged to pal around with his friends in our backyard, our pool."

"Honey," Bob says, trying to calm her down. "It was business. It was just going to take a few minutes."

"So our *daughter*, our ten-year-old, comes out to be with her father and what did you do?" Vickie plunges on as if Bob hadn't spoken. "What did you say to her?" She turns to me without waiting for a response. "He tells Lizzie, *orders* Lizzie, I should say, to get back inside the house and leave him alone."

"You know, Vickie, there's more than one way to . . ."

"You didn't say that?" Vickie asks.

"You just take things out of context, that's all," Bob says, shrugging. "All the time, actually. Well, a lot of the time."

"So I march out," she goes on.

"You got that one right," Bob mutters.

"I *try* talking to him," Vickie says.

"In *front* of my friends," Bob complains.

"In front of your *business partners*," she corrects. "And you say to me, what?"

"Go on, Vickie," he waves her on. "Go ahead."

"In front of the whole group he says, 'Vickie, you turn around and get yourself back into that kitchen and leave us alone.' Right?" She starts to cry. "Only his exact words, believe me, weren't that nice. Not *nearly* that nice, were they, Bob? In fact, I think you'd agree that your *exact* words were rather crude. Humiliating even." She turns away, hurt and disgusted. "But they were supposed to humiliate me, weren't they, Bob? I mean, that was the point?"

"Listen Vickie, you . . ." he tries.

"Don't start," she warns. "Don't even go there. There is *no* excuse . . ."

"I know, honey, but . . ."

"I hate it, Bob," her voice rises. "You understand? I *hate* it! You *cannot* talk to me that way!"

Bob wheels on her. "And Vickie, how about you don't *dress me down* in front of my friends, okay? How 'bout that? Like I never said that before, right? If you want respect, okay, so let's talk about it going both ways. You got something to say to me, pull me aside . . ."

"I'm sorry, Bob," she interrupts. "Really, I am. But your *daughter . . .*" she begins.

"Oh, cut the crap, Vickie!" Bob shoots back at her, furious. "You're not sorry and you damn well know it. You're not even a little bit sorry. But I'll tell you what, honey. You *will* be sorry, get that? You most definitely will be sorry if you don't knock this off."

"Oh, are you *threatening* me?" she fumes, turning toward him. "Is that the deal now? You and I have now dropped down that low? Okay, Bob. Go for it. What exactly do you have in mind? I mean if I'm going to . . ."

"Okay, *stop!*" I yell at them both. "That's *enough*." They each look up at me, blank. "Maybe you two can go on like this," I explain, "but I'm getting a headache just listening to it."

I had no interest in allowing the two of them to just escalate, clobbering each other in front of me the way they do perfectly well at home without my assistance.

What's easy to lose in the snarl of their bickering is that, underneath the tangle, Vickie has a legitimate request—that Bob be more of a father to Elizabeth. Clearing away all the dust they kicked up, that desire is at the heart of their conflict. Yet it's hard to imagine how two people could speed further away from the matter at hand. Like many couples, their "discussion" so quickly turned into a plate of spaghetti that one could hardly remember what they were supposed to be arguing about. Who remembered anymore what the issue was?

While it is true that their manners could use some brushing up, the main difference between Vickie and Bob and other couples I work with is little more than an issue of style. Some couples pound away at each other with rocks, while others blow poison darts so neatly that there hardly appears to be blood. But whether our demeanor is rough-hewn or sophisticated, in heated moments, few of us manage to stay any better focused on our real wishes than Vickie and Bob were able to. And fewer still find a way to get their wishes met. Why is it so difficult, when talking to someone who loves you, to simply get what you're after? Watching Vickie and Bob, the answer is clear.

We lose our way.

Instead of staying focused on our goals, we get sidetracked by one or some combination of five losing strategies. We have not successfully navigated *the crunch*.

What Is "the Crunch"?

When dejected Elizabeth turned to her mom, Vickie experienced the crunch—the discrepancy between the relationship with Bob that she wanted and the one she had. We all have to deal with the crunch, in ways large and small. It is a central aspect of being intimate. Some people deny that there even is a crunch in their relationship. They pretend to be perfectly satisfied. This, as we all know, is a tedious lie. Other couples visit the crunch quite regularly. Bob and Vickie seemed to own it. When faced with the crunch—with the raw experience of our unmet needs—most of us do not consistently push all the way through to a successful solution for one fundamental and simple reason: We stop trying.

You may *act* like you are looking for a solution. You may even trick yourself into believing that you are. But any objective observer could see in a heartbeat that, just like Vickie and Bob, far less savory strategies have taken possession of you.

The First Losing Strategy: Needing to Be Right

Even when Bob and Vickie calm down, it still looks as though they're bashing away at each other. Instead of focusing on Elizabeth and her needs, their debate centers on the burning question: Which one of them was "out of line"? Bob, for speaking disrespectfully, or Vickie, for meddling? They each feel the need to be right, marshalling their evidence and arguing their case, two lawyers before the court. "Do you think it's *right*," Bob asks Vickie, "would you call it *respectful*, to give your husband a tongue-lashing in front of his business associates?"

"Maybe you should think about whose tongue lashed who," she replies.

Vickie and Bob would sound the same at home with nobody watching. Like many couples, they try to "resolve" their differences by eradicating them. Faced with contrasting views of what happened, the way to end the argument, they think, is to determine which version is the more accurate. They are in an objectivity battle: "You and I can settle our differences by establishing which of the two versions of what happened is objectively the correct one."

The problem with this strategy is, of course, that each person is certain that he or she is right and yet somehow, annoyingly, for some utterly irrational and perverse reason, the other stubbornly refuses to see it that way. Instead of being a battle for the relationship, it is a constant war about who is right and who is wrong.

In another session with Vickie and Bob, the need to be right shows itself again. Vickie complains that Bob drives too fast. He's aggressive, tailgates, and blares his horn at drivers who get in his way. "I can't tell you how embarrassing it is," she confides to me. "I mean, we're not *teenagers*. But that's not what's most important, of course. What's really important is that we're not safe."

Not surprisingly, Bob has a different idea. "I'm a New Yorker," he announces. "Born and bred. We're *all* aggressive there. But we *know* how to drive. In Florida, some geezer cuts in front of you and then drops to ten miles an hour just to stick his butt in your face; it's *incompetent*."

And so, as the crowd hushes, the sides are staked out: Is the problem aggression, or is it incompetence? Like the ball in a tennis match, the argument shoots back and forth:

"Bob, even coming here this morning you were driving over seventy," *Vickie volleys*.

"Honey, the speed limit was sixty-five," *Bob returns.*

"But you were way too close to the car ahead of us." *A corner shot.*

"Vickie, have I ever gotten into an accident?" *An unexpected lob.*

"No, but how many speeding tickets have you gotten?" *Straight down the line!*

"Well, yeah, but that was before I got the radar detector." *Ah, Bob looks a little shaky on this one. His defense is faltering.*

"How many, Bob?" *Vickie presses her advantage.*

"Three, maybe four?" *Bob tries.*

"*Five*, Bob. There were *five*! *I'm* the one who pays the insurance bill." *Vickie fades back. It's a drop shot and . . . score! The crowd goes wild!*

This is the forensic approach to tough problems. Let's lay out the evidence and see where it takes us. Bob and Vickie are trying to solve their issues by using the scientific method.

Here's the real deal on being right:

RULE: OBJECTIVE REALITY HAS NO PLACE IN CLOSE PERSONAL RELATIONSHIPS.

Objective evidence is fine for solving a crime or for getting the buses to run on time. But, please, don't try it at home. From a relationship-savvy point of view, the only sensible answer to the question "Who's right and who's wrong?" is *"Who cares?"* The real issue isn't whether Bob is aggressive or whether the driver he curses is incompetent. The real issue is that Vickie makes herself crazy whenever her husband gets behind the wheel. I tell Bob that he has a choice: *"You can be right or you can be married. What's more important to you?"* Whether or not Vickie's feelings were, as Bob put it, "grounded in reality," they were plenty real enough for her. So, Bob could either start slowing down or his wife could start taking cabs. Which was Bob's priority: asserting his right to drive as he chose or helping out his unhappy partner?

The seductive thing about trying to convince your partner that you are right is that a lot of times you are, in fact, right. And proving just how right you are can be a tough temptation to walk away from. But relationship grown-ups understand that being right is not the real point. Finding a solution is.

GETTING DRUNK ON INDIGNATION

At its most extreme, being right becomes self-righteous indignation. It's no longer that *I* am angry; it's that *you* are a jerk. There's a world of difference between saying, "I'm really mad," and saying, "I'm really mad because you are such an idiot!" I call it *staying on your side of the line*. It's the difference between fighting fair and being mean, the difference between expressing yourself and shaming someone you love. In our culture, self-righteous indignation is more than tolerated; it's celebrated. It is personal empowerment's big hit record: "Stand back. I'm madder than hell. And I ain't gonna take it no more!" If being right is compelling, self-righteous indignation can be downright intoxicating. And like drink or drugs, although it may feel good at the time, the consequences of indulgence can be serious.

Here's the real deal on being right, which often degrades into self-righteous indignation: *It is always toxic in personal relationships and often dangerous in public life.* You will never find a solution from a position of self-righteous indignation for the simple reason that you're not seeking one. You're too busy looking down your nose at your partner to care. Letting go of the need to be right is a core principle of relationship empowerment:

RULE: MOVING INTO RELATIONSHIP EMPOWERMENT MEANS
    LEARNING TO LIVE A NONVIOLENT LIFE—
    NONVIOLENT BETWEEN YOU AND OTHERS AND
    NONVIOLENT BETWEEN YOUR EARS.

Scolding your partner as if you were his mother, passing judgment on him, humiliating him—these are all forms of psychological violence. There's no excuse for it, and fortunately there's no need for it either. *Relationship empowerment teaches you how to honor your own experience while at the same time respecting your partner's.* That doesn't mean it's always warm and fuzzy. But there's a world of difference between assertively standing up for yourself and aggressively putting your partner down. You can do one without yielding to the other. In chapter six, I will show you exactly how to do that. But for now, I want you to do this: *Understand that the need to be right eats away at intimacy. You can make a commitment to stop self-righteous indignation, no matter what the provocation.* If you're mad, say, "I'm mad!" not, "You're bad!" explicitly or implicitly. You can be angry; you can defend yourself. But lose that outraged, offended stance. It's toxic to the relationship and it's toxic to your own well-being. If you read this book and follow only this one suggestion, I guarantee that your life will be substantially transformed.

Bob and Vickie

Let's go back to Bob and Vickie on that day in my office when they were discussing Bob's behavior toward his family, so that you can see what giving up being right looks like:

I explain the difference between a strategy of being right versus a strategy of making peace with each other. I use the topic at hand—the way Bob spoke to his wife and daughter.

"Bob," I say. "Vickie wants you to have a close relationship with Elizabeth. Is that something you'd like as well?"

"Of course," he agrees. "I *do* have a good relationship . . ."

"Okay," I interrupt. "Can I give you some coaching?" He nods. "If somebody's asking you to do something," I say, "and you're already doing it, don't argue with them. Just say, 'Sure.' Now, what does that cost you? You're already doing it anyway."

"Okay," he says, turning to Vickie with a big smug smile. "Sure!" he pronounces enthusiastically.

"Very good, Bob," I say, playing along with his clowning. "Now, look. Vickie thinks that the way you talked to Elizabeth and the way you talked to her was out of line. Do you disagree with that?"

"No," he answers. "I already talked to Lizzie about it."

"Oh, you did?"

"Sure I did. I knew it was outta bounds. I already apologized to her. I told her I was stressed out from traveling and that I was really, really proud of her and I thought her recital went terrific."

"Wow," I say. "Not bad." He shoots Vickie a look. "Did you tell Vickie you did that?" I ask.

"Yeah," he answers, and then, "Well, maybe. No," he says finally. "No, I guess I didn't."

"Uh-huh. And now what do you think of the way you talked to your wife?" I ask.

"Totally over the line," Bob answers quickly and emphatically. "Inexcusable. I completely lost it. I'm sorry."

"Have you said *that* to Vickie?" I ask.

"Well, maybe not yet," he answers.

"Uh-huh," I say. "So, what? You're waiting for just the right moment?"

He shrugs. "I dunno."

"Can I tell you why I think you haven't apologized?" I ask.

" 'Cause I'm a schmuck?" Bob ventures. I have to laugh.

"Well," I say, nodding. "I guess. Basically, yeah. The way I would have said it is that your pride got in the way."

"Well, I didn't want to give her the satisfaction," he says. "If that's what you mean."

"Yeah," I agree. "That's it."

"So maybe now?" he suggests.

"Perfect," I answer. "You got it."

"Okay." He turns to Vickie. "Vickie," he says. "My darling, lovely wife. There was and there is and there never shall be *any* excuse for me to talk to you like that. It was disrespectful. It was vulgar. It was crude. And I truly am very sorry."

" 'And I won't do it again,' " I suggest to him.

"I never say never," he replies.

" 'I'll do my very best not to speak like that to you again,' " I try a second time.

"That's true," he says.

"Say it," I tell him.

"I will do everything in my power to speak to you with the respect you are due. One hundred percent," he tells her.

"I just hope, Bob, that you understand . . ." Vickie starts, but I block her.

"Vickie," I say. "Your husband just gave you a gift. The gift of his humble apology. Where I come from, when someone gives you . . ."

"Bob," she cuts me off. "I accept your apology. I do. Thank you. And I hope you mean it when you say that you'll work on this."

"You know, Vickie," Bob says, "it'd be a lot easier for me if you . . ." I can feel him begin to wind up.

"Bob," I cut him off. "You did great. Don't screw it up."

"Okay, okay," he replies. He takes a breath and offers his wife a big smile. "You're welcome," he tells her. "You're very welcome."

"Great," I interject quickly, before either of them can get in the way of their own success. "That's *that*. Now, let's move on."

The Second Losing Strategy: Controlling Your Partner

"I could be happy if only you'd . . ." "You know, if you really loved me you'd . . ." "Honey, what you need to do is . . ."

When we're in the crunch, along with the seduction of being right, another common losing strategy we fall prey to is *control*. When you're in control mode, you try to minimize the discrepancy between what you want and what you have by "getting" your partner to behave the way he ought to. File this one under the heading "Good luck!" Like all of the losing strategies, control—nutty as it may be once you step back and look at it—is hard to resist, particularly when the qualities you're trying to instill in your partner are the very ones he demonstrated during the early part of the relationship—back when you were first falling in love, or, said differently, back when he was on his best behavior.

WHY IS CONTROL SO COMPELLING?

To understand the allure of control, we need to place it in the context of every relationship's fall from grace. We all fall in love with someone we think will mend the unhealed places we carry inside, someone who, at the very least, will help us avoid them. And yet, devilishly enough, we all somehow wind up with a partner who is exquisitely designed to *stick the burning spear right into our eyeball.* How this happens no one really knows. "How could I have *known* that David would turn out to have an alcohol problem just like my dad?" "Molly never *once* lost her temper with me before we got married. How could I have ever guessed she'd turn out to be a rager like my mom?" In decades of practice, I have heard sentiments like these innumerable times. How could you possibly have known? The honest answer is, I have absolutely no idea. It is the *mysticism of marriage.* Over the course of your dating years, dozens of potential partners sailed into view, many of whom would never have triggered your deepest hurts. And none of them even blipped on your screen.

RULE: WE ARE DRAWN TO PEOPLE WHOSE ISSUES FIT PERFECTLY WITH OUR OWN IN A WAY THAT GUARANTEES A REENACTMENT OF THE OLD, FAMILIAR STRUGGLES WE GREW UP WITH.

WE ALL MARRY OUR UNFINISHED BUSINESS

We all choose our mothers or fathers. We all *become* our mothers or fathers. Consciously you think, "With *this* person I can finally be happy!" Unconsciously you think, "Ah-hah! A *player in the old familiar game!*" The mad, inspired thing about real love is that we all marry our unfinished business. And we think we're the only ones who do! You may believe, in your foolishness, that the couple to the left or the right of you isn't going through their version of exactly what you're going through. You're wrong. You may think that a good relationship doesn't bring up to the surface every hurt and anger you've ever carried inside. But it does.

**RULE: A GOOD RELATIONSHIP IS NOT ONE IN WHICH THE RAW PARTS
OF OURSELVES ARE AVOIDED. A GOOD RELATIONSHIP IS ONE IN
WHICH THEY ARE HANDLED. AND A *GREAT RELATIONSHIP* IS
ONE IN WHICH THEY ARE *HEALED*.**

The most spectacular news is that the wounds of our past *can* be healed
in our relationships, just as we dreamed they might be, only not in the
way we imagined they would be. By mastering the art of relationship empowerment, we use the magic of connection to heal ourselves as we
learn to change *ourselves, not our partners.* This is a hard lesson to assimi-
late. When faced with the crunch, our first and deepest instinct is to do
everything in our power to "get" our partners to behave. Our understandable, naïve, and utterly dysfunctional dream is that our partners will give
to us whatever we most missed in our childhoods, that which we most
yearn for now as adults: For him to be kind if your father was harsh. For
her to be honest if your mother was manipulative. For him to be emotionally available if both of your parents were distant. The deeper our
early pain, the more we are triggered, the more desperate we are to control the situation. We feel a knee-jerk response to *make* a partner responsible, or *get him* to stop being so angry, or *win back* the attentiveness he
showed at the start. Whole magazines are devoted to "how to get him
to" be more open, more romantic, sexier. Here's the real deal on control:
It's an illusion. Short of outright coercion—holding a gun to someone's head—no one "gets" anyone to do anything. Which, unfortunately,
doesn't mean that you won't try.

Your attempts at control can be either direct or indirect. The other
word for indirect control is manipulation. While there are always exceptions, men tend toward direct control and women tend toward
manipulation.

The first two losing strategies, needing to be right and controlling
your partner, can combine to produce a *benevolent despot.* When men
adopt this stance, they tend to be explicitly professorial and patronizing.
When women adopt this stance, they tend to be the power behind the
throne: "A man is the head of the family. But the woman is the neck. And

the neck moves the head." For both sexes, when you combine needing to be right with control, you always assume that you know what's best for your partner better than he does. It is always "one-up" and intrinsically condescending. Women have been quite vocal in their objections when men are patronizing in this way. But men are not insensitive either. They know when they are being managed rather than squarely dealt with, and by and large, they don't like it. This is a big part of why men mistrust women, and understandably so.

Whether it's direct or indirect, bullying or benevolent, control is always a losing strategy. Even if you succeed in getting your way, you have won the battle but lost the war. Whether your partner shows it or not, no one likes to be controlled. Unless your mate is a happy masochist, he will either rebel eventually or else settle into a lifetime of resentful martyrdom. In either case, you can count on payback. Control is the only one of the five losing strategies that actually *is* an attempt to get more of what you want. But it's a dismal failure for the same reason that tyranny always eventually fails. No one thrives when deprived of liberty. Oppressing someone may lead to compliance, but it will never engender health or love.

The Third Losing Strategy: Unbridled Self-Expression

I must confess that the third losing strategy, *unbridled self-expression*, is one of my personal favorites. It sounds like this: "Hey, let me tell you in precise, lurid detail just exactly how miserable you made me by your shortcomings. *I need to vent!*" Psychotherapy has been a major aider and abettor of what I have come to call the barf-bag approach to intimacy ("Here. Hold this for me, will ya? I feel better now!"). As a child of the 'sixties, I remember being part of the movement to break free of our parents' constricted culture, wrestling our way out into the wide-open entitlement to "spontaneously" say or do just about anything, anywhere, to anyone. Here's the real deal on venting: When you are hurt or angry, spewing is not being authentic; it's being a brat.

The nutty idea here is that "holding back," not being "open and hon-

est," with each other will create a roadblock to the achievement of perfect intimacy. This is utterly naïve. First of all, intimacy is *not* perfect.
How could a relationship between two imperfect human beings ever be
perfect? Real intimacy is born precisely out of the impact of your human
imperfection with mine and how we both handle that maddening, en-
dearing, challenging, and creative collision. A completely honest and
open relationship is nothing I want to witness: "Honey, as sexy as I think
you are, I need to tell you that I've always been more attracted to your sister. Geez, it feels great to get that off my chest!" How would you like
hearing a friend say *that* to his wife one night when you were out with
them for the evening?

The idea that one's feelings are either expressed or suppressed is a direct inheritance from the work of Sigmund Freud. Freud, who wrote at
the same time that the steam engine was revolutionizing our world, pictured the human mind as a giant hydraulic machine, with feelings getting "dammed up" over here, "building up pressure," and eventually,
"leaking out" over there. Unreleased feelings, like steam, burst through
their containers to "erupt" into neurotic symptoms.

Let me reassure you: You will not die if you don't express yourself
whenever a thought pops into your mind. Furthermore, venting is not an
inalienable right. You can vent, or you can move toward solution. Which
is more important to you? I'm not saying that expressing yourself is always a bad thing, but I am saying that it must be done very carefully and
thoughtfully. Also, expressing yourself, even if done well, will not by itself get you more of what you want. In order to do that, you have to let
your partner know what you're asking for and then do your best to help
him get there. What you need to understand about unbridled self-
expression is that *telling your partner precisely and in no uncertain terms
how horrible you feel about his behavior is probably not the most effective
way to engender a generous response.*

Marlene and Rowland: "How Could You Do Such a Thing?"

With her blond hair pulled back, her blue jeans and boots, forty-three-year-old Marlene looks more than fit; she looks chiseled. She sweeps into my office with the commanding grace of an expert horsewoman, which is exactly what she is. Most of her adult life she and her husband, Rowland, have raised horses, shown them, and sold them. While Marlene and Rowland are both New Englanders, born and bred, they have the weathered faces and deep physical strength of people raised out in the open. Yet within a few moments of our third session, Marlene's sturdy body collapses in on itself as she sits on the couch and bursts into wild, uncontrollable crying. It's heading toward Christmas, she manages to explain, and all she can think about is the Christmas that lying Rowland had spent with his hateful young mistress. "I know I shouldn't," Marlene cries, "but I can't get them out of my head. Every time I try to do any of the things that *we've* always done. Our family. Getting a tree. Buying food. Buying wine for our friends. *Anything*. I just . . . ," wracking sobs stop her for a minute, "I see *them*! I see them together. And I just can't . . . It's so *painful!*" Still in tears, she turns on her husband. "How *could* you? What the hell were you thinking, Rowland? I just don't . . . How could you get up from her bed and come home to me, to our children? How does one *do* that? What kind of monster can do that? And you say that you love me?"

"I'm sorry, Marlie, I . . ." Rowland tries, but his words only incite her.

"Didn't you *know*?" she hurls at him, frenzied, screaming. "Didn't you know what a *spectacle* you were making? How you *humiliated* me? Yourself? Didn't you *care* at all?" She collapses again, crying furiously. "I can't . . . I just . . . Rowland, I want you to hold me. I feel so alone. But when you touch me I'm just . . . I'm *repelled*. It's disgusting to me; it's *disgusting*."

"Marlene," I cut in.

"Help me," she says, still bent over, her face covered in tissues. "I don't want to be like this. Tell me what to do."

"Okay, I will," I say. Leaning toward her feels like pushing into a storm. "Marlene," I say softly, "you have to stop." She pauses.

"Stop?" she asks. "Stop what?"

"All this," I answer. "The crying, and the yelling, and the venting."

"When?" she asks, raising her head, looking stunned. "When exactly would you like me to stop?"

"Now," I answer. "Right now."

Marlene's reactions would have been perfectly understandable, and I would not have moved to help her contain them, had Rowland's infidelity been a few weeks ago, or months ago, or perhaps even as far back as a year. But in fact, Rowland's affair had occurred close to eight years earlier. Marlene is like an inflamed wound that refuses to heal. Her level of rage is simply no longer appropriate to a betrayal, as horrible as it was, that took place close to a decade ago. She takes this in, head up, no longer crying, her cheeks still wet with tears.

"But my therapist, Evan," she says, both annoyed and genuinely confused. "Evan says it's *good* for me to get it all out. He says that sucking everything in and not expressing myself was one of the things that contributed to Rowland's having an affair to begin with."

Inwardly, I can feel myself groan. I know her therapist and I respect him, but I'd bet the ranch that there had been a miscommunication. A phone call quickly established that Marlene's therapist, as I'd suspected, was emphatically *not* encouraging her to keep herself whipped up in such a state, nor to go after her husband in rage. But in this, I was lucky. Because a lot of therapists, to be frank, would have supported Marlene's "honest expression" in just the way she'd imagined. Therapy, no less than feminism or codependency programs, has often encouraged personal empowerment and devil takes the hindmost. Research shows that two partners who each engage solely in individual therapy in order to deal with a marital issue have an extremely high rate of divorce. One recalls the famous split-screen scene in Woody Allen's *Annie Hall*. "I can't stand it," Woody's character complains to his shrink. "I'm lucky if we have sex three times a week." "I hate it," Woody's girlfriend complains to her shrink on the other half of the screen. "Sex. Sex. All the time, sex. He wants it at least three times a week!" "That's terrible!" each therapist exclaims to his patient. "How can you *live* like that? You need to *say something!*"

Unlike the other four losing strategies, which have no place at all in a healthy relationship, I do support *constructive* self-expression. But I'd like you to consider the act of sharing every subatomic particle of your displeasure with your partner as something akin to lighting a stick of dynamite. It can be extremely useful in the right circumstance. But, please, do yourself and your relationship a favor and use it very, very thoughtfully.

The Fourth Losing Strategy: Retaliation

"Don't get mad, get even," reads a chipper little slogan we could probably all live without. In the early 'seventies, during the heyday of the smiley face and other such saccharine emblems, one of my clients walked into his session wearing a button that declared: "If you love something, let it go! If it doesn't come back . . . *hunt it down and kill it*." Revenge is such a familiar part of our humanity that none of us needs anyone to explain much about what it is. But it may be useful to think for a minute about *why* it is—and why it's so hard to resist.

First of all, let me state that if you think you never engage in retaliation, you're probably fooling yourself. Retaliation can be writ very large, as large as killing someone. But it can also be very small, and easy to disown:

"Do you love me, honey?"

"Yeah, sure. Hey, where's the paper?"

Like control, retaliation can be *direct*:

"You think I'm mean, Marvin? Well *everyone* says that *you're* mean. The only reason you have any friends at all is because of your *money*."

Or it can be *indirect*:
"Did you like making love last night, darling?"
"It was fine."

The clinical term for indirect revenge is *passive-aggression*. Passive-aggression is the covert expression of anger through *withholding*. I explain passive-aggression to clients by telling a joke my teenager once shared with me: The masochist says to the sadist, "Hit me!" And the sadist smiles and says, "No." In direct retaliation, you say or do something nasty. In indirect retaliation you *don't* say or do something you should. The first is mean; the second is mean-spirited.

Generally, we turn to retaliation after the first three losing strategies fail. "Oh, yeah? Well, if you won't admit that I'm right, you won't let me control you, and you don't care about my feelings, well, then, take *that!*" Far and away, the most prevalent underlying dynamic of retaliation is *offending from the victim position*. Adopting this stance, one thinks: "If you hit me, I get to hit you back twice as hard, with no shame or compunction because, after all, I'm your victim." Whenever you offend from the victim position, you wind up in the absurd position of being a perpetrator who feels like he's being victimized even as he attacks.

Here's the real deal on retaliation: *Almost all perpetrators see themselves as victims.* You would think that batterers, to pick an extreme example, would feel, in the moments that they lashed out, pumped up, powerful, dominant. But anyone who works with them will tell you that universally when they strike, they feel inside that they are the wronged party, that their partner has betrayed them, or abandoned them, or assaulted them first. O. J. Simpson—who, no matter what your thoughts are about the murder, was indisputably a wife beater—had the audacity to declare himself a "battered husband."

I believe that offending from the victim position accounts for 90 percent of the world's violence. Whether the form it takes is a cold silence or an unkind word between two partners, or it's the act of a disenfranchised, angry criminal who feels entitled to violate our civil code, or a seemingly endless cycle of violence between fractious countries or ethnic groups, violence at all levels is fueled by the righteous anger of the victim. And standing up to our thirst for revenge, no matter how "justified" it might feel, is a large component of learning to live nonviolent lives. You and I may not be equipped to bring peace to the Middle East, or even end civil strife in our communities. But we can start by committing to resist the temptations of retaliation; we can bring peace into our own bedrooms and living rooms.

Here's something we tell our children and too often forget as adults: Just because someone has hurt you does not give you the right to strike back. There is a difference between self-defense and reciprocal attack. We all understand this; it's even a point of law. If you're mugged, it's obviously your right to immobilize your attacker. But then, after he's down, if you were to continue to hurt your attacker, *you* could be brought up on charges of assault.

While the human impulse to hit back is often so fast and so visceral that it's difficult to control, most of us do manage to contain our impulses when it comes to physical retaliation. But far too often, we give ourselves permission to lash out verbally. Humiliating, ridiculing, telling your partner what he should or should not do—these are all aspects of verbal abuse, and they *have no place whatsoever* in a healthy relationship. In chapter four, I describe some specific measures that you can take to prevent verbal, as well as physical, abuse, measures designed to protect you from retaliation, and to protect your partner from you. But, as with self-righteous indignation, you can start *right now* by making a commitment to take retaliation—physical and verbal, direct and indirect—off the table. If you're mad, say so, but *don't act it out.*

Oddly enough, underneath all the retaliatory nastiness to which we human beings seem prone, there might actually lie a buried desire to heal. Retaliation, at its core, may represent a perverse wish to communicate, to make the one who hurt us feel what they made us feel—so that they might understand, and be accountable. Harnessing that deep wish is the goal of a growing legal movement named *restorative justice,* in which victims confront their abusers in forums that make healing possible for the one and true accountability and reparations possible for the other. What this group of lawyers and statesmen practice in the public world is what we must realize in our personal lives.

The Fifth Losing Strategy: Withdrawal

Like retaliation, the fifth losing strategy, *withdrawal*, can be writ large or very small. It can be as shocking as someone stalking out of a marriage or as gradual as a slow decline in the frequency of lovemaking. When withdrawal is meant to be punishing, it overlaps with passive-aggressive retaliation. But withdrawal can also be motivated by a distaste for retaliation, or a general fear of conflict, a mistrust of closeness, a reluctance to be vulnerable, a sense of futility, or just plain fatigue.

You can withdraw from the *entire relationship*, drifting further and further apart. One client told me, "John and I just started leading more separate lives. He had his interests. I had mine. He had his friends. I had mine. Eventually, there simply wasn't much left to bind us together."

You can also withdraw from *specific aspects of the relationship*—stop sharing your feelings, or stop sharing yourself physically—so that one or more of the five areas of intimacy—intellectual, emotional, physical, sexual, and spiritual—starts to dry up between you and your partner. You can tiptoe around your partner, fearing his volatility, thinking him either too fragile or two explosive to handle stressful issues. Or you can withdraw discussion and negotiation about one particular issue, such as child rearing or money, because you "know" in advance that you "won't get anywhere."

WHAT IS THE DIFFERENCE BETWEEN WITHDRAWAL AND MATURE ACCEPTANCE?

Not "butting heads" with your partner because you're convinced that it's futile to try can look like mature acceptance. After all, real relationships are not perfect and you will not get everything you want. But real acceptance and the pseudo-acceptance of withdrawal are emphatically not the same, and confusing the two can lead you and your relationship into a lot of trouble. Real acceptance feels like a *choice*. Earlier I said that while we all long for perfect relationships that we think will complete us, in fact, it is the collision of each other's imperfections that provides our real healing. In a grown-up relationship, when it becomes clear that, for now, a certain want or need of yours will not be fully met no matter how many different strategies you try, you run through a *relationship reckoning*. You ask yourself: Are enough of my needs being met in this relationship to make grieving those wants and needs that will not be granted worth my while?

Phyllis and Doug: You Can't Always Get What You Want

Like a lot of women—by some estimates, as many as one in four—Phyllis had a history of sexual molestation. Doug knew that when they married. And he knew that it was bad, that her trauma had left some indelible marks. In sessions together Phyllis spoke of being the recipient of not one, but several sexual assaults in her lifetime, beginning—as early as age seven or eight—with inappropriate touching by her grandfather, and including a gang rape as a teen and a date rape in college. Like many survivors of such intrusions, Phyllis's relationship to sex was extreme. There were periods in her life of hypersexuality, but in intimate relationships she eventually began to shut down. As I routinely do in such cases, I helped the couple by helping Phyllis regain a sense of sexual control, even power. In the short run—and for as long as she felt she needed it—Phyllis was completely in charge when it came to sex. She chose when, what, and where—the whole nine yards. She even experimented, with my blessing, with tying Doug to the bedposts—not to engage in S & M, or anything else exotic, but to reassure herself that she was absolutely, physically protected from the threat of invasion. I also encouraged her to experiment with her own sexual power, a force of which she was understandably frightened. She learned to tease her husband. She learned that she had the right to arouse him and leave him frustrated, just for the hell of it. In other words, she began to recover what healthy women don't need to think about—the capacity for play.

Phyllis did well, and equally to the point, Doug did well in allowing her this much-needed control, and their sex life began to recover. If this were a fairy tale or a Hollywood movie, the punch line would no doubt be a report of their wild, uninhibited nights together. But real life is seldom that pat. Phyllis began to relax as she learned to trust her control, but she did not relax enough to hand equal control over to Doug. Doug had a normal sexual desire for flexibility in their lovemaking. Sure, he was happy to at times yield to her wishes. But he also fantasized about having a partner, as he'd had in the past, who would be turned on by yielding to him at times, a woman who now and again enjoyed being "ravished," as he put it. Being the recipient of that kind of healthy sexual aggression might have been fine, even arousing, to someone else, but not to a woman who had been sexually injured. Phyllis was simply too wounded to be able to distinguish between being "ravished" and being raped. Whenever Doug grew too aggressive, Phyllis's fear and anger got triggered. Phyllis committed to doing more trauma work, but in truth, as far as I could see, Doug wasn't going to have an uninhibited partner, eagerly surrendering to him, anytime soon. If he wasn't prepared to deal with that limitation, he should reconsider being with this particular woman.

With a little help, Doug moved from feeling like a deprived victim to feeling like a grown-up man. How did he feel about not having a sexual partner as uninhibited as he'd wished for? Bad. But not nearly as bad as he would have felt if he lost the woman he loved. And not as bad, he came to realize, as he would have felt if he'd kept pressuring Phyllis to go beyond her own wishes. With coaching, Doug asked himself the ten-thousand-dollar question: Is there enough for me in my marriage to Phyllis to make grieving the loss of a totally uninhibited sexual partner worth my while? His answer was an emphatic no. And so he *owned* his choice to be with her as a choice and not an unfortunate imposition.

Like all the people I coach, he learned to tolerate the pain and disappointment he experienced without seeing himself as a victim. Doug came to wholeheartedly embrace the many blessings between himself and Phyllis, not just in the other four areas of intimacy but in their sex life as well, a terrific sex life overall even if it didn't exactly conform to his image or meet every single one of his needs. This is true acceptance. It is the cultivation of an "attitude of gratitude."

Where Doug easily might have gone — in fact, where he was headed when I first met him — was withdrawal, feeling hurt, angry, frustrated, and ultimately resigned. Doug might have paid lip service to his pals about "having to compromise"; he might even have fooled himself into thinking that he believed it. But he'd be lying.

RULE: THE DIFFERENCE BETWEEN ACCEPTANCE AND WITHDRAWAL IS
   RESENTMENT.

The Doug I first met would not have done the work of letting go of some of his needs in order to embrace the rest. That Doug would have moped, sometimes openly, sometimes internally. *If you have tried everything to get a need met and it's clear that it is not in the cards, you must take ownership of your choices. Either move into acceptance and relish the gifts you are given, or realize how important your need is and deal with it.* Perhaps you need more, or a different kind of, help. Perhaps you need to issue an ultimatum: "If you can't pledge to monogamy, that's your choice, but I will no longer be here." Perhaps you need to consider ending the relationship altogether: "As much as I love you, I've decided that I cannot in good conscience subject either myself or our children to your volatile anger and verbal abuse." In any case, remember that no one has a gun to your head. There is only one person responsible for the choices you make.

WITHDRAWAL VERSUS RESPONSIBLE DISTANCE TAKING

Just as there is a big difference between withdrawal and acceptance, there is also a big difference between unhealthy withdrawal and a healthy need for space. Many people, especially men, assume that as a relationship expert, I always support increased closeness between partners. Not so. There's a technical term for a union of unadulterated closeness: psychotic fusion. Real relationships are an endless negotiation between closeness and distance. Both are important. But there are responsible ways to take distance and there are irresponsible ways to take distance. Withdrawal is irresponsible distance taking. It is unilateral, and without functional communication—the one who withdraws is either silent or screaming. By contrast, *responsible distance taking* is neither unilateral nor provocative.

RULE: RESPONSIBLE DISTANCE TAKING ALWAYS INCLUDES TWO
ELEMENTS: AN *EXPLANATION* AND A *PROMISE OF RETURN*.

You don't, for example, just slam out of a room during a fight. You call a "time-out," letting your partner know that you're going to cool off for a while and come back when you are ready. Instead of answering the question "Do you want to talk?" with "No," you say, "No. Here's why. And here's when I can," or "Not now. I just got home from work and I need to unwind a little. Let's talk after we put the kids to bed." Most "nos" can be considered a form of distance taking, and relationship-savvy partners learn to say no responsibly, as in "Thanks for asking, hon. To tell you the truth, the last thing I want to do right now is talk about my day at work. But give me a half hour or so to zone out and check the news, and then I'll be happy to hear about your day."

No.

Here's why I'm saying no.

And here's my alternative proposal.

Whether it's taking time to cool off, politely declining an invitation, or simply taking some time for yourself, responsible distance taking is an exercise in self-care that also respects the relationship. Withdrawal may be an attempt at self-care as well, but by being one-sided, poorly communicated, and often at least a little retaliatory, it's no form of self-care I'd recommend.

Both responsible distance taking and acceptance allow you space while still remaining accountable and engaged in the relationship. Withdrawal, by contrast, always causes a rupture, large or small, in your connection to each other. And severing your tie to your partner will never lead to fulfillment.

Of the five losing strategies, withdrawal is the most blatant example of not getting what you want because you've stopped trying. Clearly, you cannot get more of your needs met by withdrawing them. And the cost of withdrawal is the loss of passion. When you stop telling the truth to your partner, when you find yourself saying, "It's not worth the fight," know that you are on a slippery slope. This is particularly important for women who are tempted to "keep the peace" by sliding into acquiescence, that twentieth-century strategy of our mothers and grandmothers. *If you carry one shred of resentment, either do the work of full acceptance or go back to the negotiation table and fight for what's important to you.* But don't try to be a marital martyr; you won't pull it off. We moderns aren't really built for noble self-sacrifice. Don't give in to a false sense of compromise. In the long run, you won't like it. And you won't be the only person in your relationship who will pay for it.

At the core of relationship empowerment lies the belief that taking good care of yourself *is* taking care of the relationship. You don't really want to withdraw your needs, your ideas and feelings, out of frustration, anger, or hurt. And a sensible partner doesn't want that for you, because he loves you, certainly, but also out of a sense of enlightened self-interest. Because a sensible partner understands that the withdrawal of truth, the withdrawal of one partner's real needs, even when masquerading as acquiescence or generosity, will hurt both of you in the long run.

What Is Your Losing-Strategy Profile?

Each of us has his or her own unique blend of losing strategies — a *losing-strategy profile*. You can be 30 percent wrapped up in needing to be right, 50 percent in unbridled self-expression, and 20 percent in retaliation. Or you can have a characteristic two-step, such as moving first into control and then, when that doesn't succeed, into withdrawal. I say all this by way of illustration. You don't need to be so fussy and precise in your own self-assessment; just get a flavor of your characteristic temptations when you are in the crunch.

Chapter Two
Practice Section

A Trial Run: Assessing Laura and Bill

I'll quote from a real couple I encountered and leave blank spaces here and there for you to fill in with your guess at each partner's losing agenda at the time:

I am conducting a workshop on relationship skills in Mason City, Iowa, the model for "River City" in the musical *The Music Man*. Instead of asking for seventy-six trombones, I ask for a volunteer couple willing to present to the audience a "little problem." Sixty-one-year-old Laura promptly shoots her hand up. Her husband, Bill, stays seated next to her, looking bemused. I ask them to stand.

"I'd like to describe an argument Bill and I had the other day," Laura begins, a bit breathless.

"Okay," I say. "All right with you, Bill?"

"Well, I guess," he answers. "Won't really know till we get there."

"Fair enough," I answer, turning to Laura.

"Well, we were at my sister's, last Sunday," she begins. "We often spend Sundays there and Bill doesn't much like it. He's usually pretty good about it, but sometimes he gets grumpy. Anyway, this last Sunday we were there and . . ."

"Hey, wait a minute," Bill interrupts. "That's not really the start of the story. You know it begins before that. _____

Laura looks contrite. "You mean the tickets?" she says more than asks, and then proceeds before he can answer. "Bill had purchased tickets to our school's football game," Laura says.

"Tell him how many," Bill says to her. _____

"What difference does that make?" she asks.

"I just think he should know, that's all," he replies.

"Four," Laura clarifies, getting annoyed. "For us and another couple, friends of ours."

"Tell him who was playing. I mean, why we were going," Bill says, growing frustrated as well. _____

"Our nephew was playing," Laura says, looking embarrassed. But then her annoyance gets the better of her. She turns on Bill. "Look. If you're so unhappy with the way I'm telling this story, why don't you just go ahead and tell it yourself?"

"No," he answers. "You're the one who volunteered, I didn't. I support your telling the story. I just want you to do it right." _____

Now Laura is visibly flustered—and angry. "Bill, either leave me alone or tell it yourself, okay?" she says.

"Laura," he answers patiently. "You don't need to make such a big deal out of it. Just go on." _____

"We were," Laura says, trying, "we were there at my sister's . . ." And then she collapses. "Gosh darn it, Bill!" Laura throws herself back into her chair and bursts into tears. "This is what you *always* do! I can't . . . I just cannot go on like this!" And then Laura falls silent, leaving Bill standing in front of a few hundred people. _____

Bill pokes her a few times and bends down, desperately whispering to her, but Laura, head in hands, will not budge.

Did you guess their moves? Bill is about being right and in control. I read Laura as trying to be moderate in the face of Bill's provocation and holding her own for awhile, until it all gets to be too much for her. Then she throws herself into a withdrawal that has a large measure of retaliation in it. Did this fit with your assessment?

SELF-ASSESSMENT

This is a journaling exercise. Get out your notebook and jot down what you remember of a recent argument between you and your partner. As much as possible, try to recall, sentence by sentence, how it escalated. Whatever you don't remember, *make up*. In fact, if you don't have a specific memory, you can make up a fight from scratch that you feel would be a typical example of how it goes between you.

Now, just as you did with Bill and Laura, annotate the fight with your best guess at *your* losing strategies.

What does this teach you?

Does this example leave out a typical losing strategy of yours that should be included in your profile? If so, include it.

Note:

If you have difficulty articulating your losing-strategy profile, explain the concept to your partner and ask him to give you his humble opinion about your profile (not his!). His thoughts should not be taken as the truth, but as data for you to consider. (Asking your partner to help profile you, by the way, is an excellent strategy for piquing his interest.)

If you haven't already, you may now write out what you see as your partner's losing-strategy profile.

Note for readers who are doing this without their partner's participation:
   Do *not* share your partner's profile with him at this time. Don't do
   anything with it just yet.

Note for partners who are using this book together:
   Share with each other using these steps: Partner A first listens to what
   his partner has written about him, and then shares what he has written about himself. How well do the two descriptions match? Then
   Partner B takes a turn. Remember that your partner's description of
   you may or may not have anything to do with your own. Do *not*
   argue about it. Just take it in as information about how your partner
   sees you, right or wrong.

EXPERIMENT WITH CHANGING YOUR STRATEGIES

This is an alternating-day exercise.

   For ten days, *every other day will be a magic day.* On *ordinary days,*
you *must* use your typical approach (your losing-strategy profile) on no
less than four issues of negotiation or conflict that arise—at home, work,
or school. On *magic days,* however, your powerful magic enables you to
use a completely new approach. You may experiment with new moves
that you think might be more successful. Or, just for the hell of it, you
may adopt a different set of losing strategies, just to see what they feel
like. But on magic days, you cannot do the same old same old.

   Remember, as with feelings, negotiations don't need to be big. You
can negotiate who sits where at the table, or who tells the joke. We negotiate in tiny ways all the time. And so, on non-magic days, you approach
negotiations by resorting to your favorite losing strategies. On magic
days, however, a powerful spell enables you to try a completely new approach. You might experiment with new, more effective, moves. Or you
might adopt a different set of losing strategies, just to see what they feel
like.

   Journal at the end of each day about what you've learned.

Chapter Three

Second Consciousness

STEPPING OUT OF YOUR BAD DEAL

Do Your Losing Strategies Affect Only You?

There's a saying in family therapy that most couples have the same fight over the course of forty or fifty years. These seemingly endless, irresolvable repetitions are like children's Chinese finger puzzles: The harder you pull, the tighter they get. They are *vicious cycles* that dig us in deeper and deeper, eating up, over the years, more and more of the goodwill and connection we start off with. Looking at the five losing strategies, it's not difficult to see that none of them will succeed at getting you more of what you want. But I'm afraid that their effect on your relationship is more pernicious than just that.

RULE: THE APPEARANCE OF ONE PARTNER'S PARTICULAR BLEND OF
   LOSING STRATEGIES IN A COUPLE'S TRANSACTION OFTEN
   TRIGGERS THE OTHER PARTNER'S LOSING STRATEGIES.
   THE PARTNERS' LOSING STRATEGIES THEN REINFORCE
   AND EVEN INTENSIFY ONE ANOTHER.

As part of their training in marriage therapy, it is common to teach students how to articulate a couple's "stuck place" by using the phrase *the more, the more*: "The more he Xs, the more she Ys. And the more she Ys, the more he Xs." I call the vicious cycle that a couple faces over and over again their *bad deal*. It's as if both partners have agreed to play out for all eternity reciprocal roles that get neither of them anywhere.

The following profiles illustrate how two different couples are caught up in bad deals.

Ethan and Kendra

Months of Kendra's depression have driven Ethan crazy. His patience gone, he finds himself angry, even screaming, at what he sees as her helplessness. Despite the fact that Kendra has found and is using both talk therapy and medication, neither has helped very much. In time, Kendra and her doctor will probably find effective treatment, but meanwhile Ethan's anger leaves Kendra only feeling worse and more powerless to change.

The more Ethan gets angry, the more Kendra gets immobilized.

Ethan and Kendra could be described as being caught in a *Scolding Father/Helpless Child Deal*.

Rebecca and Lonnie

Rebecca has always been jealous, but after Lonnie's affair, she has become obsessed with the fear that he might lie to her again. Each night Rebecca grills Lonnie about his whereabouts, searching for inconsistencies in his stories. Over and over again she catches Lonnie hiding something that he thinks will upset her—that his business took him to his ex-mistress's neighborhood, for example, or that a close colleague of his ex-lover called him about something. Lonnie explains that he doesn't always "fess up" to these innocent situations because he knows Rebecca will "be a nightmare" if he does.

The more Rebecca interrogates her husband, the more he conceals the truth.

Rebecca and Lonnie could be described as being caught in a *Controlling Mother/Bad Boy Deal.*

Where Does Your Bad Deal Come From?

While it might not be readily apparent, the vicious cycle most couples find themselves stuck in *replays some aspect of the relationships they grew up with:*

Ethan and Kendra

Ethan's mother radiated resentment throughout much of Ethan's life; she was a perennial angry victim of her husband's slow, degenerative battle with M.S., *just as Ethan now radiates resentment about Kendra's battle with depression.*

Rebecca and Lonnie

While Rebecca had no reason to doubt her father's fidelity, he did twice lose a small fortune in reckless speculation. He made back all the money that he'd lost the first time, and more, but he never recouped his losses the second time. He lived out the rest of his days a modest, salaried employee, broken in spirit and henpecked by his wife, who insisted on a minute accounting of his every expenditure, *just as Rebecca insists on a minute accounting of Lonnie's whereabouts.*

None of these four individuals is a terrible person. Ethan feels horrible about his growing impatience with Kendra. Lonnie wishes he'd never had his affair. And Rebecca knows she's "over the top" with her control and intrusion, even as she seems unable to stop. These are not bad people; *they are ordinary people caught in bad deals.*

The painful dramas they each grew up with spill into their marriages with the seeming inevitability of a classic tragedy. Their relationships are crowded with ghosts.

Ethan and Kendra: A Good Man Behaving Badly

At the end of one session I ask Ethan and Kendra when their next appointment will be, and their response to this seemingly straightforward question is revealing. Ethan asks Kendra to answer and Kendra begins rummaging through her voluminous, disorganized purse, bumbling and apologizing as she searches for her calendar. Finally, in frustration, Ethan growls, "Oh, just *forget it*," and tells me he'll call when he gets back to his office.

"Ethan," I say, "can I ask you a question?" He nods. "How did it get to be Kendra's job to know the appointment date?" He just stares at me for a moment, not comprehending.

"I . . . I don't know," he finally sputters. "I . . . these things just happen in relationships, don't they? I do certain things; she does certain . . ."

"She keeps the calendar?" I ask.

"Around certain things," he replies.

"Because she wants to?" I press. "Because she's good at it?" They both laugh.

"Well," Ethan says, "actually, no. She's not very good at it at all."

"That's what I thought," I tell him. "You seem like the super-organized one to me. Are you happy with the job she's doing?" They laugh again.

"You mean am I usually as pissed off as I was just then?" he asks.

"I wouldn't say you were pissed off, actually," I tell him. He looks at me, waiting, and I let him wait a few beats. "*Disgusted* is what I'd say you were, Ethan. *Contemptuous.*" He starts to talk, but I cut him off. "What's striking to me is that you don't just do it yourself . . ."

"Well, I . . ." he begins.

"It's important that she learn to be competent?" I venture. "Or, it's not fair for you to do everything?" I watch him become more vexed by the second. "Even though she doesn't do it right, does she? Not quite right." He leans forward to answer, but I turn my attention to Kendra, who has begun, very quietly, as if fearing to disturb us, to cry. "Just how 'not right' are you exactly?" I ask her.

"Very," she answers in a small voice. She sniffles, dabbing her face with an oversized wad of tissues. All of a sudden this sexy, very cool-looking young woman seems to be about eight years old.

"So, this is the part where I say, 'And how frequently are you "not quite right"?' And then you say . . ."

"Always." Tears fill her eyes again and trickle down her face. "He wasn't like this at first," she says, as if to apologize.

"Well, *you* . . ." Ethan starts but then bites back his words. I wheel on him.

"She *what*?" I ask. "She wasn't like this either? She wasn't so helpless? So needy? She wasn't so repulsively, annoyingly sick?"

"And the point of all this is?" he asks, superciliously.

"How contemptuous of your father was your mother?" I ask.

"I don't know. We've been through this."

I ignore him and turn to Kendra. "How contemptuous of . . ."

"She was *horrible*. It made me *ill*." She looks at her young husband, finally angry. "I couldn't believe the way she spoke to him."

"This isn't about your depression, is it, Kendra?" I ask. "You couldn't do much that was right *before* the depression, could you?" Again, she cries. "Could you?" She shakes her head.

I lean back and look at Ethan, who perches on the edge of his seat as if he's dying to talk but has nothing left to say. We both look at Kendra as she cries. "This is bad, Ethan." I inform him. "I think it's really pretty bad."

"What is?" he says.

"How mean you are," I say. He physically recoils.

"I don't *think* of myself as mean," he responds slowly, no longer fighting me.

"That's because you don't know what normal is," I tell him. "You grew up with mean. You drank it in with your mother's milk. How old are your kids?" I ask.

"Two and five," he responds.

"You have to deal with this, Ethan," I say. "They're young and cute now. But it's just a matter of time until they start not being right by you, do you understand? You're going to turn this meanness on them too eventually. I guarantee it."

"He already has," Kendra blurts out. Ethan doesn't answer.

"We have to stop this, Ethan," I tell him. He opens his mouth but nothing comes out. Then he nods his head. "You're a good man," I say. "I felt that right away. A good man behaving badly." Now, finally, his eyes begin to fill. "Go on and feel it," I tell him. His cries are spastic, their sound tight and strangled. "Open the back of your throat, Ethan. Don't choke it off like that."

It Isn't the Lyrics; It's the Beat

Ethan and Kendra illustrate a crucial principle of relationship practice.

RULE: COUPLES DON'T *HAVE* PROBLEMS; THEY *ARE* PROBLEMS.

It is true that Kendra's sudden, biological, and very real depression stressed their relationship. And to the unschooled eye, it would seem obvious that Ethan's impatience and Kendra's sense of helplessness were perfectly understandable reactions to her condition. But Kendra's depression did *not* cause the vicious cycle in which helplessness evokes contempt, which evokes more helplessness. If anything, constant reiterations of this unhappy dance probably contributed to, and most certainly now prolong, her depression. The critical thing to understand is that you could drop just about any issue into the Cuisinart of this couple's Scolding Father/Helpless Child Deal and the ensuing dynamic would look the same. Because what partners do with *this* stressor will be pretty much what they do with *every* stressor.

> RULE: YOU THINK THAT YOUR RELATIONSHIP WILL IMPROVE ONCE
> PARTICULAR STRESSFUL ISSUES, LIKE MONEY, PARENTING, OR
> SEX, "GET RESOLVED." BUT IT'S ACTUALLY THE OTHER WAY
> AROUND. YOU'LL BE ABLE TO SUCCESSFULLY TACKLE TOUGH
> ISSUES ONLY AFTER YOUR RELATIONSHIP IMPROVES. YOU
> MUST CHANGE YOUR USUAL APPROACH, YOUR DANCE—
> YOUR BAD DEAL.

Life's stressors rarely determine a couple's dynamic. Your relationship's dynamic will determine how well, or how poorly, you'll handle life's stressors.

In my encounters with couples over the years, I have been amazed at how pervasive and how stubborn each couple's repetitive dance tends to be. You could tell Ethan and Kendra that they were both about to lose their jobs, or you could just as easily write them a check for three million dollars. *The circumstances don't matter.* In either situation, sooner or later Kendra would appear overwhelmed, incompetent, and apologetic, and Ethan would respond with impatience and disgust.

> RULE: AS CHILDREN, WE LEARN WHAT WE LIVE. IN OUR ADULT
> RELATIONSHIPS, WE LIVE OUT WHAT WE'VE LEARNED.

Why Do You Re-create Your Own Family?

At the simplest level, we re-create the relationships we grew up with because they are what we know. Ethan "knows" how to be a frustrated partner feeling trapped by a mate's illness. It's a way of being connected, *a template for relationship*, that he experienced every day growing up. And Kendra grew up as the "star" of her family while her mother suffered with incapacitating bipolar disorder. When Kendra went off to college she hit the wall and collapsed, experiencing her first bout of depression. From that point on, Kendra adopted her mother's old role of helplessness. Like Ethan's frustration, Kendra's dependency was a model of what a relationship looked like—a helpless woman paired with a caretaking man, a way of being related that Kendra had lived with every day.

Just like Ethan and Kendra, each of us adopts stances in our relationships—losing strategies—without questioning them. To us, they are *normal* because they were the "norms" we grew up with. "You mean retaliation isn't normal?" says the child of a rager. "You say that everyone doesn't withdraw and make their own life when they're unhappy with their spouse?" says the daughter of two walled-off old Yankees.

RULE: THE BAD DEALS WE EXPERIENCED AS CHILDREN BECOME
　　　OUR MODELS FOR "HOW ONE DOES IT," OUR UNQUESTIONED
　　　INTERNALIZED TEMPLATES FOR RELATIONSHIPS.

Are We Doomed to Keep Repeating the Same Patterns?

No. Because beyond the unconscious search for the familiar, another reason pulls us into the old drama: our desire to get out of it. At a more spiritual, mystical level, *we pick partners with whom we can re-create whatever it was that was relationally dysfunctional in our formative years out of a deep-seated impulse to heal it.*

RULE: WE ARE DRAWN TO PARTNERS WHO MEET TWO CONDITIONS:

　　1. The person's character is *similar enough* to that of one or both of
　　　　our parents' that, with this person, we can re-create our most
　　　　familiar and most unresolved childhood drama.

> **2. The person's character is *dissimilar enough* from that of our parents' that, with this person, the old drama carries within it *the potential for a new and healthier outcome.***

How can you attain the new, healthier outcome waiting inside your relationship? How can you, like Ethan, learn to break the enchantment of behaviors that pull you away from your deepest wishes, allowing you to free yourself, transform your marriage, and spare your children?

You must change your relationship to relationships.

There is an old alchemical saying, "The laws of nature are like a miller's wheel. And they will grind you to powder—*unless you learn to be the miller.*"

How Do You Work a Relationship?

RULE: YOU CANNOT ATTAIN A NEW, SOPHISTICATED WAY OF BEING IN A RELATIONSHIP USING OLD, UNSOPHISTICATED METHODS. IF YOU WANT A RADICALLY DIFFERENT, FULFILLING RELATIONSHIP, *YOU MUST KNOW HOW TO SHAPE IT.*

We've all heard the clichés about how we bring baggage, "unfinished business," into our relationships. But what does that really mean? The "baggage" we carry into our relationships is the relational dysfunction, the unhealthy ways we have of being related—being helpless like Kendra, or scolding like Ethan. To say that we "have issues" is just another way of saying that we have things to learn about how to connect in healthy ways. Our areas of immaturity always represent unfinished business, incomplete conversations, with one or both of our parents, because it was they who should have guided us toward the relational maturity we now lack as adults. Wherever that guidance was lacking, we will feel "unfinished." And we are right to feel that way.

What does it mean, then, to feel finished? It means that we were functionally parented. It means feeling that we got from our parents what we deserved and needed in order to be healthy. Kendra needed her parents to help her feel a sense of worth and loveableness, independent of her performance in the world. They didn't cherish her that way and she now has trouble cherishing herself that way; she is prone to low self-esteem and, consequently, to depression. What she needed, deserved, and did not get from them was acceptance. No less than Kendra, Ethan also failed to get the wisdom that one can be cherished and vulnerable at the same time. But Ethan took the other side of the dance. He became contemptuous of human frailty, just as his mother had been contemptuous of Ethan's ill father. As adults, Ethan and Kendra are now like two shards of broken pottery that fit together perfectly.

Why would Ethan and Kendra pick each other? As I've said, at the simplest level because their dance is so familiar. But at a deeper level, it's because each wants from the other the thing that he or she deserved and did not get. Kendra desperately wants Ethan to love her despite her occasional lapses into incompetence. She desperately wants to be loved for herself and not her star performance. And Ethan wants just as desperately to be relieved of the burden of caretaking. Growing up, he tended to the physical demands of his ailing father and, even more, to the emotional demands of his resentful mother. Whether he admits it or not, Ethan longs for someone to tend to *his* needs for a change, and he is furious with Kendra for not doing so. The sad irony for this pair is the same sad irony for most of us:

RULE: IT IS THE URGENCY OF YOUR WISH TO "GET" FROM YOUR PARTNER WHAT YOU SHOULD HAVE HAD BUT DID NOT GET FROM YOUR PARENTS THAT DRIVES YOUR LOSING STRATEGIES AND GUARANTEES FAILURE.

If, like Kendra, your father was emotionally unavailable and you struggle with feeling unlovable, then why in the world do you keep picking men who are unavailable? Why don't you just settle in with a nice fellow who adores you? The reason is that he doesn't count. It's too easy. Obviously such a man either doesn't know who you really are or he's of no real account, because of course any real man of substance and acuity would know, just as your father knew, that you weren't quite good enough. *Convincing* him that you are good enough, winning him over, *that* would finish the unfinished conversation with your father. Now, at last, you think, you can esteem yourself because *he* sees you as worthy. Or perhaps now, at last, you have found the magic bullet that can cure your irrational mother (wife) so that she will finally be healthy enough to give you that love you've always wanted. Or now, at last, you've found just the right move to stop your raging father (husband) from abusing you. He sees, finally, what a worthy creature you are. A drunken mother fuels one partner's endless scheming to "get" his mother/wife sober. A passive father fuels another's compulsion to "get" her husband/father to finally protect her . . . and on and on and on. We hit the piñata this way and that, trying to get at the candy we've always known lies inside. But we are deluded. Whatever it is that we wanted from them then came and went a long time ago. It's far too late for anyone to give it to us now. We are no longer children. The only person who can learn to make up for what wasn't there—the only person who can finally give you the missing skills and love you so yearn for—is yourself.

RULE: TRY AND WISH AS WE MIGHT, AS ADULTS, NO ONE ELSE CAN RE-PARENT US. WE MUST LEARN TO RE-PARENT OURSELVES.

We *think* we will be healed when we wrest from our partners the particular form of care we crave. *That*, we think, will complete the uncompleted conversation. But our ambition always fails; we have no better luck with our partners than we had in the past with our parents. Because our healing doesn't come when we replay the old failing drama and finally win.

Our healing comes when we replay the old failing drama and *finally stop trying.*

Our healing comes not when we finally succeed at righting the wrong, being told what we were never told, loved as we were not quite loved. *Our healing comes when we give up.*

RULE: YOU NEED NOT STEAL WHAT YOU ALREADY OWN.

Our relational healing comes as we learn to give to ourselves that which was not given, so that we can turn to our partners not as longing, frightened, or overburdened children, but as freestanding adults wanting to share with another adult. Perhaps you married your mate to steady you, or to be successful for you, or to give you value, abundance, culture, standing, or friends, or to stop you from drinking or start you having fun, or simply to give you the gift of not draining you dry. And all of these things are wonderful; they're great—as *gifts*. But they're poison as obligations.

As you move into relational health, you no longer need your partner to make up for your own areas of immaturity. You don't need your partner to never become overly dependent because you've learned how to say no. You don't need his validation because you've learned to feel worthwhile inside your own skin. I am not saying that all of your immaturities will go away, or that all the old voices in your head will just stop. Our vulnerabilities and childish reactions will always be with us. But *we've stopped foisting them off, like bothersome children, for others to deal with.* The buck stops here. *You stop asking your partner to heal you and start seeing your relationship as the crucible in which you get to heal yourself.*

As a Grown-up, How Do You Work a Relationship?

You start thinking relationally, systemically. You are not *above* your relationship working *on* it, the way a mechanic works on a car. You are working on yourself *inside* the relationship. You are a part of the system. You move within it. You move with humility.

You cannot directly control your partner, and you cannot directly control how the system operates as a whole. You can't control the out-come. The only part of the relationship that is under your direct control is you—and that is on a good day. *Give up the mad agenda of "getting" your partner to change and try changing yourself instead.*

RULE: WHILE YOU CANNOT DIRECTLY CONTROL EITHER YOUR PARTNER OR YOUR RELATIONSHIP, YOU MAY BE ABLE TO *INFLUENCE* THEM BOTH BY EXPERIMENTING WITH RADICAL NEW MOVES OF YOUR OWN.

In its broadest terms, this is such simple common sense that all of us know and use it. We all know that the odds of our mate granting a particu-lar favor improve if we show up for a surprise dinner at his favorite restaurant, just as the odds will shrink if we show up an hour late, scream at the children, and then berate him. But for most of us, our occasional use of this principle is crude. We either use it to be manipulative or we use it without giving it much thought. *Our relationship to our relation-ship tends to be passive.* We get what we get from our partners and *then* react after being disappointed. This is a child's approach to relationships. As an adult, we take responsibility for doing what we can to *actively shape* the relationship as we go along. As you adopt relationship practice, the question "What could I do to help make this better?" starts to be-come a way of life.

What Is Relationship Practice?

The foundation of relationship practice is the insight that, just as people don't have problems, they *are* problems, a good relationship isn't some-thing you have but something you *do*. And it's not something you do once or twice in big ways but rather something you keep doing day by day, minute by minute throughout your life. Your partner says something. In the following instant you have choices to make. Your response can be mature or immature, artful or spontaneous, thoughtful or thoughtless.

Relationship practice occurs—or doesn't occur—in that split second before you choose. Will you run your response, or will it run you? Will you
be under the miller's wheel, or will you be the miller?

Relationship practice is very akin to a mindfulness practice. In *this*
second, in front of you *right now*, will the actions on your side of the seesaw be conscious or automatic? The automatic response is, of course, the
one you learned, the one that fuels your part of your vicious cycle. The
cultivated response is novel.

More than simply a set of techniques, relationship practice is nothing less than a new level of awareness, a *second consciousness*.

What Is Second Consciousness?

Kevin and Dominique

Kevin comes home from a hard day's work still carrying the stress of the
day. His partner, Dominique, meets him at the door in a fury. Kevin
didn't do *this*; he didn't do *that*. Just like Dominique, Kevin grew up in a
family in which rage was an ordinary occurrence. His first instinct, his
whoosh—that visceral reaction that comes over him like a wave in an
instant—is rage. In the past Kevin's rage would be met with Dominique's, and the more one spun out of control, the more the other did.
But Kevin and Dominique have begun relationship practice. Just as his
fury sears through him, another voice, a new consciousness, sounds in
Kevin's head shouting, "*Wait! Kevin, STOP!*" followed by, "*Breathe.
Breathe deep. Good. Now, let's see if there's a different way of responding.*"
And Kevin does try a new response. "Dominique," he says, "I'm not
speaking disrespectfully to you. And I want the same in return." And, lo
and behold, Dominique stops. Kevin can almost feel the weight of Dominique's newly cultivated second consciousness, like a foot on the
brake of her revved-up engines. Dominique's whole body is ramped up,
ready to fight. But she, like her partner, settles back down. "Okay," Dominique says. "I'll try it again." Later Kevin tells me that Dominique

looked so adorably earnest, brows bent in concentration, that he would have given her anything.

Your *first consciousness* is your knee-jerk reaction: "To hell with *me*? Well, baby, to hell with YOU!" Or, "You seem angry. Oh, no! What did I do?" "You have a problem? I'll call you later." "You're sad? Hey, did ya hear the one about . . . ?" It's the habitual response you learned growing up, the one that seems so spontaneous and normal, the one that fuels your half of your bad deal. That ingrained response feels altogether natural, immediate, physical, and unstoppable. You can think of it as the miller's wheel ready to grind your relationship into powder unless you become its master. How can you do that? By actively cultivating a smarter, more mature, and more skilled part of you—a new voice, like Kevin's, that restrains your old reactions and offers new ones. In a word, an adult.

RULE: WHEN IMMATURE PARTS OF YOUR PERSONALITY BECOME
   TRIGGERED—EITHER THE WOUNDED, OVERWHELMED PART
   OF YOU OR THE DEFENSIVE, ENTITLED PART—IN YOUR MIND'S
   EYE, TAKE THAT CHILD IN YOUR LAP, PUT YOUR ARMS AROUND
   HIM, LOVE HIM . . . *AND TAKE HIS STICKY HANDS OFF THE*
   STEERING WHEEL.

Relationship practice means learning to bring the adult part of yourself into your relationship along with the less-mature parts as you interact with the people you care about. It means the development and use of *second consciousness* in *this* moment, *right here*. In this moment when, as with Kevin and Dominique, every muscle and nerve in your body is screaming to do the same old same old—fight, flee, or fix—and, through sheer force of discipline and grace, you lift yourself off accustomed track A and place yourself, kicking and screaming, onto new track B.

Your journey toward health and a great relationship consists of strings of such moments. The more such moments there are, the stronger and more effective your second consciousness becomes, and the further along you are in your practice. It's as simple as that.

What Gets in the Way of Second Consciousness?

Ghosts. Your baggage. And that's why learning to become relationally empowered has the power to heal you. It teaches you not how to banish your ghosts, but how to manage them. What gets in the way of the development and use of second consciousness is the grip of first consciousness. It's quite straightforward. What gets in the way of mature responses are immature ones. Like the heroes of thousands of mythic journeys, in the heat of the moment, we lose our way. We stop remembering who we are and to whom we're speaking. We become entranced. How do we wake up? How can we break the spell of old wounds and old enemies, long since gone but still with us?

We must disempower our ghosts.

Core Negative Images—The Ghosts Inside the Machine

Arjun and Maya

With her thick reddish-brown hair, dark eyes, and soft skin, Maya is a striking young woman. Her husband, Arjun, is rail thin and balding even though he's still in his twenties. With his big black-framed glasses and high forehead he screams *academic*, and indeed he teaches advanced engineering at one of Boston's universities. It was Arjun who first contacted me. He described his relationship with Maya as "a very good marriage on the brink of disaster."

"Have you worked much with Indian couples?" he inquired early on in our first session. As a matter of chance, I had, and told him so. "And how would you describe traditional gender relations in our culture?" Arjun pressed. I took a deep breath, thinking that this was going to be one of those make-it-or-break-it moments in our work together.

"I'd call it patriarchy squared," I ventured.

"Not at all! Not at all," he hastily replied. "Patriarchy *cubed*, at the least." And then he leaned back and smiled.

As enlightened as Arjun might have imagined himself, however, he was far from enlightened enough for his wife.

"I don't *care* what you think," Maya yells at him, stomping her foot on my office carpet. "We already *know* what you think. There is no shortage of people who have been apprised of your views." The issue is whether or not to allow their kids to watch television. Arjun is adamant. There is no need for it. There is far too much violence. It will destroy their capacity for imagination. It will render them passive and stupid.

Maya is no less intransigent. Their two boys, now six and seven, are old enough to want to watch sports. Television shows are a part of their peers' vocabulary, their everyday talk. Does Arjun want his kids to be the only ones in their school who don't even know what *American Idol* is? *Must* he brand them as marginal outsiders? But, of course, the argument isn't really about the issues at hand. It's about their bad deal.

"You don't *listen* to me, Arjun," Maya complains. "You make such a show of your modernity, our 'egalitarian partnership,' until there's any actual disagreement. *Then* you're no different than the men you make fun of. No, you're worse. At least they're not *hypocrites*!"

Arjun turns on her sternly. "Maya," he warns. "I don't like you speaking to me like this."

"You foolish man," she says, and laughs, though not warmly. "You don't *like* my speaking to you like this? You confirm my exact point."

"Maya, I think you're being unfair," Arjun tries again, clearly beleaguered. "I do try to listen, we just don't see…"

"Yes, right," she interrupts, her voice goading, sarcastic. "And whenever we don't *see* . . . then *we* do what *you* want, isn't that so?"

"No." He smiles back, containing his annoyance. "No, that is not so."

"Name one instance . . ." she challenges.

"School . . ." he begins.

"*School?*" Maya yells, incredulous, incensed. "School? So, okay Arjun, that was your *father's* decision, not yours."

Arjun loses all pretense of containment. He turns to her, furious. "First of all, he is paying for it," he says, ticking off points on his fingers.

"Should I care about that?" Maya tries interrupting, but Arjun rolls past her.

"Second," he ticks off, "you *wanted* that school, Maya."

"Was it my first choice?" she shoots back.

"Did you not say you'd feel great about our boys going there?" Arjun tries.

"Was it my *first choice*?" she repeats.

"That's it!" Arjun throws his arms up in mock defeat. "Maya, that's *it*! *Nothing* I do is enough for you!" he screams.

"That's because you *don't do enough*!" she screams right back at him.

"Okay, okay," I interject, trying to stop them. "Maya, stop."

"Sure. Sure. It's useless anyway. He never listens."

"Maya, please . . ."

"You're the one who doesn't listen," Arjun yells, coming in under me. "You're the one who's too *stupid* to appreciate what I give you . . ."

"Stop it!" I say again. "*Both* of you."

They fall silent for a moment, chastened, pouting.

SHADOWBOXING

The problem with trying to help Maya and Arjun stop arguing with each other is that they actually *aren't* arguing with each other anymore; they're arguing with each other's ghosts. By the time they move into "You always" and "You never," they no longer address their real partner but rather a caricatured version of that partner. Arjun *does* listen to his wife, although perhaps not as often or as well as she'd wish. And Maya *does* appreciate Arjun's many efforts to be fair and sensitive to her, although not as much as he'd like. Instead of building on these strengths, or even acknowledging them, the well-oiled tracks of their usual contest slide them further away from resolution and even from remembering who they really are to each other. They are no longer actually fighting with each other, but rather with each other's *core negative image*.

RULE: A COUPLE'S REPETITIVE FIGHT REMAINS UNRESOLVED
BECAUSE NEITHER PARTNER TRULY ENGAGES WITH THE
OTHER, BUT RATHER WITH *HIS WORST FANTASY ABOUT THE
OTHER.* AS WITH LOSING STRATEGIES, EACH PARTNER'S
NEGATIVE FANTASY LEADS TO ACCUSATORY AND DEFENSIVE
BEHAVIORS ON BOTH SIDES THAT ONLY FURTHER CONFIRM
THEIR FEARS. *OUR NEGATIVE FANTASY IS THE ENGINE THAT
DRIVES RELATIONSHIP VICIOUS CYCLES.*

What Is Your Core Negative Image?

Your core negative image—or CNI—of your partner is that vision of him that you feel most hopeless and frightened about. You say to yourself, in those furious, or resigned, or terrified moments, "Oh my god! What if he really *is* . . . ?" (You can fill in the blank.) What if he really *is* a vicious person? What if she really *is* a cold-hearted witch? A betrayer? An incompetent? Constricted? Selfish? Your CNI of your partner is your worst nightmare. It is who your partner becomes to you in those most difficult, irrational, least-loving moments.

Maya thinks Arjun is a hypocritical tyrant who never really listens to her or treats her with true respect. Arjun thinks Maya is insatiable and relentless; nothing he does is ever good enough for her. The first and most important thing to notice is the way that each of their CNIs calls forth and reinforces the other's. Each CNI is like Brer Rabbit's Tar Baby: The more you fight against it, the more stuck you get. Every time Arjun asserts that Maya is unappreciative, Maya feels dismissed and not listened to. And each of Maya's complaints about feeling unheard reinforces Arjun's conviction that nothing he does will be enough.

By now, it should almost go without saying that each of their CNIs is a direct carryover from their childhoods. Remember the idea that our repetitive bad deal represents a fight we never finished, a wish to get from our partners something critical that we didn't get growing up? While Arjun may, in his quiet way, be more of an autocrat than he likes to admit, he pales in comparison to Maya's father, who ruled his family with an iron grip. After years in the United States, Maya's mother, who never once disobeyed her husband, grew even more quietly vitriolic than she'd been back home. It was up to her first American-born daughter to have the knock-down fight with her father that really belonged between the two adults. Maya desperately longs for Arjun to listen to her as her father would not.

Arjun's mother loved and nurtured him. For her, anything he did was wonderful. His father was just the opposite. For him, truly, nothing was good enough. Arjun desperately needs Maya to approve of him as his father would not.

Both Arjun and Maya have married their fathers. And in their worst moments, endlessly and irresolvably, each sees the other with the same anger and with the same sense of hopelessness that they each felt toward their father. But, in fact, they are wrong. It is true that Arjun can be dictatorial and that Maya can be unappreciative—but only in their worst moments. Unlike each other's real fathers, at their best, each of them has much more to offer.

Remember the rule that said that each of us chooses a mate enough like what we grew up with to enable a re-creation of the old struggle—to be heard, to be appreciated—but at the same time enough unlike what we grew up with that the old drama might have a new outcome? Here is that moment: when CNI meets CNI. The moment of challenge, and opportunity.

How Can You Use Each Other's CNIs for Good?

There is an old Wampanoag saying: To find your unique strength, look deep into the heart of your worst enemy. Left to themselves, partners' CNIs will at best create logjams and at worst, fester and poison the relationship. But for many couples, learning how to work with each other's CNIs has proven to be the single most transformative aspect of relationship empowerment work.

RULE: YOUR PARTNER'S CNI OF YOU CAN SERVE AS YOUR
RELATIONSHIP'S COMPASS. *CNIs ALWAYS POINT IN THE
OPPOSITE DIRECTION FROM YOUR GOAL.*

What follows are five strategies for using CNIs:

1. Make each other's CNIs explicit
2. Acknowledge the truth in each other's CNIs
3. Identify CNI-busting behaviors
4. Use CNIs as your compass
5. Set up dead-stop contracts

An Important Note:

These strategies are intended only for those readers whose partners have joined them in reading this book and doing these exercises. Do NOT attempt to share this material with a partner who is uninterested in or resistant to learning relationship practice.

Even for those who are working toward relationship empowerment together, if you think that sharing the material that follows may lead to serious upset, wait until after you've read about and have begun to practice boundaries. You may return to these strategies then. If you feel that sharing the material that follows may lead to explosiveness in your relationship, do the exercise with help and support from a trained professional.

STRATEGY 1: MAKE EACH OTHER'S CNIs EXPLICIT

Step One: Sit down with your journal and write, in no more than a paragraph or two, your CNI of your partner—how you see your partner as being when he is at his all-time, absolute, most despicable, most impossible worst.

Step Two: Write, as honestly as you can, what you imagine your partner's CNI of you is.

Step Three: See if you can identify the resonance of your CNI to your childhood experience growing up. Here are some questions you could ask yourself:

- Does my CNI of my partner remind me of, or have some of the same characteristics as, one or both of my parents?
- Does the behavior connected to my CNI of my partner remind me of behavior that existed in my childhood?
- Did I see anyone behave in these ways? If so, who was it? What did he or she do, and to whom? And what did that person do?
- Did anyone behave in those ways toward me?
- Did I behave in any of those ways without anyone stopping me?
- When I see my partner through the spectacles of my CNI of my partner, how do *I* behave?
- Did I see anyone behave in these ways? If so, who was it? What did he or she do, and to whom? And what did that person do?
- Did anyone behave in those ways toward me?
- Did I behave in any of those ways without anyone stopping me?
- When I see my partner through the spectacles of my CNI of my partner, what is it I most want him to understand?
- What must he change?
- What is it that I most want from him?
- Does what I want from him remind me in any way of something I wanted from one or both of my parents?

Step Four: Write what you imagine your partner's answers to Step Three would be—not what he would say, necessarily, but what you see as true.

Step Five: In a safe and respectful manner, realizing that you are sharing each other's realities (which may be very different), share the material you generated in Steps One through Four. Journal about what you heard and your reactions to it, and speak to each other about it.

STRATEGY 2: ACKNOWLEDGE THE TRUTH IN EACH OTHER'S CNIs

This next strategy can be enormously liberating for both of you, and it has the power to substantially change your usual dance.

As I said earlier, when our partners confront us with their CNIs of us, we almost universally react to the fact that their CNIs are distorted and caricatured. In other words, we argue with them. We often see the very fact that they think such nonsense about us as proof positive that we are correct in our CNIs of them—as in "You only think that of me because nothing is ever enough for you!"—and then we are off to the races.

Instead of denying the truth of your partner's CNI of you, I want you to try a radically new approach. Imagine that your partner's CNI of you is not, as you've been thinking it was, completely fabricated and nutty. Instead, consider it as *an exaggerated version of you at your very worst.* That CNI doesn't remotely acknowledge who you can be at your best; it doesn't even acknowledge who you usually are. In fact, it doesn't even accurately describe you at your worst, but offers instead an exaggerated version of even that. Having acknowledged all that, try on the idea that the CNI, exaggerated and limited as it might be, is nevertheless *essentially true.* Your partner's CNI doesn't describe someone else; it's you. It's how you can be when the most immature parts of yourself have grabbed hold of the steering wheel. Your partner's CNI of you is a super-bright, high-contrast photograph of your fault lines. You work hard not to fall. But when you fall, this will be where you go.

Words cannot convey the power that comes when you stop denying the truthful aspects of your partner's CNI of you and *join him* in his concerns about them.

Arjun and Maya

"You are right, Maya," Arjun, in a later session, after much coaching, confesses to his wife. "I can indeed be far more traditional than I style myself as being. It is easy to be egalitarian in matters that don't cost me much. And furthermore," he intones, speaking with gravity and formality, "I must tell you that often when you try to point out how authoritarian I am being, I know full well that you are right. I huff and puff and call you ungrateful precisely because I know that you are right, and either I am mad about it or I just want my way."

"Or both," Maya suggests.

"Maya," I say, teasing her, "do you think Arjun might do well enough on his own with this?"

"Point taken," she says, bowing her head.

"And I must tell you that you are right also, Arjun," Maya says later on. "Rather than praise what you do give to me, I often criticize you for all that you do not. I don't want to be a shrew anymore, Arjun. I know too well what that does to people."

STRATEGY 3: IDENTIFY CNI-BUSTING BEHAVIORS

Each partner takes a page in his or her journal and draws a line down the center. Write as headings "CNI-Confirming Behaviors" on the left-hand side of the page and on the right, "CNI-Busting Behaviors." Write a bulleted list of behaviors your partner has or could engage in that you would experience as further proof that your CNI of your partner is in fact true. Then write a bulleted list of behaviors your partner has or could engage in that you would experience as evidence that your CNI of your partner is in fact not true. Share these lists with each other.

STRATEGY 4: USE CNIs AS YOUR COMPASS

Your partner's list of behaviors that serve to either support or dispute his CNI of you is the most direct set of operating instructions for your relationship with him that you will ever receive. Use it. Know that every time you behave in ways that come close to his CNI of you, you will likely trigger upset in him. That doesn't mean that there might not be occasions when you choose, for any number of reasons, to behave in CNI-confirming ways. But it is to say that you'd best be prepared for the fallout whenever you do. More important, I want you to understand that any-time you behave in ways that are emphatically different from your part-ner's CNI of you, ways that are the opposite of his expectations or that are found on his CNI-busting list, your behavior will most likely reassure your partner, feel good to him, and, at the most profound level, touch something deep inside him. Because in those moments you will in fact be giving him what he didn't get growing up, what he longs for and finds it hard to believe in.

These acts of kindness are *not obligatory.* And they do not take the place of your partner's own healing. But they are merciful. They are gen-erous. If your partner can take them in, they will fall on his soul like warm, cleansing rain.

STRATEGY 5: SET UP DEAD-STOP CONTRACTS

Of all the techniques of relationship empowerment work, the use of *dead-stop contracts* is without doubt the simplest and most direct way to transform the playing out of your usual repetitive bad deal into a mo-ment of healing for both of you. Because they rely on both partners' co-operation and because they demand a fairly high degree of discipline, dead-stop contracts are geared for couples on the higher end of the troubled-to-healthy spectrum. They are a more refined version of *time-out* contracts, which I will describe in detail in chapter four. While help-ful at times for all relationships, time-outs are especially needed for helping turn bad relationships into good ones, while dead-stop contracts are especially useful for turning good relationships into great ones.

The dead-stop contract itself is an agreement to interrupt the vicious cycle of CNI-meets-CNI. The agreement goes like this: "If I feel, rightly or wrongly, that you are behaving in ways that reinforce my CNI of you—if I feel, for instance, that old, horrible feeling of being bossed around by you—I will signal a dead-stop. And you agree in advance that whenever you hear that signal, understanding that your behavior is CNI-triggering, you will come to a dead stop—*whether you agree with my per-ception or not.*" Let's say, for example, that my CNI of you is that you're

a big bully. Whether I am nuts for feeling bullied by you in this particular instance or not, you agree, upon hearing my signal, to stop whatever
it is you are saying or doing *on a dime*. Instead of continuing, you agree
to turn to me and say your version of "I'm so sorry. I don't mean to bully
you. Forgive me. Is there anything I can say or do right now that might
help you feel better?" On my side, I promise not to use this as a moment
to give you a hard time but rather to appreciate your effort and move on
as quickly as possible.

Arjun and Maya

Arjun agrees in advance that whenever he hears Maya say "autumn," he
will know that she feels unlistened to. In the past, of course, her complaint would have triggered a rebuttal on his part followed by complaints
that, once again, she didn't appreciate how much he was giving her,
which would have left her feeling even more unlistened to, and on and
on. But now, even if Arjun thinks that he *has* been listening to her, even
if he thinks that she is certifiably crazy or that she is deliberately or mali-
ciously misusing the dead-stop contract just to manipulate or abuse him,
none of that matters.

RULE: WHEN YOU AGREE TO USE A DEAD-STOP CONTRACT, NOTHING
    SHORT OF PHYSICAL SAFETY TAKES PRECEDENCE OVER YOUR
    GOAL OF STOPPING YOUR REPETITIVE PATTERN. NO MATTER
    WHAT YOU THINK YOUR PARTNER MAY BE DOING, YOU PLEDGE
    TO HONOR YOUR SIDE OF THE CONTRACT.

Arjun understands this rule and so, upon hearing the word "autumn," he
immediately stops what he's been saying, apologizes, affirms his intent to
respect his wife, and asks if there's anything more she would like from
him at the moment.

Because Maya now understands that her husband's CNI of her is
that she is unappreciative, she has made a quiet vow to herself to be *emphatically appreciative* of Arjun's good efforts in such moments and to

leave it at that. In a session soon after their first use of this contract, Maya fills me in on the details. "Is there anything else I would like?" she reports herself as having replied to Arjun. "Only that my husband should understand how grateful I am to have such a dear and extraordinary man as my partner." Beside her, Arjun blushes pink even at the retelling of the story, while Maya, observing his discomfort and pleasure, can't help but laugh, making him blush all the more.

Maya and Arjun made their new interaction look easy, but there were actually a number of critical turning points. Instead of passively tolerating a build-up of resentment, Maya attempted to *shape the relationship* by letting Arjun know, in a respectful way, that she felt unhappy with the way he was treating her. Instead of getting defensive, Arjun honored her feelings and radically shifted his behavior. And finally, instead of criticizing how Arjun had behaved, or asking for more from him, Maya deliberately chose the CNI-busting response of emphatic appreciation. Both partners replaced old knee-jerk reactions with more functional new learned responses. Instead of the escalation of CNI meeting CNI, they engaged in the healing of second consciousness meeting second consciousness. And they turned what would certainly have been in the past one more instance of miserable argument into the light, warm experience of success. Watching Maya laugh at her befuddled husband that day in my office, I couldn't help but think to myself that the more Maya teased, the more Arjun blushed. And the more he blushed . . .

Now, *that* seemed like a deal they could live with.

Practicing Solo

If, for the moment at least, your partner has no particular interest in learning this material or practicing these skills, it is hard to imagine how you could share your CNI of him in a manner that wouldn't evoke a lot of hurt defensiveness, and I'd advise you to not even consider it until after you have read further and have mastered some skill in speaking relationally. This should not stop you, however, from using much of this material yourself. If you are honest with yourself, I'll bet that you can imagine fairly accurately what his CNI of you is, and that you can even come up with a useful description of your bad deal, your repetitive dance. Since your partner has not agreed to this practice, you have no right to request that he honor a dead-stop contract with you, but you can offer to honor one on your side. If Arjun had no interest in this work, for example, nothing would have prevented Maya from saying, "Arjun, you've told me many times that you feel that I can be unappreciative. I would like to remedy this. You could help me by letting me know in the moment that it occurs, whenever you feel this, and I promise whenever you do to stop and change my behavior." How often does one get an offer like that from one's partner?

RULE: IT IS ALWAYS WITHIN YOUR POWER TO DISRUPT YOUR
      REPETITIVE DANCE, *NO MATTER HOW YOUR PARTNER
      RESPONDS.* IF YOUR PARTNER RESPONDS WELL, YOU HAVE
      THE OPPORTUNITY TO TRANSFORM YOUR VICIOUS CYCLE
      INTO A CHARMED CIRCLE—NEGATIVE REINFORCING NEGATIVE
      BECOMES POSITIVE REINFORCING POSITIVE. THAT'S THE BEST
      OUTCOME. BUT EVEN IF YOUR PARTNER CLINGS TO THE OLD
      PATTERN, *YOU HAVE THE ABILITY TO STEP AWAY.* YOU CANNOT
      SINGLE-HANDEDLY SHIFT YOUR RELATIONSHIP FROM A BAD
      DEAL TO A GOOD DEAL, BUT YOU CAN SINGLE-HANDEDLY
      STOP YOUR BAD DEAL IN ITS TRACKS BY CHOOSING HEALTHY
      BEHAVIORS FOR YOURSELF.

Chapter Four

Are You Intimacy Ready?

CLEANING UP

Summary

The chapters you've read so far have been principally concerned with helping you understand what's gone wrong in your relationship, why you may not be as satisfied as you'd hoped to be.

Chapter one laid out a broad overview, placing your particular relationship in the context of this moment in the history of marriage, and it explained why we all need a new set of rules that match our new twenty-first-century expectations.

Chapter two introduced you to the idea of the *crunch*—the experience, large or small, of discomfort stemming from the discrepancy between what you want in your relationship and what you have. Relying on any one of the *five losing strategies* guarantees that your goal of getting more of what you wish for in your relationship will not come to pass. You learned to identify your particular *losing-strategy profile*, and what you imagined your partner's profile might be as well.

Chapter three started to pull things together for you. You were shown how each partner's losing-strategy profile fits with the other's, creating the couple's characteristic vicious cycle, the fight they return to over and over again. The childhood roots of this ever-repeating drama were shown, and you began to see that it is precisely to throw us into the old drama that we choose the partners we do—in part because we are drawn to familiarity, but also because we are drawn to the possibility of healing so that the familiar struggle might finally be resolved. That healing comes not when we change our partners, but when we use the crucible of our relationship to experiment with changing ourselves. Doing so demands the development of a new consciousness, through which you can master the art of relationship practice.

Chapter three also introduced you to the idea of *core negative images*, and gave you the means to identify your and your partner's CNIs of each other and use them rather than being used by them.

You are now firmly on the new path toward establishing and sustaining a great relationship. As in all great endeavors, however, like all mythic quests, there are a few tasks to complete before setting off, challenges that you must master in order to be fit for the journey ahead. You must prepare your environment. And you must prepare yourself. This chapter and the next address each of these actions in turn.

Prepare Your Environment: Cleaning Up

RULE: IN ORDER TO WORK TOWARD A GREAT RELATIONSHIP YOU MUST HAVE A SANE, SOBER, AND SAFE PLACE IN WHICH TO DO THE WORK.

Your team won't get very far in your pursuit of intimacy if either or both of you has:

- An untreated psychiatric condition
- An untreated issue of self-medication
- An untreated "acting-out" disorder (either sexual or aggressive)

Why Must Individual Psychiatric Disorders Be Treated First?

If you or your partner is struggling with an issue such as depression, anxiety, phobias, or obsessive-compulsive disorder, you owe it to yourself and your family to get—or insist that your partner get—help. There is simply no way your relationship is going to get healthier when one of you is in a state of emotional distress. The great news is that the field of mental health has come a long way, and most psychological conditions can be significantly improved with the right care. Treatment for depression, for example, has been shown to be 90 percent effective. Yet only two in five depressed people ever get help. The implication of these statistics taken together is heartbreaking, not just for the sufferers themselves, but also for the people who love them. Neglecting to get treatment is your individual choice if you live alone, but once you elect to create a family, getting help is no longer a decision that impacts only your life. It is your responsibility to be the best spouse and parent you can be. In order to accomplish that, to be a truly valuable team player, you must first be a reliable, healthy individual.

If you are the one who has been reluctant to get help, understand that your unwillingness inflicts unnecessary suffering on those around you. And if you are the partner of such a person, you should know that a spouse and parent in disrepair affects everyone in the family. *You have an absolute right, even an obligation, to insist on health in your family.*

WHAT CAN I DO TO HELP MY PARTNER OVERCOME AN UNTREATED PSYCHIATRIC CONDITION?

Some people hesitate to confront their mate's emotional difficulties for fear that it will "set off" the person and "make things worse." That might be true in the short run, but I don't think you have much choice. It is rare for these conditions to get better all on their own, and in many cases, they only grow worse. The difference that treatment brings to the quality of your family's life makes it well worth the effort, even if it triggers some conflict. It is far better for your children to see healthy argument as part of dealing with a tough issue than for them to watch an adult operate as an emotional drag on the whole family.

Other partners may feel shy about nagging, or "doing too much" for their hesitant mates. They have taken to heart the advice that a person has to "do it for himself." That's all well and good in principle. But my advice is to put principle aside and *do whatever it takes to get your partner in front of a mental health professional.* Even if you need to make the calls, screen the potential therapists, and make the initial appointment, I suggest you do it. When dealing with a partner who may be struggling with an untreated psychiatric condition, how your partner gets to a mental health professional matters far less than what happens after he gets there.

HOW CAN YOU HELP A RESISTANT PARTNER?

Even if your partner steadfastly refuses to see a therapist individually, that need not deter you. In such cases, *you* can go ahead and book an appointment for couple's therapy.

Jamie and Gloria

Thirty-eight-year-old Gloria says to Jamie, her husband of eleven years, "Jamie, honey. I've noticed that you've been drinking more these last few months. You've been complaining a lot about stress. The kids tell me that you've been more irritable with them and you've certainly been more irritable with me. I know you have been under a lot of strain at work, but, honey, you know I don't think that's all there is to it. Now, Jamie, depression runs in your family, and I think it's worth checking out. You just haven't seemed to be your old self. Now, I know you don't think you have a problem and you say you won't see someone. But, you know what? We have a problem as a couple, then, because I don't want to keep living this way. I have booked a couple's therapy appointment for the two of us in about three weeks, and Jamie, I need for you to come to it with me. This is serious."

How do you find a reliable therapist? Several potential resources are listed in the Resources section at the end of this book. Once you have the names of a few therapists, call several and ask for a phone consultation. Spend a little time talking with each of them. Lay out your concerns, and, just as Gloria did, be sure to detail the specific symptoms—changes in attitude or behavior—that cause you anxiety. If you listen carefully to how the therapist responds to you, you should get a feeling for whether he or she will take your concerns seriously, or whether the therapist is too arrogant or disconnected to credit the information you give.

A professional evaluation may reveal that your partner is in a better state than you thought. Be open to such reassurance. But if your suspicions turn out to be true, then it will be important for you to have found a clinician with spine enough to back you up in your insistence on treatment.

RULE: IN YOUR INITIAL SCREENING OF THERAPISTS, BE EXPLICIT ABOUT THE SUPPORT YOU ARE LOOKING FOR AND THEN CAREFULLY ATTEND TO THE WAY HE OR SHE ANSWERS.

Don't be afraid to be blunt, as in, "I strongly believe that my husband suffers from obsessive-compulsive illness. I'd be delighted to be wrong. But if your evaluation proves me right, and if he doesn't want to admit to it or deal with it, what sorts of things would you say to him? How would you handle it?" A therapist who is willing to take a clear and firm position in such matters may not be all that easy to come by. But the last thing you want is to go through the pain of getting your partner there only to have the professional cave. So take your time and find help that will really help.

Once you're both at the appointment, do your best to give the therapist specific data so that:

a. **the diagnosis can be as clear as possible, and**
b. **the therapist will have enough concrete examples to challenge your partner's denial about his condition and need for help.**

Once you've done all the hard work of finding a good clinician, getting your partner to the appointment, and giving the therapist everything you can to help out, then the ball is in the therapist's court. If you've chosen well, the therapist won't drop it.

What Is Self-Medication?

In order to prepare for the work of building a great relationship, the first clean-up item you must attend to is untreated psychiatric conditions. The second concerns issues of *self-medication*. Trying to work on a relationship while lugging along a self-medication problem is like putting one foot on the gas while the other stomps on the brake. You can rev up the engine all day, but you ain't going nowhere. As a brake is to acceleration, self-medication is to working on your relationship—they cancel each other out, and nothing moves.

WHERE'S THE LINE BETWEEN USE AND ABUSE?

The difference between the *recreational* use of something and its *abuse* as a form of self-medication is very clear. When you are in a state of emotional health, you use something like alcohol to enhance your good feelings. You have a glass or two at a party and feel looser, more social, and a little bit euphoric. Why do you do it? Simple enjoyment. But when you are someone who self-medicates, your goal is to boost baseline feelings inside that are not okay. Because it doesn't feel all that great to be in your skin, you turn to something like alcohol not for enhancement, but to right yourself, to bring yourself up from feeling bad. You have developed a *psychological dependency*.

Many people assume that if you don't have a *physical dependency*, if you can choose not to indulge when you want to abstain, then you are in the clear. But it's not that simple. *Self-medication does not mean that you can't do without whatever it is that makes you feel better. It's that you can't be very happy without it.* When your "drug of choice," the object of your dependency, is flowing, you have a sense of self-worth and well-being. All seems right with the world. But if there's a crimp in the line between you and whatever you're depending on, you go through a self-esteem, well-being crash. That crash can feel like emptiness, loneliness, depression, jaggedness, anxiety, coldness, or blackness.

While dependency on substances is widely recognized, less well known are *process dependencies*, in which the person turns not to a thing, like alcohol or drugs, but to an activity. The best-known process dependency is compulsive gambling. But you can use virtually any gratifying activity compulsively. You can spend; you can engage in high-risk behaviors; you can overindulge with food or television; or you might be a workaholic.

One process dependency getting a lot of press these days is *sexual compulsivity*. If either of you is sexually compulsive, you self-medicate with sex, sexual arousal, or the prowess of sexual seduction. Your acting out may or may not include an ongoing affair. Most probably you'd be carrying on a string of affairs or one-night stands, perhaps seeking prostitutes, Internet partners, or pornography. If you are in the grip of sexually compulsive behavior, you need help. There are AA-type meetings for sexual compulsivity and a growing number of counselors trained to assist you.

The importance of self-medication for our purposes is simply that whenever a partner turns to a process or substance for comfort, that person is *not* turning to you, and vice versa.

For the relationally empowered, our union is the vessel that holds us. It is the crucible for our own change and growth. It gets awfully hot in

there sometimes, but we need to stay steady and work it through together.
If every time the temperature rises beyond your comfort zone you or your
mate scoots off to the fridge for a cold one or a quick trip to the mall for
a shopping spree, you won't face the challenges that you need to master.

Misery Stabilizers

Misery stabilizers are the things people turn to instead of turning to each
other, staying engaged, and facing their issues. Like steam valves, they
bleed off your discontent, staving off a crisis but cementing your lack of
fulfillment as well.

Most of the couples who come to see me are one step away from divorce. Virtually all of them have been unhappy for years, and many have
run through one, two, or even six stabs at therapy. The first thing I look
for in such cases is the list of misery stabilizers, because in situations of
chronic displeasure, one or both partners have probably been turning for
comfort or vitality to someone or something outside the relationship. If
they weren't, the pain and loneliness that characterizes a long-standing
dissatisfactory relationship would probably have been too hard to bear.
We turn away from each other, choosing to numb the pain in lieu of ad-
dressing its cause.

RULE: TURNING TO MISERY STABILIZERS IS ONE FORM OF THE
    FIFTH LOSING STRATEGY, WITHDRAWAL. A PARTNER WILL
    NOT FULLY ENGAGE, AND REAL INTIMACY WILL BE SEVERELY
    COMPROMISED, IF MISERY STABILIZERS ARE NOT DEALT WITH.

HOW CAN YOU AVOID THE STALEMATE OF MISERY STABILIZERS?

From my perspective as a coach trying to help people have great relationships, the most difficult thing about misery stabilizers is that, in a way,
they often work. The Catch-22 of using misery stabilizers is that you get

just enough satisfaction to be able to stand a situation you'd be better off challenging.

Men tend to use workaholism, substance abuse, risk taking, gambling, food, exercise, television, the Internet, and sexual compulsivity. Women tend toward love dependence through overinvolvement with their children, food, prescription drug abuse, spending, exercise, "busyness addiction," and love dependence on a romantic adult.

In order to get the juices flowing in your relationship, you and your partner need to kick out the props that hold you in stasis. *Let your relationship go into crisis.* Deal with your own discomfort. If removing your stability props throws you into depression or anxiety, then fix it, don't mask it. Of course, the idea of doing without is frightening and unappealing for most of us. You or your partner may need support, even professional help if the dependency is significant. But the very reason we are reluctant to give up our props is the reason we should. Doing so throws us into a confrontation with each other, and with the unresolved aspects of our relationship that we've been far too comfortable avoiding.

Decades of work with couples have taught me that just because someone is miserable by no means necessarily indicates that he wants to change. I call this being "comfortable/miserable," and ask my clients, "You can be comfortable or you can have a great relationship; what's more important to you?" If you're serious about changing your relationship, you need to cut back or altogether stop anything that emotionally removes you from the reality of it. Put away your diversions. Turn around, face your partner—and deal.

Irma and Gil

Twenty-four-year-old Irma is physically stunning. She has been Gil's lover for almost four years, and she's been drinking heavily for at least three of them. Gil, fourteen years Irma's senior, is handsome, rich, and demanding. He could have his pick of beautiful mistresses, and he's not above reminding his girlfriend of this. And yet despite the jet-setting life they lead, the boats and travel and glamorous friends that Gil provides,

Irma has been in a tailspin. With my help, she confronted her drinking problem, and now, newly sober, she confronts Gil:

"Gil, I have no sexual desire for you anymore. But to tell you the truth, after the very beginning, I don't think I ever did. It's not that I haven't found you attractive. It's that sex has always been about you. Your fantasies. Your gratification.

"You're rough with me, Gil. And selfish. I went along because I was mostly drunk. I didn't mind, but I didn't like it. I want to love you like a real woman. If you want a doll, there are a lot of women out there who will play that game for you. But I won't anymore."

Listening, I am in awe of Irma's clarity and newfound courage. She fully expects Gil to leave her, but instead, to her amazement, he breaks down and cries. Not only was this Irma's first step toward real health, it turned out to be Gil's first step in dealing with his toxic, grandiose use of people and his sexual compulsivity. Irma's sobriety opened a path toward real connection for both of them.

Making It Safe: Stop All "Acting Out"

The first two "clean-up issues" were untreated psychiatric conditions and problems with self-medication. The last issue that must be addressed before deep work on the relationship can begin concerns danger.

RULE: IF EITHER OF YOU IS PRONE TO ACTING ON YOUR SEXUAL OR
    AGGRESSIVE IMPULSES, THE RELATIONSHIP IS SIMPLY NOT
    SAFE ENOUGH FOR REAL INTIMACY. IN ORDER TO BE ABLE TO
    ENGAGE WITH EACH OTHER, YOU MUST FIRST REMOVE THE
    THREAT OF RETALIATION OR HIGH-RISK BEHAVIORS.

Sexual acting out includes any current affair. You cannot work on your relationship while having another one on the side. In my practice, if one of the partners is ambivalent about the marriage, I ask that he or she commit to working on it intensely for three to four months. If, after the end of that time, no change has occurred, the person is free to go. But during the period when we are working together, neither partner can have contact with another romantic figure. This is true for physical affairs and also for *emotional affairs*, in which a partner has all the intrigue of infatuation without ever getting physical. Being involved in a platonic romance does not diminish the impact of degrading your primary relationship.

THE THREAT OF AGGRESSION

Aggressive acting out includes any retaliation against a partner that poses a real danger to that person or to the family. It could be a credible threat to take away someone's children, to hurt someone professionally, or to withhold needed finances.

Aggression includes anything physically harmful or even intimidating, such as standing too close to someone or throwing things. I will not see couples in therapy when there is a threat of physical violence. If someone is physically assaultive, he needs treatment on his own, such as joining a batterer's group or anger-management program. I believe it is unethical to place a woman in the dangerous position of facing possible physical retaliation if she dares to tell the truth. Usually treatment of uncontrolled rage occurs in groups. You might also elect to work with an individual counselor. But if you do, be certain to choose one specifically trained in the area of domestic violence. Generic therapy will not help.

WHERE IS THE LINE BETWEEN ANGER AND ABUSE?

To deal with abuse realistically, we need to understand what it is and what it isn't.

I draw a distinction between three types of interpersonal behaviors:

1. Functional
2. Abrasively dysfunctional
3. Abusive

You can behave annoyingly, even repugnantly, without actually abusing anyone. You can be ditsy, or self-centered, or ungenerous. Your behavior can be downright gross. While there is a myriad of behaviors repugnant enough to burn out a relationship, they may still fall short of outright abuse. The line separating unappealing behaviors from abusive behaviors is your line, the one that should be standing between you and the person taking liberties with you.

Behaviors are abusive when they violate your psychological self, when they cross your internal boundary. These boundaries are universal and are not determined by your partner. In the next chapter I discuss psychological boundaries in detail, but for now, I want you to have a guide for determining what is and what is not a psychological boundary violation.

Psychological Boundary Violations

Yelling and screaming

Name-calling:

     Any sentence that begins with, "You are a . . ."

Shaming or humiliating:

     Communicating that someone is a bad or worthless person. Shaming behaviors include ridiculing someone, mocking, being sarcastic, humoring, or being patronizing.

Telling an adult what he or she should do:

     Unless you're someone's boss, therapist, or advisor, you have no right to tell another grown person what he or she needs to do. That's intrusive. The same is true for dictating what someone should think or feel. And it's even more intrusive to tell someone what he "really" thinks or feels, as in, "You're not disappointed; you're angry."

Making contracts and then breaking them

Lying

Manipulating:

     Deliberately falsifying information, or dishonestly changing your behavior, in an attempt to control your partner. For instance, hamming up a feeling: "Don't worry about me; I'll be fine out here in the rain. You go have a good time."

IF IT'S NOT ON THE LIST, IT DOESN'T EXIST

Here's the great thing about having a list of abusive behaviors: If a particular behavior of yours does not appear on it, the behavior isn't abuse. If someone is calling it abusive, however, the chances are good that the behavior in question isn't anything to brag about. Remember, you can avoid abuse and still act horribly enough to wreck a relationship. But, having said that, there is still a difference between behaviors that are obnoxious and those that are injurious.

I sometimes tell verbally abusive couples that they must separate for a time if it seems that they just can't stop assaulting each other. I strongly encourage verbally abusive couples, even if they need to separate, to keep working on their relationship and to continue with couple's therapy. These are not couples that necessarily need to break up; they just need a break.

I *insist* that verbally abusive couples separate if the fights occur regularly where children witness them. Children live in a magical, unbounded world. Research shows that, emotionally, even older children make little distinction between abuse that is observed and abuse aimed directly at them.

While instances requiring separation over the issue of verbal abuse are not rare, they are not typical. The vast majority of the couples I work with learn how to stand up to abusive behaviors and defeat them. These couples quickly master a very simple technique that is not at all hard to understand but does take some discipline to use. Once this technique is learned and practiced, it has the power to stop verbal abuse in its tracks.

TIME-OUTS: A VIOLENCE CIRCUIT BREAKER

RULE: THE BEST DEFENSE AGAINST VERBAL ABUSE IS A FORMAL TIME-OUT.

While you have probably heard of this technique and possibly even used it with your children, time-outs work equally well with "unruly" adults.

When either partner calls a time-out—by saying the word "time-out," by using the "T" hand signal, or by using any agreed-upon sign—*the interaction comes to an immediate stop.* The spoken or gestured signal is understood by both partners to be an abbreviation of the following words:

> "Dear partner, for whatever reason, right or wrong, I am about to lose it. If I stay here and keep this up with you I am liable to do or say something stupid that I know I'm going to regret. Therefore I am taking a break to get a grip on myself and calm down. I will check back in with you responsibly."

Notice that the time-out is always taken from an "I" position, never from a "you" position. It's a singularly bad idea to tell your partner that *he* is being a brat and that *he* needs a time-out. *You* take it. This is the main difference between time-outs and dead-stop contracts, in which you signal your partner to change his behavior to disrupt the interaction. Scrupulously couching your time-out as *your* issue has the distinct advantage that no one can argue with you about it. Telling your partner that he needs a break, by contrast, virtually guarantees an argument. The other advantage to a time-out is that cooperation from your partner is not necessary. Once the contract has been agreed to in advance, either partner has the right to leave the interaction whenever he or she chooses, and should not be stopped.

HOW MUCH TIME SHOULD YOU TAKE?

The default interval for a time-out is twenty minutes. You can specify something else if you like, but if no time is specified, twenty minutes is when you need to check in. Checking in does not necessarily mean getting back together. You can check in—either in person or by telephone—and tell your partner that you need more time. With each extension, the time-out interval gets longer. The recommended length between check-ins is:

- Twenty minutes
- One or two hours
- Half a day
- A whole day
- Overnight

Most people won't need that much time. But some will.

Alice and Stan

Alice and Stan both came from raging families, and one's fury almost always triggered the other's. They have had wild, screaming fights that sometimes lasted for days. About three sessions into their treatment, Stan describes a previous Saturday in which he and Alice had both "started up." But this time Stan did something different; he called a time-out. Stan went for a cup of coffee and called Alice after about twenty minutes. "Hi," he said. "Wanna stop fighting?" Alice responded to this offered olive branch with, as she herself describes it to me, "an icy blast from hell." "Okay, Alice," Stan had replied. "I'm gonna go to the coffee shop, read the paper. Whatever. I'll call in an hour." An hour later . . . same question, same response. Stan ran some errands. That afternoon was more of the same. Stan called a friend and went to a movie. The fight that had begun at about nine in the morning drew to a close around seven that night. "Alice, I'd really like to stop fighting," Stan told her, and this time, at last, he heard a big sigh on the other end of the line. "You really are an asshole," Alice had replied. "But it's not worth it, is it? Come on home, Stanley. It's *safe*. Psychowoman is restrained for the moment."

"I knew right away by her tone," Stan told me. "It really didn't matter what she said."

Alice grins. "I had him with 'You really are an asshole,' " she says, laughing.

Later on, both Alice and Stan marked the turning point of their relationship to that disciplined, lonely Saturday in which Stan traded several days of screaming at each other for one day spent alone. Stan also said that for the first time in his life, he'd found that he was able to resist the lure of *offending from the victim position*. Alice's verbally abusive behavior was *not* answered in kind. Stan's use of time-outs turned out to be a positive development for their relationship, but most important to him was his experience of finally gaining leverage over his own habitual response. Whether things worked out with Alice or not, for the first time ever, Stan was able to control his anger rather than having it control him.

RULE: WHEN RECONNECTING AFTER A TIME-OUT, YOU MUST TAKE A TWENTY-FOUR-HOUR MORATORIUM ON THE SUBJECT THAT TRIGGERED THE INITIAL FIGHT.

After the time-out is over, whether it's twenty minutes or an entire day, when you move back into contact with each other do not discuss the topic that started you off. If you do, you run a great risk of just getting wound up again. You can, and should, talk it over after twenty-four hours, but not before. If you find that either or both of you winds up calling for a time-out every time a particular subject is discussed, this should indicate to you that, for now at least, you and your partner are unable to navigate that particular topic on your own. Either let go of the issue altogether or get some help with it. While it may seem obvious, let me also say that the frequent need for a time-out whenever any serious issue is broached also indicates the need for help.

COMMIT TO A LIFE WITHOUT VIOLENCE

Time-outs represent a contract in which you both agree in advance that your commitment to end physical and/or psychological violence in your family is unflinching, and that someone's right to leave a potentially abusive confrontation is sacrosanct. As relationship grown-ups, you have come to appreciate that no problem will ever get solved until both parties put retaliation aside. Nothing other than immediate safety takes precedence over ending retaliation as a technique in your relationship. Whatever the topic at hand, if either or both of you becomes abusive, drop it. If there are kids, leave them, or, if you need to, take them with you. Go to another part of the house and close the door. If your partner dishonors your contract and refuses to leave you alone, get out of the house. And if your partner physically bars you from leaving, then call the police. I mean that. Very few people need to experience having the cops called more than once before they get the message that you're serious. Here's what you must understand: *Nothing short of a life-or-death emergency is more important than ending violent behavior between you.*

There is no excuse for abuse.

Period.

The extraordinary news is that, by using just this one instrument, time-outs, you can stop all abusive behaviors right now, today and from this day forward.

WHAT IF YOUR PARTNER JUST CAN'T CONTROL HIS ANGER?

If that's really true, then your partner should be locked up somewhere, because he's dangerous. But over decades of practice, I've almost never known that to be true, although it is often claimed and can indeed feel as though it were true. You or your mate may claim that your anger takes over so quickly and utterly, or that your partner's behavior has been so hurtful and wounding, that you just "can't stop yourself." It is important that you are clear on this point: What you or your partner is saying about this is simply not true. I tell men or women who use this line of reasoning, "There is, in fact, a very small group of people who truly cannot control themselves. By and large, they are in mental institutions or in jail." If a partner persists in the notion that his anger simply overpowers him, I say this: "Imagine that a state trooper stopped you for speeding on your way to the most important business meeting of your life. Your whole career, thousands and thousands of dollars, rests on this deal. Now this officer is a real SOB; he's deliberately rude and keeps you waiting forever just out of spite. Every muscle and nerve in your body is dying to tear into him. But do you think that you would? Of course not! The consequences would be too great. You know what we call that? Controlling your anger. Guess what? If you can do it *there*, you can do it *here*. Those very sick people who truly cannot control themselves can't control themselves *anywhere*. No one *selectively* loses control."

I will concede that there may be moments when, were you to stay and keep talking, you might not be able to stop yourself from getting nasty. But you *always* have the option of keeping your mouth shut, turning around, and leaving. If you or your partner is one of those rare people who truly does have a very hard time restraining anger, then get professional help. But, please, no matter what, make a commitment to do whatever it takes to *stop inflicting your anger on others*. When anger overtakes you, walk away. And there is equally no justification for the recipient of verbal abuse to just stand in the jet stream of someone's cruelty and tolerate it. It's not much better for your children to witness your lack of self-protection than it is for them to witness your partner's lack of fundamental respect. Ask yourself, "What kind of model am I presenting to my kids?" Both the aggressor and the recipient must learn to break the pattern and walk away. The bottom line is that you come to realize with unshakable conviction that there is no earthly reason you should tolerate cruelty anywhere in your life. There is no reason to dish it out and no reason to subject yourself to it. Ever.

Full-Respect Living

After years of working with clients who have arrived at my door with the widest range of human experience imaginable, I have come to believe that ordinary people can learn to practice *full-respect living*. In this new way of living, you don't have to deny or attempt to repress your varied, sometimes ugly, human feelings or shy away from conflict, or even intense anger at times. But you make a deep commitment that, no matter what, the line separating anger from disrespect—from contempt, control, retaliation, or punishing withdrawal—is never crossed again. And you are equally passionate about removing yourself and your children from harm's way. For years, I have helped couples move into what has been, for most, the radically new psychological landscape of nonviolent living. Do they achieve perfection? No. But over time and with hard work, for every single couple that commits to this path, the baseline shifts. Respectful behavior becomes the norm, while taking liberties comes to represent the rare exception. And the lives of those many couples that have learned to practice full-respect living have been utterly transformed.

My message to those couples was the same message I now have for you. You have the capacity to move your relationship to a level of safety and solidity, openness and tenderness, that leaves the norms of our current society in the dust. Cleaning up is just the first step toward getting there, but it is a necessary first step. You can do it. You can push back against the lure of retaliation, or the entitlement to take liberties. And you can demand respectful treatment in all your dealings with others, just as you give the same.

Time-outs are an everyday manifestation of that life-changing pledge. The tool of a time-out begins as a simple contract between you and your partner that acknowledges the priority of treating each other respectfully. As you learn to put that contract into action, a concrete practice grows, one that brings your commitment to full-respect living into the world.

At any given moment, whether your partner honors the contract or not, your commitment to end your participation in actions that are disrespectful to you or to anyone else places the power to stop emotional violence clearly and forcefully in your own hands—now, and for the rest of your life. *Use it.*

What Should I Do If My Partner Doesn't Want to "Clean Up"?

If your partner thinks he doesn't have a problem, or blames you or some other outside source for it, or, for whatever reason, refuses to handle any of the three clean-up issues responsibly, then you have to ask yourself some soul-searching questions. The three domains we're talking about— psychiatric conditions, self-medication, and acting out—are serious matters. Your response to any of these should be *realistically proportionate* to the severity of the problem. I don't want you to overreact to a moderate problem, or underreact to a significant one. Be honest with yourself about your usual style of reacting to difficult situations. Do you tend to be overdramatic or minimizing? Take that into account as you weigh this question: How disruptive to your relationship is your partner's behavior? It's one thing for you and your partner to disagree about how much television is good for the relationship; it's quite another if he feels entitled to scream at you on a regular basis in front of the kids. For psychiatric conditions, the devil is in the details. Can you live with a partner who's afraid of flying? Probably, if he has a cocktail or a sedative and still gets on the plane. Would you be happy with someone who insists that you both take only trains or ships, and never fly? Some people would be willing to do that, others wouldn't. Would you want to be with a partner with manic-depressive illness, who stubbornly refuses to take medication and who occasionally thinks that terrorists have taken over the airports? I wouldn't wish that on anyone I cared about.

The same principle holds true for issues of self-medication. If your partner's compulsive penchant for exercise means that you hardly ever see him, that is a real problem. And if the two of you can't work it out, perhaps consulting a marriage therapist once or twice wouldn't hurt. But this is obviously a different order of problem from a wife whose husband comes home, polishes off a few stiff cocktails and then wine with dinner only to "fall asleep"—which is a genteel way of saying that he passes out—every night. Your exercising absentee partner presents a different order of problem than this "functional" alcoholic husband, or a partner who can't stop gambling, get off the Internet, or keep his hands off other women. If you don't trust your own judgment, talk to a trusted friend, seek professional help, or find the appropriate self-help group in your community.

Chapter Four
Practice Section

Your Misery Stabilizers

Here is a list of common misery stabilizers. Feel free to add to the list if necessary:

Alcohol or other drugs	Including prescription drugs.
Workaholism	A sustained workweek of 60 hours or more, and/or your performance determining your sense of worth.
Love dependence	Using the warm regard of someone outside the relationship to supplement both your own low self-esteem and also the missing intimacy you crave. May lead to either sexual or emotional affairs.

Sex   Includes porn; Internet sex; one-night stands; paid sex; affair(s), both physical and emotional; and inappropriate flirting.

Food   Turning to food for psychological comfort or reward.

Gambling   Includes irresponsible, reckless investing.

Risk taking   And other unusually high-intensity activities or situations.

Spending   Overspending, compulsive shopping, or finding missing vitality in buying.

Television   A rampant form of self-medication, particularly among men. Soothing oneself with the passivity of watching. Vicarious enlivenment and company.

Computer   Similar to television. May be an aspect of someone's sex addiction.

Children   A particular example of love addiction. When your kids perform for you, parent you, or are your peers; when they supply you with the meaning, comfort, or company missing in your adult relationship(s).

Exercise   Wonderful in moderation but may be used as an escape, as a needed "endorphin high," or as an aspect of love and/or sex addiction.

Busyness   Never allowing yourself to be still long enough to feel much or make real contact with others.

Other

YOUR ASSIGNMENT

Make a list of your misery stabilizers (if you have any). Organize the list by order of severity:

- recreational (moderate)
- self-medicating (problematic)
- addictive (needs treatment)

Do the same for your partner.

Do speak frankly to your partner about your own use of misery stabilizers; however, do *not* speak at this time about your experience of his use.

Your Boundary Violations

Overview: There are two types of boundary violations, physical and psychological.

Physical boundary violations include touching another person in any way he or she doesn't want and doesn't consent to, or threatening to do so. Those threats can be explicit or nonverbal—slamming or throwing things, standing too close to someone, or getting into his face. Physical boundary violations also include getting into someone's personal space—going through the person's drawers or e-mail, or eavesdropping without the person's permission. A subcategory of the physical boundary is the *sexual boundary*. Anyone has the right to determine exactly when, where, how, and with whom he or she will be sexual. *Psychological boundary violations* always represent an assault on the integrity of someone's personhood; they are actions that fundamentally disrespect the other. The list includes:

1. Yelling and screaming
2. Name-calling
3. Shaming or humiliating
4. Telling an adult what he or she should do, think, or feel
5. Making contracts and then breaking them
6. Lying
7. Manipulating

YOUR ASSIGNMENT

Make a list of any physical or psychological boundary violations you have been guilty of.

On a scale of 1 to 5, with 1 being the least and 5 the most, assign a number to each of your actions that reflects its frequency and intensity. Ask yourself, "How big a presence is this behavior in my relationship?"

Do the same for your partner.

Note:

> *Do* speak frankly to your partner about your behavior; however, do *not* speak at this time about your experience of his.

EXPERIMENT WITH YOUR MISERY STABILIZERS

This is a three-step experiment.

Step One:

> After alerting your partner about your experiment, pick two of your most important misery stabilizers and do without them for ten days. If possible, abstain altogether. If it's impossible to do that—as is the case, for example, with food or work—for ten days cut back your use or involvement to a level that nine out of ten people would call healthy and moderate. You should imagine that your group of ten is on the conservative side, but not extreme.

Step Two:

> Take out your notebook and write no more than fifteen minutes each night for ten days about the effect of your cutting back. Write about how you feel about yourself, the impact of your cutting back on your relationship, and any impact that you observe on your family.

Step Three:

    See if you can find a health buddy, a friend who would be willing to support you in your relationship practice and talk things over with you. Write out questions you may have about the experiment, and discuss them with your buddy.

    You may resume use of your misery stabilizers if you wish at the end of this period.

EXPERIMENT WITH TIME-OUTS

This is a three-step experiment.

Step One:

    If he will listen, talk to your partner about the concept of boundary violations. Ask him to share his thoughts about your violating behaviors (not his!). Explain the idea of time-outs. Tell him that you are experimenting with a commitment to full-respect living, and invite him to contract with you for the use of time-outs. If he does not agree, tell him that, in the interest of not treating him disrespectfully, you are going to take time-outs for one week, whether he chooses to or not. Do your best to help him understand that you are trying to protect him from your immature behavior. If you are alone in this, practice taking time-outs for one week, *after* you've had time to recover fully from your experiment with misery stabilizers, above. If you are both onboard, let your kids know that you, the adults, will be trying out a new tool to help you get along. Unfortunately, while a child may ask for a time-out, the decision to grant one or not rests with the adult. But kids can ask if they want; they can also suggest a time-out for a parent!

Step Two:

    As with the first experiment, journal about your experience every day for no more than fifteen minutes. Do time-outs make things better or worse? Cool things down or heat things up as you opt out of your usual participation? What, if any, effect is this practice having on your partner and your kids? What discomfort does it bring up in you?

Step Three:

As in the first experiment, use your health buddy to support you and to talk things over with. Write out questions you may have about the experiment, and discuss them with your buddy.

You may *not* give yourself permission to engage in abusive behaviors after the experiment is over. However, you can resume your normal life and make it less of a central focus if you so choose.

WHAT WOULD IT FEEL LIKE?

This is a journaling exercise. First, sit or lie quietly in a private, peaceful room and take a few deep, relaxing breaths. Imagine that six months ago both you and your partner ingested a magic pill. The pill totally and permanently stops all boundary-violating behaviors, both physical and psychological.

Write: What, if any, changes have occurred in your relationship over the last six months?

Write: A letter to your partner expressing your thoughts and feelings about your six months together since taking the magic pill.

Chapter Five

Get Yourself Together

HEALTHY SELF-ESTEEM AND BOUNDARIES

Summary

Chapter four walked you through the task of *cleaning up,* the first of two challenges you must face in preparation for setting off on your journey toward a great relationship. Dealing with *untreated psychiatric conditions, issues of self-medication,* and *problems of acting out* clears the decks for transforming your life as a couple. You made a list of your *misery stabilizers,* along with what you see as your partner's, and you began to think about what changes, if any, you thought were needed.

The second task to complete in preparation for your journey toward intimacy focuses deeply and exclusively on the one and only part of your relationship over which you have any direct control: you. Before you can ask your partner to step into deep connection with you, you need to be a person with whom someone could connect. To become fully *intimacy ready*, you must have at least some mastery of two indispensable *self-skills*:

1. Good boundaries
2. Healthy self-esteem

Good Boundaries

Full-respect living means honoring the right of all human beings to be treated with the fundamental decency they deserve while at the same time affirming your own right to the same, your right to assert your wants and needs, and your right, if necessary, to remove yourself from harm's way. Some of the techniques you've been introduced to so far translate the principle of full-respect living into an everyday practice. Dead-stop contracts, time-outs, and, most directly, your commitment to nonviolent living (taking boundary-violating behaviors off the table) are all means by which your commitment to a new way of life can start to become a reality. All of these techniques are aspects of having good boundaries, which is not surprising. Because the development of healthy boundaries is virtually synonymous with living respectfully.

IS THERE MORE THAN ONE BOUNDARY?

Yes. In this, as in so much else, I follow recovery pioneer Pia Mellody, who distinguishes between one's *physical boundary* and one's *psychological boundary*. Having a physical boundary means that you respect others' physical and bodily space as well as insisting that they respect yours. Accordingly, you do not touch someone without his consent. You don't get physically closer than he wants you to. You don't engage in intrusive actions such as going through his drawers or his e-mail, or eavesdropping.

Your *sexual boundary* is one specific example of your physical boundary. Having a sexual boundary means that you understand that all people—including you—have the right to determine whether and how they will touch or be touched for the purposes of sexual arousal and release. In other words, you have the right to say no. In my early years as a couple's therapist, I naïvely assumed that any reasonably well-educated person would naturally have such an understanding, but I don't make that assumption any longer. I have been amazed at how many partners— more often men—feel that it is their right to be sexually serviced when they want to be. And how many women perform a mental calculation that tells them that it will be "less trouble" to "keep the man happy" than it would be to deal with the pouting or irritability that will follow if they don't? There is a place for asserting one's desire for *the two of you* to have a healthy and satisfying sex life as a couple, but that's different from demanding gratification. On the other side, there's a place for saying, "I'm not turned on this particular second but I know if we get started, I'll get into it." There's even a place for being generous sexually as well as in every other way. But there's a difference between all of these and feeling coerced. I tell the men I work with that the price they will pay in the long run for not respecting sexual boundaries is the drying up of their mate's real desire for them—not infrequently to the point of their being thoroughly disgusted or repulsed by the partners they no longer give in to.

RULE: FEW THINGS DIMINISH ONE PARTNER'S DESIRE FOR SEX MORE EFFECTIVELY THAN THE OTHER PARTNER'S DEMAND FOR IT.

Mackenzie

When I think of the toll that the absence of a sexual boundary exacts on a couple, I usually picture people in their mid-forties or beyond. But Mackenzie was a bright twenty-five-year-old graduate student just finishing an advanced degree in anthropology. On site in the Sahara, underneath the wide African sky, her steamy relationship with an older student sounded at first like the stuff of romance, until it grew clear that the steam traveled in only one direction. Back in the States for the summer, Mackenzie found herself so troubled and confused about the relationship that her parents suggested she consult with me.

During the course of our one conversation, Mackenzie allows that she isn't "really all that attracted to Logan anymore"—in fact, to be honest, she feels pretty disgusted, which seems like a shame to her because they're perfect together in so many other ways. She admits, with some embarrassment, to wondering if she might just be "frigid."

It doesn't take long before Mackenzie reveals that she'd always "felt not all that great" about "the sex part" of their relationship. "It seemed pretty much to be all about him," she admits. I imagine that "all about him" refers to the common female complaint about a male partner not taking much time, not caring nearly as much as he might about giving her pleasure. I did not imagine that it referred to her lover's insistence on sex several times a day, every day, and most often in public or near-public settings that could easily have led to their embarrassment or even to potential harm to their careers given that they were on a job site. "Logan gets off on danger, I guess," Mackenzie observes.

"And you?" I ask. At first, she says, she was willing to go along; in fact, she liked experimenting with the feeling of sexual surrender. But "the game got tired fast," she admits, "especially when it started feeling like it wasn't a game to him."

What troubled Mackenzie was that she had never voiced an objection. Furthermore, when she finally did speak up just before coming home, Logan was more than willing to honor her wishes. But somehow, even though Logan "was being great about it," she found herself "turned off" to him. In short order, it seemed clear to me that Mackenzie really just wanted someone's permission to break it off, which is just what I gave her.

At twenty-six, with no kids and her whole life ahead of her, Mackenzie's willingness to "just go along," and the dampening of desire that followed, seemed more like a learning experience than a tragedy. But she was lucky to learn this lesson early on. For women who find themselves utterly turned off to the husbands that they've spent decades with, the fathers of their children, the consequences of "just going along" are less easily dismissed.

The issue of sexuality brings into clear focus a more general principle.

RULE: WHEN WOMEN TRY TO USE TWENTIETH-CENTURY ACQUIESCENCE IN TODAY'S RELATIONSHIPS, THE FIRST CASUALTY IS MOST OFTEN PASSION.

As with sex, so too with the four other domains of sharing: intellectual, emotional, physical, and spiritual. *If you don't stand up for your needs, you begin shutting them down, often feeling like a resentful victim.* The most reliable long-term sexual stimulant is the ability to be truthful.

What Is Your Psychological Boundary?

Your *psychological boundary* is to your psyche what your skin is to your body. It's where you end and the world begins. And just like your skin, it has two functions: it *contains* you and it *protects* you. Imagine your psychic "skin" as being like an orange rind. Like the covering of an orange, your psychological boundary has an inside and an outside: The outside, protective part of the boundary shields you from the world; the inside, containing part shields the world from you.

Containment means your capacity for restraint. The containing part of your psychological boundary (the inside of the rind) stops you from leaking your "stuff" out onto those around you—your rage, your anxiety, your sexuality, your certainties about right and wrong. It stops you from acting out your inappropriate impulses. I said earlier that techniques like dead-stop contracts and time-outs were aspects of practicing good boundaries. To be more precise, these techniques strengthen the *containing part* of your psychological boundary. Clamping your mouth shut, taking a time-out, or walking away from a fight are excellent examples of how to build strong containing muscles. Generally, the more un-contained the environment you grew up in, the weaker those muscles will be and the harder you'll need to practice.

> RULE: FULLY DEVELOPING THE CONTAINING PART OF YOUR
> PSYCHOLOGICAL BOUNDARY IS A NECESSARY PREREQUISITE
> FOR CLOSENESS, BECAUSE WITHOUT IT YOU WILL BEHAVE
> INAPPROPRIATELY, OR EVEN OFFENSIVELY.

Someone who needs work on the containing part of the psychological boundary will be vulnerable to indulging in the boundary-violating behaviors we discussed earlier. People with a weak containing part of their psychological boundary will be intrusive. They are prone to the losing strategies of control, unbridled self-expression, and retaliation. When you commit to the practice of full-respect living, you stop making excuses for uncontained behaviors—either yours or anyone else's.

WHAT IS THE PROTECTIVE PART OF YOUR PSYCHOLOGICAL BOUNDARY?

The *protective part* of your psychological boundary (the outside of the rind) protects you from others' intrusion just as containment protects them from yours.

> RULE: FULLY DEVELOPING THE PROTECTIVE PART OF YOUR
> PSYCHOLOGICAL BOUNDARY IS A NECESSARY PREREQUISITE
> FOR CLOSENESS, BECAUSE IT ALLOWS YOU TO BE
> *CONNECTED* AND *PROTECTED* AT THE SAME TIME.

People for whom the protective part of the internal boundary (the outside of the rind) is weak or nonexistent are prey to any idea or emotion that someone they're close to throws at them.

Sheryl: "Do I Look Fat?"

"I'm just *so reactive*," twenty-year-old Sheryl tells me, arranging her long, thin frame on the couch, legs tucked under, bushy black hair pulled back in an unruly ponytail. "Okay, look," she confides, "Chris says to me, 'Hey, ya know, baby, you might wanna think about gettin' to the gym, ya know? Don't wanna get *squishy* on me, do ya baby?' " She looks up at me. "Do I look fat?" she asks, sincerely.

"Sheryl, you're a *runner*," I remind her. "You look like a trim runner."

"See, but what that son of a bitch *did* was . . ." She starts to cry. "He *knew* this would get to me. You tell me, why in the *world* would I . . . ?" Tears choke her words. "Do you know what I did?" she goes on. "I went to Weight Watchers. Okay? So, how sick am I? I went to freakin' Weight Watchers! You know what they did? They *threw me out*! They told me that, first of all, losing more weight wouldn't be good for my health—I mean, I'm sure they just *assumed* that I was some psycho anorexic, which I sort of *am* in a way, I guess. And then—here's the killer—they tell me they would in *no way* put me into one of their groups because it would only *discourage* the people who really needed it. Can you *believe* this? So now I'm a *health hazard*? I'm a freakin' Weight Watchers *reject*? How big a loser is *that*?"

Despite my best efforts, I laugh, and then she laughs, and then neither of us seems able to stop. "Cool." She sneers between gulps of air. "This is *so* cool. Even my *therapist* thinks I'm a clown."

"Listen, Sheryl," I tell her, "you're not *pathetic*; you're just desperate . . ."

"That feels *so much* better," she cracks.

"No, listen, will you? You're desperate for a functioning boundary," I tell her.

"Desperate for a functioning *boyfriend* is what I'd say," she whines.

And then we get to work.

———

Sheryl was like a room with a wide-open gap where a door should have been. Anyone could saunter into her psyche and do pretty much what they liked. "Fat? Sure, okay. If you say so." And she wasn't vulnerable to just her boyfriend Chris. If one of her roommates got sad, she got distressed. Anxious? She grew fearful. She was altogether too porous. When people speak of being "thin-skinned," or "too sensitive," they probably mean that they lack a protective psychological boundary. When someone feels wounded that "you could even think that of me," he is in boundary failure.

HOW DOES THE PROTECTIVE PART OF YOUR PSYCHOLOGICAL BOUNDARY WORK?

Using the protective part of your psychological boundary simply means that, as you listen to the material being presented to you, you ask yourself whether or not it seems true. Say, for example, that your partner complains of your treating him, upon occasion, with coldness. You listen; perhaps you ask for clarification or for some examples. And then you ask yourself, "Does this seem true to me?" The important phrase in that sentence is "to *me*." You're the judge. Remember, there is no place for "objective reality" in personal relationships, so you have to decide as best you can. If what you're hearing seems true, or if some portion of it seems true, you let *that* in, and only then do you have feelings about it. But if what you're hearing honestly strikes you as untrue, or part of it seems untrue, you keep *that* out. Imagine the person's assertions about you going *splat* on your psychic windshield like an egg sliding down a plate of glass. You say to yourself, "That's about him; it's not about me."

Your partner's inaccurate images of you are just his projections, the products of his imagination. You needn't get wound up about them. And you needn't become high and mighty either, because you have the good sense and humility to appreciate that getting things wrong, imagining all sorts of nonsense, is just what we humans do in close quarters. You don't get bent out of shape or injured-feeling, because you know full well that you're perfectly capable of making up an equally unjustified bunch of absurdities about him in the next ten seconds.

WHAT DOES CULTIVATING SUCH PROTECTION DO FOR YOUR RELATIONSHIP?

When you don't have a protective psychological boundary, your environment—whomever you're with—will determine your psychic "temperature." Positive people will cheer you; sad people will bring you down. If someone's angry, you'll either get angry back or crumble. In all of these cases, you have little capacity to stay rooted in your own reality in the face of someone else's.

In his film *Zelig*, Woody Allen plays a character suffering from the ultimate case of poor boundaries. The protagonist literally, physically, morphs into a version of whomever he's talking to. Within seconds he becomes obese, then a cowgirl, next an African American. At one point he becomes Woodrow Wilson.

When you have a poor protective psychological boundary, you are in a constant state of emotional vulnerability. If you are fighting with your partner, for example, and he says something negative about you, you will immediately and invariably start feeling bad—not just about him, but about yourself as well—even if what he's saying is totally untrue. You lack the means to keep his negativity at bay. Without a protective psychological boundary, the only way you can make yourself comfortable is by *stopping the upsetting stimulus.* In order for you to feel right again, you have to either "get him to stop saying that" or else leave, removing yourself from the disquieting material. *Your only options are the two losing strategies of control or withdrawal.* By providing protection, your psychological boundary allows you to stay *engaged* with what's being said, without the need to stop it or run from it.

Having a healthy protective psychological boundary allows you to self-regulate. You remain appropriately constant whether the environment around you is hot or cold. And this newly developed capacity to self-regulate, independent of changes in your environment, releases you from endless, seemingly uncontrollable reactivity. You don't need to feel hurt; you don't need to fight back; you don't need to "get" your partner to see things differently; you don't need to be defensive; you don't need to run away. In fact, you no longer *need* to do anything. Protected by your internal boundary, you have the miraculous new freedom to simply stand still and be present, or said differently, to utterly transform your relationship.

WHAT ABOUT PEOPLE WHO ARE TOO BOUNDARIED?

So far we've been focusing on individuals with a poor or even with a nonexistent psychological boundary. But what about the other side of the equation, those who suffer the consequences of being overly protected? These are people who live their lives behind *walls*.

A healthy psychological boundary is supple. You stay actively engaged with the speaker and what that person is telling you, while at the same time letting in only those things that seem true. When you're behind a wall, you take in nothing. You are not engaged with the speaker; in fact, no matter what you may look like from the outside, you're not actually listening at all. You are shut up in a closed fortress that no one can breach.

When you are boundaryless, you are connected but not protected.

When you are behind a wall, you are protected but not connected.

Neither condition is intimate.

The number of things we can use as walls is simply astounding: walls of silence, walls of words, walls of anger, intoxication, preoccupation, charm, humor, condescension, helpless fatigue. I've even spoken to guys about hiding behind walls of TV clickers!

The one and only circumstance in which using a wall is appropriate is when you're on the receiving end of someone's abuse and you can't, or choose not to, remove yourself. You're stuck in a full airplane and your partner's being a jerk to you. Or you're in a car with him ten minutes away from the dinner party you're both attending and he's directing his anger at you. Then, and only then, you can choose to use a wall in order to protect yourself. And even then, you must soften your wall back into becoming a pliant boundary the minute the abuse stops. In what other circumstance is it healthy to operate behind a wall? None.

Emma and Jake

Emma and Jake, now in their mid-sixties, have been coming to my lectures and seminars for years. They jokingly refer to themselves as relationship empowerment groupies. They hardly look the type. For almost thirty years, Jake was the police captain for a small but tough little town up on Boston's north shore. With his completely shaved head, handlebar mustache, linebacker body, and South Boston accent, Jake never fails to delight when he speaks. "It takes a man with *balls* to be sensitive" is one of his many mottos. Jake's moment of truth came a dozen years or so earlier. Here's how Emma describes it in a recent workshop they attended:

"So, I came home late one afternoon, early evening. I teach high school freshman English, which in itself is an oxymoron to begin with. Freshmen don't speak English. Anyway, back then Jake didn't either. Most of the time, anyway. You know, it was the usual, 'Hello. How are you? How was your day?' And there Jake would be trying to unwind, which I understand, reading the paper or watching the news or a game. And I'm getting responses like 'Umm-hmm,' 'Oh, yeah, honey. That's nice.' And so I start slipping in little things to annoy him, like 'Yeah, and then I told that cute gardener down the street to stop by.' But I might as well have been talking to a plant. I just couldn't take it after a while. Even when we'd be off by ourselves, on vacation or what have you, it wouldn't be much different. There'd always be something, TV or a book or something. He'd go out fishing with his buddies. *That* would be fine. But trying to make plans with *me*, trying to talk about our kids, our values, it'd be, 'Everything's fine, Emma. The kids are fine. Lighten up.'

"So one evening I come home and I've had a really bad day, depressing; it's depressing some days, what these kids live with. And I say to him, 'You know, Jake, you're not the only one here with a tough job. I appreciate your need to get away from it all. But I have needs too. I support you when you need it.' And so, this is what he does, this is what Jake always did when I would complain about him. He takes his paper and gives me this look, and then he goes into the bathroom, because he knows I won't disturb him there. The throne room. And I don't. Jake told me his first wife used to knock down the door on him, which, I must say, I now have come to appreciate. But I don't do anything wild like that. What I do is, I slip this little piece of paper under the door. I used his police report form," Emma grins, " 'cause I knew that would get him. Misusing department supplies. And what I said on this paper was:

"To My Dear Beloved Jake. You can:

–Talk to me about what we need to do to start having a real relationship

–Pack your f—ing bag and get the f— out!

Please let me know your decision by 3 p.m. so that I can make suitable arrangements."

Emma stops speaking, as if this were the end of her story.

"So, he chose to stay?" one of the participants asks.

"Nope." Emma smiles and shakes her head. "No, he packs up a bag and storms out. Right?" She nods at Jake for confirmation. "He stayed away for three days," Emma says, leaning forward, as if to confide. "He was *testing my mettle*," she almost whispers. "And we had two little children at the time, mind you. But I didn't call him that whole time. I cried and cried, I remember. But I just *knew* not to pick up that phone. And then he came back."

"I was just at Emma's brother's place, two blocks away," Jake interjects. "It was ridiculous. I might as well have been in a pup tent out back in the yard."

"Anyway," Emma goes on, "he puts down his bag and he says, 'Okay, Emma. So what do you want me to do?' "

"What did you say?" someone asks.

"What *could* I say?" Emma answers. "What would *you* say? I told him I loved him and that it was like the sun coming out after years of clouds, didn't I say that?" she asks Jake, who nods. "Just like the sun. And then we started doing things like this workshop. I honestly don't remember how I even found things like this back then. But somehow I did."

"And I'm a better man for it." Jake looks proudly at Emma. "Although," he adds, "I was already into this stuff from work. People skills kinda thing. Working with inner-city youth and so forth. I just needed to bring some of it back home with me, that's all. I learned to leave work at work, but bring my work skills back home."

"Hey, that's a great line," I comment. " 'Leave work at work but bring your work skills back home.' That's good, Jake."

"Hey, you like it? It's yours," Jake tells me. "Don't even bother giving me credit. I don't care. I don't make speeches anymore. I'm *retired*."

LEAVE WORK AT WORK BUT BRING YOUR WORK SKILLS BACK HOME

Those skills at home of which Jake was justifiably proud all started off when he agreed to put down, or turn off, the things he'd placed between himself and Emma. He didn't hide behind walls at work. He would never just ignore another cop, or a citizen, or even a common criminal, the way he routinely ignored his own wife. And, being a fair man and an honest one, Jake admitted as much once Emma "brought it to his attention."

HOW CAN YOU TEAR DOWN SOMEONE'S WALLS?

You can't. And you're better off not attempting to. Furthermore, I don't recommend your trying to tear down your own walls any more than your partner's. Walls are just the flip side of boudarylessness. Neither state leads to health or to intimacy. Many people, including some therapists, don't understand that the "cure" for being walled off is not simply "opening up."

RULE: THE CURE FOR BEING WALLED OFF IS DEVELOPING THE PROTECTION OF A FUNCTIONING BOUNDARY.

I want you to respect walls. They're there for a reason. *Partners who live behind walls are just boundaryless people who've learned to protect themselves crudely.* Take down their walls and you get unshielded boundarylessness—which is precisely why they won't let you do it. People who live behind walls don't need talk of more openness; they need reassurance that they will still be able to protect themselves as they get healthy, but in more nuanced ways.

RULE: BOTH BOUNDARYLESSNESS AND WALLS BLOCK REAL CONNECTION. AND THE SOLUTION TO BOTH OF THESE SEEMINGLY OPPOSITE CONDITIONS IS THE SAME: CULTIVATING THE SUPPLE PROTECTION OF A FUNCTIONING BOUNDARY.

Healthy Self-Esteem

We hear all the time that "you can't love someone else unless you love yourself." But we rarely stop to think about why that is, or even what those words really mean. The psychological term for the ability to love oneself is *self-esteem*. There are a lot of misconceptions about this influential concept, even among professionals. So let's begin with a clear definition:

> Self-esteem is your capacity to recognize your worth and value, despite your human flaws and weaknesses. Your value as a person isn't earned; it isn't conditional; it can't be added to or subtracted from. Your essential worth is neither greater nor lesser than that of any other human being. It can't be. Self-esteem is about being, not doing. You have worth simply because you're alive.

Self-esteem comes from the inside out. Thinking otherwise is a delusion. We understand this fundamental ethic in theory. It is the central

principle of democracy itself: "All men are created equal." We understand the essential equality of all human beings in times of crisis. Medical
triage, for example, is based on a patient's need, never on his or her status.
Privileging one patient over another would constitute a serious breach in
medical ethics. And yet, despite its being central to our morality and the
very bedrock of our form of government, somehow most of us manage to
all but obliterate the vital truth of essential equality when we think about
ourselves.

Instead of a spiritual clarity assuring us that no one is fundamentally
better or worse than anyone else, our lives are ruled—day by day, hour
by hour, even minute by minute—by the confusion of believing that we
must justify our existence, that we must earn our worth every day, and,
even worse, that our value or its lack will be coolly judged against a back-
drop of unending competition. Today you may be superior to your neighbor, but by tomorrow you may find yourself outdone.

We have been hoodwinked into thinking that a larger house, a
trophy wife, or anything that provokes the envy of others actually makes
us more important as people. This is the American Dream. Not only
will our *lives* be transformed through material success, but our very *selves*
will be transfigured. The "good life" will do more than make us happy:
It will give us the meaning and inner substance we lack.

To say that modern culture pushes us away from the wisdom of
healthy self-esteem is a wild understatement. It is more accurate to say
that our culture *runs* on unhealthy self-esteem. The feeling of inade-
quacy, and the dream of its cure through acquisition, is the fuel that
drives our economy. We are constantly barraged with the message that
simply as ourselves, we are not enough. We're too fat; we're too dumb;
our sex lives could be better; our dishes could shine more; and, to be
frank, we could smell a lot fresher. But, ah, if we would just take this
cruise, buy that blouse, eat at the newest restaurant, we might become
one of *them*, the blessed ones, the ones who are content with themselves.

Instead of the inner strength that arises naturally from healthy self-
regard, our society feeds on three types of unhealthy self-regard:

- Performance-based esteem
- Other-based esteem
- Attribute-based esteem

PERFORMANCE-BASED ESTEEM

Performance-based esteem is a favorite among men. Its message is "I have worth because of what I can *do*." I can hit a home run, close a tough deal, earn a fat paycheck, make my partner happy. The great problem with performance-based esteem—as any honest man will admit—is that you're only as good as your last game. You can never rest. No one cares very much about how you did a few years ago. The question is, "What have you done for us lately?" And there's always someone younger, smarter, or stronger warming up, eager to eat your lunch.

For some people, *everything* becomes a performance. Their self-worth is always on the line. How well they cook breakfast, how well they drive, and, of course, their prowess in the sack determine their sense of value. These days, some men have learned to be less performance-based and consequently more relaxed. And there is a growing number of women who have recently empowered themselves to be just as performance-based and just as defensive as men. If you are a true, dyed-in-the-wool performance-based person, you are no doubt quite touchy, experiencing the criticism of virtually anything you say or do as a threat. Performance-based individuals live in a fraught and not very pleasurable world in which the focus is always on the struggle of getting, rarely on the enjoyment of having.

OTHER-BASED ESTEEM

Other-based esteem has been favored among women. It is the belief that "I have worth because you think I do." The "you" in that sentence could be family, friends, or colleagues, but, of course, it most often means "you, the man I care about." Pushed to an extreme, other-based esteem becomes *love dependency*, in which someone's lack of the ability to cherish herself is supplemented by her partner's warm regard for her. His esteem of her becomes a drug on which she is dependent in order to feel good about herself. The vulnerability inherent in basing your sense of value on another person's opinion is obvious. The lengths that people will go to in order to hold on to someone's regard can be truly sad, even frightening.

Chris and Samantha

To Samantha, a research technician who hailed from a hardscrabble working-class background, Chris, the biologist who managed the lab she worked in, seemed a thing of splendor. Good-looking, well educated, intelligent, Chris appeared to her from the start "to be out of my league." And she was amazed at her good fortune. At first, she didn't mind that Chris wanted to keep their relationship "under wraps," given their status at work. She didn't mind that, in short order, their routine consisted of Chris coming over now and again, drinking heavily, and herding her into the bedroom. It took a few months before Sam figured out that Chris was married, which he at first denied. Even then she somehow managed not to think about Chris's wife or children. But she did think about having him all to herself. She knew the way to capture him was through sex, and she began pushing herself farther into extreme behavior hoping that he'd find it impossible to let go of her. She surprised him at work with sexual favors; she began calling his cell phone and leaving provocative messages even when he was at home with his family. Sam found herself lying about contraception in the hopes of getting pregnant and then lying about being pregnant, only to then have to lie about getting an abortion. Within six months of meeting Chris, Sam had become someone she could no longer recognize.

Soon after their inevitable breakup, after Chris had changed his phone number, arranged for her to be transferred to another lab, and refused to ever see or talk to her again, Sam found herself one night with a half-empty bottle of vodka in one hand and a full bottle of tranquilizers in the other. That was her moment of "bottoming out." Instead of doing herself in, she called a friend who knew all about her tough childhood and who, luckily, knew a few things about love dependency herself. Her friend got her to A.A., and to a therapist who really helped. Samantha did the trauma work necessary to begin ridding herself of the burdensome shame she'd absorbed from her parents' poor treatment of her. She began learning the practice of cherishing herself, instead of depending on someone she idealized to do it for her. Her first attempts to feel abundant inside rather than empty seemed ludicrously ineffective to her. But over time Samantha got stronger. And then, brick by brick, she built herself into a relational adult able to share herself with another.

I saw Samantha from time to time in workshops over the course of a few years. Sometimes she looked great, other times not so well. But then her healing work seemed to gain traction. You could hear the hard-won maturity in the way that she spoke. You could even feel in her the beginnings of joy. About two years after our first meeting, Samantha appeared at a workshop trailing a charming young man she identified as her fiancé. A few months after that, I heard from her therapist that Sam's husband had been promoted at work and transferred to the West Coast. Sam was pregnant, the therapist told me, and by all accounts, she seemed radiant. I remember congratulating her dedicated therapist and thinking how different Sam's life might have been without their work together, comparing how she was when I'd first met her and how she seemed now. When you deal closely with issues of abuse, trauma, and addiction, you come to terms with the fact that sometimes we lose. But then again, I remember thinking as I pictured Samantha, more often we don't.

ATTRIBUTE-BASED ESTEEM

While performance-based and other-based esteem seem to be favored by one sex or the other, *attribute-based esteem* is used equally by both. Its message is "I have worth because of what I *have*"—a big car, big muscles, a rich husband, a child at an Ivy League school. Everywhere we turn, the accoutrements of class and status promise that owning the right things, having the correct social standing, will render us "people of distinction."

But no matter how exclusive the club you belong to, the person you bring to it will still be you. Learning to whack that golf ball around may make you a better golfer, but it can never make you a better person. Neither that generous gift to charity nor that awful crime committed against your neighbor affects your fundamental worth as a human being, not for good and not for ill. Behaving generously is laudable and behaving criminally is reprehensible; we can even call one person *morally* superior to the other; but neither is *essentially* superior. Understanding this brings a great sense of internal stability, one might even say peace. Not that you check your brain at the door. Of course, you feel great when things go well and poorly when they don't. But there is a firewall between such ups and downs—your *unchanging birthright to remain a dignified human being*.

GRANDIOSITY: THE OTHER SELF-ESTEEM DISORDER

In the latter half of the twentieth century, the pursuit of personal happiness became such an intense cultural focus that it rose to the status of a collective obsession. The drugs and insurrection of the 1960s gave way to the human potential movement, to spirituality, stock options, and personal trainers. Psychotherapy of all types, support groups, and the exploding self-help industry all held out the same promise—that we could feel better about ourselves. This thunderous stampede toward feeling good effectively drowned out the voice of a small question: "What's so terrible about feeling bad now and again?" Our collective drive to feel good about ourselves over the last several decades has obscured the fact that you could just as accurately define healthy self-esteem as feeling proportionately bad about the bad things you have done.

RULE: HEALTHY SELF-ESTEEM REQUIRES AN APPROPRIATE AMOUNT OF SHAME.

Too much shame pulls you into a "one-down" position, engendering feelings of inferiority. But too little shame pulls you into a "one-up" position, engendering feelings of superiority. Both states are unhealthy, and *both* need correction before effective work on your relationship can take hold.

You cannot love someone from either the one-up or the one-down position.

For fifty years, psychotherapy has given an enormous amount of attention to the task of helping people come *up* from the one-down state of too much shame, but comparatively little attention has been paid to helping people come *down* from the one-up state of too little shame. The psychological term for the feeling of shameless superiority is *grandiosity*. Understanding and learning to work with issues of grandiosity—in yourself and in your partner—is one of the least-recognized and most potent skills needed for creating and sustaining great relationships. Why? Because, while an overabundance of shame may hurt you, the shameless behavior of grandiosity can do great harm to the people around you.

WHAT IS GRANDIOSITY?

To be grandiose is to feel superior, one-up, godlike, to see oneself as worth more than another person or group of people. You are being grandiose whenever you look down your nose at the man down the street, the woman who goes to another church, the poor people across town— whenever you say to yourself, "I'm not *that* kind of person." Grandiosity means regarding someone judgmentally, not for what he may have done but for "who he is." It whispers phrases to us like "He's a loser," "She's disgusting," or "I have lost all respect for him," to say nothing of less-savory phrases like "That asshole (bitch, moron)," or even racial or ethnic slurs.

Grandiosity can also pull you into a one-up position by making you feel that you're special, the best, above the rules. You're entitled to park in no-parking zones, fix traffic tickets, retaliate when angry, manipulate when you feel like it. Grandiosity may even lead you to consider yourself above the law.

In its most extreme form, grandiosity moves beyond sanity itself and produces delusions of grandeur. You are the messiah; you can fly. You are not only above the rule of man, but the bonds of nature itself.

Frank: Paranoids Rarely Get Lonely

Frank is a twenty-three-year-old grad student in one of Boston's high-prestige colleges. He has struggled with and been medicated for manic-depressive illness since adolescence. About two weeks before I first met him, he decided to declare a self-prescribed "med holiday." He now views this choice as having been a singularly bad idea. Restabilized by medication, Frank tells me, almost nostalgically, about his recent manic high.

"I was obsessed with Susan Sarandon, the actress. I rented all her movies. I saw her as the embodiment of The Life Force," he intones, half making fun of himself, half not so sure. "In her lines, there were embedded messages meant just for me. Other people wouldn't get it, but she knew and I knew." He falters for a moment. "I have to tell you, even now . . ." He shakes his head, trying to get clear.

"It was all such high drama," he muses. "People out to get me. Some mission from The Life Force. Like a thriller. Everything I did was so important, all those people watching my every move. I guess paranoids rarely get lonely. Who would have thought I rated so much attention?"

It isn't just the most extreme cases of grandiosity, like Frank's, that cry out to be helped. If we want to move into true and abiding intimacy, we must deal with *both* self-esteem issues, going one-down *and* one-up. Because every single one of us does both. If you tried to tell me that you never think or behave grandiosely, then I would *know* that you're grandiose. It's part of our human nature. I'm on a mission to take grandiosity out of the closet. In fact, I am the founder and lifetime president of the NLF—the Narcissist's Liberation Front, an organization unique in that *every* member is the founder and lifetime president.

WHAT DO YOU NEED TO KNOW ABOUT GRANDIOSITY?

While toxic shame and grandiosity are both self-esteem disorders, there are two key differences that you should appreciate:

> **Grandiosity feels good.**
> **Grandiosity impairs judgment.**

RULE: IN YOUR ATTEMPTS TO DEAL IN A HEALTHY WAY WITH A
    GRANDIOSE PARTNER, AND IN YOUR ATTEMPTS TO DEAL IN
    A HEALTHY WAY WITH YOUR OWN GRANDIOSITY, *VIRTUALLY
    ALL OF THE TECHNIQUES THAT HELP WITH SHAME ARE
    COMPLETELY INEFFECTIVE.*

GRANDIOSITY FEELS GOOD

When you are in the one-down state of *toxic shame*, you know it; you feel bad about it, and you want help. Because you're in pain, you're motivated to get out of it. But when you're in the one-up state of grandiosity—when you feel that you have the right to be indignant, or manipulative, or entitled, or unkind—half the time you're barely aware of what you're doing: You are not in a great deal of distress, and you're not, to be honest, all that motivated to change. In fact, not only does grandiosity not feel all that bad, it often feels pretty darn good. It feels *good* to let go of constraint when you're angry and blow up at someone. It feels *good* to say to your partner, "Take this stupid relationship and shove it!" It feels *good* to throw caution and loyalty to the winds and surrender to sexual seduction.

Grandiosity is intoxicating.

No matter whether it's the thrill of sexual conquest, the euphoria of drink or drugs, the dominance of rage, or the indulgence of entitlement, release from real life's constraints, being *above*, feels wonderful—at least for the moment.

A part of you might be thinking at this point, "Well, if it feels so great, what's so terrible about it?" Nothing, as far as the grandiose person is concerned—which, of course, is part of the problem.

Psychiatrist George Valliant once claimed that there were two types of people in the world: the kind of guy who walks into an elevator, gets claustrophobic, and turns green, and the kind of guy who walks into an elevator, lights up a big fat stogie, and everyone else turns green. That's the difference between shame and grandiosity. The first man in the story is too inhibited; the second isn't inhibited enough. And this brings us back to boundaries. Remember the containing part of your psychological boundary? The emotion fueling that part of your boundary is *healthy shame*. A healthy person couldn't easily bring himself to light up a cigar in an elevator because he'd simply be too mortified. But grandiosity erodes the containing function of our psychological boundary. In the words of psychiatry, it disinhibits us. *Grandiosity makes you oblivious.*

It is the impaired judgment in grandiosity that is most detrimental to intimacy, because *grandiosity always involves a blunted sensitivity to the effects of your behavior on others, to your action's potential negative consequences.* This is why traditional, nurturing therapy is largely irrelevant to people struggling with grandiosity. The deficiency is not empathy toward yourself, but, as in the case of the man in the elevator, empathy toward others. Relational sensitivity and good judgment are the missing ingredients the grandiose person needs to develop.

RULE: SHAME-FILLED PEOPLE HAVE PAIN. GRANDIOSE PEOPLE HAVE TROUBLES. THE CONFLICT IS NOT INSIDE THEM, BUT BETWEEN THEM AND THEIR ENVIRONMENT. THEY'RE NOT IN PAIN; THE PEOPLE AROUND THEM ARE IN PAIN.

Partners who ride in the one-up position rarely elect to enter therapy; by and large, they're brought. I hear from them when the "ouch" between them and someone else has grown big enough to overcome their resistance, when the unthought-of consequences of their actions come home to roost and the relational bill comes due.

Nick and Alexis: For a Few Lousy Seconds

Poor Nick. From the minute he slunk into my office, shoulders bowed, head down, I knew he was a mess. Disheveled, overweight, with a baby face under thinning hair, Nick had never stopped being his mom's little boy, even though his mother was many years gone. Nick's wife, Alexis, was tall and athletic. With ramrod-straight bearing and long hair so blond it almost gleamed white, her presence was arresting, even commanding. She seemed to me, in the opening seconds of our very first meeting, utterly out of her mind.

Words flew out of Alexis as quickly and as disjointedly as her restless, abrupt movements. She literally could not sit still, jumping out of her chair at odd moments during the session, pacing, and stringing sentences together so rapidly I found myself straining to follow. And yet my first impression of her was wrong. It turned out that Alexis was not at all crazy; she was in an acute state of shock. Her words, hurled at me, at the world, with such ferocity, told a coherent, and very sad, story. As that story emerged, I found myself riveted by Nick's expression—this man who Alexis described as a great provider, an involved father, the friend of the whole community, whose world was coming to pieces around him.

"I screwed up," Nick tells me later on in the session. "There's nothing, really, nothing more I can say. I accept it, totally. I just screwed up."

What Nick did was this: Once a year for the previous ten years, Nick and a bunch of his pals went to Las Vegas to, as he put it, "really cut loose." These were all "very good boys" for the other 360-odd days of the year, upstanding family men. Like the other wives, Alexis had figured that "cutting loose" meant heavy drinking, heavy betting, and, if she really let her imagination run wild, maybe a joint or two, maybe even a strip club. What she hadn't envisioned was prostitutes, or "escorts," as Nick preferred to call them.

The ancient Romans had Saturnalia. For one week out of the year, all bonds of propriety were released and everyone—man and woman—indulged in wild sexual orgies, returning, at the end of the holiday, to the restraint of their civilized roles. I know a number of guys who'd be thrilled with that arrangement. Nick and his pals created their own modern-day version of Saturnalia, giving themselves annual permission to relax the containment of self-control and hurl themselves headlong into sexual pleasure.

Some men would have taken their thrilling, guilty secret to the grave, but baby-faced Nick wasn't so lucky. On his last self-decreed vacation from monogamy, Nick brought back with him a virus so new he'd never heard of it. HPV doesn't kill like HIV can, but it is, nevertheless, dangerous and pernicious. It can even be transmitted through a condom. There are usually no symptoms in men, who aren't aware that they are carriers. Once it's passed on to a woman, however, the virus carries a significant risk of cervical cancer if left untreated. Alexis—who, as a child, had been the recipient of several necessary but painful and humiliating medical procedures—now found herself having her cervix cauterized once every few months. Now and for the foreseeable future.

"I can't even leave him and find someone else," she cries. "I wouldn't want to give this to someone. And who would have me, anyway?"

Alone, later on in our work together, Nick breaks down and cries. "For a few lousy seconds," he says, looking up at me, incredulous. "For what? A couple of spurts. Five, ten minutes inside that woman, max. And now look at this. Look at this. I can't believe it."

Nick might well have gone through a hundred prostitutes with no repercussions. On the other hand, one condom tear could have sent him home with life-threatening HIV. I've listened to stories like Nick's for years. I see only the devastation; the guys who don't get caught aren't the ones dragged in to see me. I'm not a puritan by any means. What I am, more than anything else, is pragmatic. Grown-ups don't play games with themselves. You face the truth, make your choices, and take your chances. But in Nick's grandiose license to step outside the bonds of his marital contract, he wasn't doing any of that. He was a fifty-two-year-old frat boy playing genital Russian roulette, with his wife as an unwitting participant.

Here's the real deal on grandiosity. It can be dangerous to your health, sometimes even lethal. It destroys intimacy. It destroys love. Every shame-less act — every offense, crime, injury, willful violation — is committed by someone in a state of grandiosity. Why do you want to practice coming down from the high of grandiosity? *Because it's the only way you will ever be happy.* I call grandiosity *the poisoned privilege.* Like a potent street drug, grandiosity relieves distress yet causes great harm, not just to you but to those who love you.

I have spoken about living a nonviolent life — nonviolent between you and others and nonviolent between your ears. The violence that occurs between you and others is always fueled by grandiosity. And the violence that occurs between you and you, the voice of that harsh critical chorus we carry inside, is shame. Being in a shame state means that you're holding yourself in contempt. And being in a state of grandiosity means that you're holding others in contempt.

I want you to notice that the emotional energy in both of these states is the same.

Shame and grandiosity, being one-up or one-down, are not primarily opposite emotions. They are the same emotion pointed in different directions.

When the beam of contempt swings inward, we call that shame. When the beam points out at those around you, we call that grandiosity. But the beam itself is fundamentally the same. We may even use the very same words to berate others that we use to berate ourselves. Relationship empowerment means stepping off the contempt conveyor belt, as it carries you toward either direction.

The work of bringing yourself down from one-up is not driven, fundamentally, by a wish to spare the other person, important as that is. It is driven by your wish to rid your own life of psychological violence. When an "idiot" cuts me off on the road, then slows down to twenty miles an hour and won't let me pass, as I look at the back of his neck with feelings of rage and thoughts of murder, I do not breathe myself back to center for *his* sake, but for mine. "*You* may not deserve this," I might think, or even mutter aloud at the maddening driver. "But *I* deserve it."

Become Truly Human

You cannot love yourself or anyone else from either the one-up or the one-down position. Come into the healthy position of *same-as*, neither above nor below. Become a human among other humans, eyeball-to-eyeball, just as frail as the next person, and just as magnificent. It is true that people get by without learning how to do this — a great many people. And their lives are often experienced as plenty good enough. But I don't want good enough to be sufficient for you. I want you to want more. I want you to insist on real intimacy and real health. They are your birthright, and the only path to true satisfaction.

HOW DO YOU USE THE RELATIONSHIP GRID?

The relationship grid is an easy tool to help you practice coming to center. It's a way of taking a mental snapshot that captures where you are any given moment, and where you need to go. The grid's design is simple: We lay out self-esteem as a vertical line with grandiosity, of course, at the top and shame at the bottom. Then we draw a horizontal line for boundaries, with being boundaryless on the right and being walled off on the left. Now, we have a cross that looks like this:

The relationship grid has four cardinal positions:

1. Boundaryless and One-Down
2. Boundaryless and One-Up
3. Walled Off and One-Down
4. Walled Off and One-Up

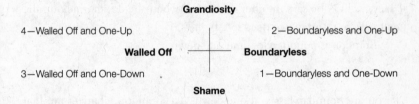

With the grid in mind, you can do a mental "freeze" and ask yourself, "Where am I? And where do I need to go?" Check your self-esteem first. "As I stand here now, am I one-up, one-down, or centered?" Do you feel deflated and shame-filled, or inflated and grandiose?

Next, check your boundaries: "How is my containing boundary? Am I uncontained, letting too much out? Or walled off, letting nothing out?" And now the protective part of your boundary: "Am I too porous, or not open enough?"

Now, quickly, without overthinking it, put yourself in the most appropriate quadrant. *Knowing where you are will instantly and unfailingly tell you where you need to go in order to come to center.*

Boundaryless and One-Down: Brandon

Brandon and Kelly are roommates in a co-ed apartment shared by six college students. One spring weekend they find themselves alone together. They eat pizza, drink beer, watch an old movie, and, to their surprise, find themselves "making out" on the battered old couch in their living room. Kelly abruptly takes off the next morning to visit her sister, leaving Brandon a ball of worry. What did he do? he wonders. Now he's ruined everything. She hates him, he's certain. The whole group of friends will be disrupted. Maybe he'll even have to move out. Memories of the previous night flood over him, and suddenly Brandon feels as if Kelly is the only girl in the world, as if her interest in him is the only thing that can save him and make him feel good again. He doesn't have her sister's number, but he can probably reach her on her cell phone. "Hey, Kelly?" he says into her voice mail when she doesn't pick up the call. "It's me. Listen, we need to talk . . ."

Brandon is boundaryless and one-down.

If you are boundaryless and one-down, like Brandon, chances are that your predominant need is for more protection and solidity. Close your eyes or look down at the floor and in your mind's eye, see the protective part of your boundary grow stronger; feel how it shields you. Let yourself relax within this circle of protection. You don't have to steel yourself against emotional upset or attack; your boundary will do that for you. All you need to do is remember it and let it do its work. You can afford to be calm, open, and curious. Breathe. Now breathe deep into your sense of shame, the source of your desperation. In your mind's eye, scoop down and bring yourself back up into *same-as*, eyeball-to-eyeball. Let yourself feel that you've come to center. Let yourself have the pleasure of knowing that you can affect your own mental state. Congratulations!

Boundaryless and One-Up: Taylor

"Did you think I wouldn't *find out?*" asks thirty-eight-year-old Taylor, incredulous, brandishing a copy of her live-in boyfriend's e-mail. "You lying, smarmy little *prick*! You thought you could pull this shit right under my nose?"

"What are you doing with my e-mail?" Brian demands.

"What are you doing contacting Julia, Brian?" Taylor replies, her voice trembling with anger and indignation. "Don't you think *that's* the question?"

Julia is Brian's former girlfriend, a young woman Taylor describes as a "needy, bloodsucking, emotional sinkhole." In the first months of living with Taylor, Brian did have some trouble extricating himself from his previous relationship. He felt sorry for Julia and didn't mind talking to her when she felt too lonely. He and Julia had grown up together, and for years they'd been good friends before their short stint as a terrible couple. He'd always looked out for Julia. But from the start, Brian's contact with his old girlfriend seemed to drive Taylor wild. Taylor had insisted that he break off all contact with her and Brian had agreed, only to renege on his contract if Julia called or wrote to him in seemingly dire straits. He just couldn't turn his back on her. Taylor seemed to find out virtually every time he wrote or talked to Julia, and his "sneaking around" only incensed her further and confirmed that he was not to be trusted. Taylor would rampage and threaten to leave. Brian would apologize and promise to stop, and all would be well until the next discovery. Of course, Brian needed to stop "yessing" Taylor and stand up for what he believed in. But he was too weak, and Taylor seemed too explosive. Brian didn't want to lose her.

Taylor and Brian are caught in a Scolding Mother/Resisting Son Bad Deal. Brian is boundaryless and one-down, and Taylor is a professional angry victim with a black belt in offending from the victim position. She honestly believes that she is the injured party and that her retaliation, which she calls expressing herself, is perfectly justified. She is utterly blind to her part in the dance, to how unreasonable she is being in controlling Brian's behavior and how inexcusable her abuse of him is.

She is boundaryless and one-up.

If you're boundaryless and one-up, like Taylor, chances are that your predominant weakness will be containment. Strengthen the inside of the boundary. Feel it pressing in against you, like a hand on your stomach, sucking it in, reining you in. If you're feeling like a big, angry victim, *stop it*. Do *not* offend from the victim position. It's not warranted, it's not attractive, and it's not good for you. Breathe and come down into same-as. Let your boundary protect you from the stimulus you got yourself so upset about. Wait until you're less reactive before thinking honestly and fairly, "Is there anything to this, or am I just ready to let it fly? Am I CNI-triggered right now? Am I battling caricatures instead of seeing the life-sized issue in front of me?"

Calm down and come down through your breathing until you feel protected and connected at the same time, until you are eyeball-to-eyeball, same-as, just another human among imperfect humans. Breathe your way down from indignation. Let it go.

Let yourself feel that you've come to center. Let yourself have the pleasure of knowing that you can affect your own mental state. Congratulations!

Walled Off and One-Down: Anthony

Short, plump, with big hair piled up high, outrageous pumps, and long brown nails, Michele is pure New York. Jiggling her foot, chewing gum, twirling her hair, and looking around, all at once, she has enough nervous energy to power the city's electrical system. And she's not just agitated; she's mad.

"Someone needs to wake Tony up and let him know that he died," she cracks with no sign of humor. Tony, slumped in his chair, just nods his head, as if confirming something to himself that he's known all along. We're in a workshop in New York in front of a few hundred people, and I'm wondering if I chose the wrong volunteer couple. "Go ahead, Anthony," Michele continues. "Talk to the man. The man's an expert. Say something."

"What's up?" I say to him. He nods, then looks away. He seems frightened.

"We fight all the time, ya know?" he says after a while. "All the time." That seems to be about the only thing they can both agree on. They fight about sex. She wants it; he doesn't. They fight about having kids. She's ready; he's not. They fight about Tony's work. He's in a dead-end construction job and wants to go to night school to become a pharmacist but somehow never manages to follow through. He smokes a little pot most days and drinks with his buddies most weekends. I ask if he thinks he's depressed, and he shrugs. "Yeah," he says. "I mean, I guess." Would he consider some medication? He tells me he doesn't like putting drugs into his body. I crack up. "You put pot and alcohol in your body all the time, Tony. You mean you don't like taking drugs that *other* people give you." He smirks and shuffles about, as if saying, "Hey, okay. You got me." He's a well-built, good-looking boy in his twenties with charm to burn. I can see how women would be willing to take care of him. But I think he's on a fast track to becoming a well-built, good-looking boy in his forties, fifties, and maybe beyond, and I tell him so. I ask him if he has any interest in growing up.

"Which entails?" he inquires.

"Getting somewhere with your life. Planning a future. Getting off your ass about night school. Cutting back on the pot and booze."

"Jeez," he says, smiling. "Anything else?"

"Some support, maybe. A therapist or a coach. Maybe a group. Something to help you get some 'oomph.' " I stop talking and Tony says nothing. We wait a while until I figure that he'd let us sit all afternoon like that. "So, what do you think?" I ask him. "Want some help?"

"I . . . I don't know," he says. "I'm not sure."

"It's a big decision, Tony," I say. "You should take some time to think it over. I'll give you two minutes." We sit in silence for what seems like forever. "So, what do you think?" I ask.

Tony nods to himself, picking up steam. "Okay," he says at last. "Sure. Why not? I'll give it a shot. Therapy. Whatever. Sure." And just like everyone else in the room, I know that he's lying.

Tony is walled off and one-down.

If you are one-down and walled off, you feel deenergized and disillusioned. Perhaps you're depressed or just resigned. You don't want contact, or you don't know how to *make* contact. You have a sense of failure before even beginning. It's too difficult, too overwhelming, or just too ungratifying. You'd rather be left alone to comfort yourself as best you can with your usual distractions. If you're like a lot of people who adopt a walled-off, one-down position, you're often passive. Perhaps you're addicted to or dependent on some substance, process, or person outside of your primary relationship.

You must have courage. Stop medicating, if you are, and rouse yourself from this state of limbo. The combination of shame and walls is hard to punch through. You have to make yourself start moving again, make yourself reengage. Your lethargy is like that horrible feeling of getting up in the morning when it's still dark and making yourself get to the gym to work out. But that's all it is. Your resistance is no more substantial and no more difficult to conquer. You fear real commitment—to a person, or work, or ambition, or everything. You fear that you will fail. Far and away the most effective remedy for such fear is simple action and repetition. *Don't stall.*

For you, in particular, "trying," "understanding," or "working on things" may be little more than sophisticated procrastination. Unfortunately, you'll have no trouble finding a therapist who will be happy to explore with you every nook and cranny of your resistance. A friend of mine once quipped, "After fifteen years of four-times-a-week psychoanalysis, I feel exquisitely lucid about precisely why I've never changed."

I believe that your decision to give up the safety of being on life's side-lines, to instead throw yourself into the game, will be no more and no less difficult before or after years of therapy. You have enough under-standing right now. And if you're waiting for your feelings to change, or for the risk to feel any less overwhelming, you may have a long wait on your hands. Get some good friends or a counselor behind you for sup-port, hold your nose, and jump.

Trust that your boundary will be strong enough to protect you, and breathe yourself up from the dead weight of shame. Reach down and scoop yourself back up to same-as. You are not a helpless victim. Try and fail, but try. Do it badly. Do it disastrously. But do it. Rejoice in small victories and build on them—one action at a time. Go.

Let yourself feel that you've come to center. Let yourself have the pleasure of knowing that you can affect your own mental state. Congratu-lations!

Walled Off and One-Up: Ashley

By anyone's reckoning, Ashley was a beautiful woman. Tall, blond, with porcelain skin and arresting green eyes, she looked like she had to be somebody's princess. And in a way, she was. Michael was fifteen years her senior, well-off, and completely entranced by her. Entranced, I came to understand, in no small measure by her audacious unavailability. Even though Michael was intelligent, accomplished, and generous to the point of doting on her, it was abundantly clear—and had been clear all along—that Ashley had never been certain that Michael was quite right for her. Michael had pressed her into marriage, their story went, then pressed her to have children. And Ashley, young, exquisite, and confused, had somehow let herself be swept along in the draw of his de-cisive personality.

To be blunt, Ashley didn't at all seem to mind the luxurious lifestyle Michael allowed her. She seemed wonderfully content with their homes and parties and charity events. The only part of her life she didn't quite care for was the man who provided it. Michael was depressed, when he should have been angry. Even when it became clear to him that his young wife had had more than one "fling," even when she stopped having sex with him and then took up residence in another part of their house, Michael saw it all as understandable. "A young woman with an older man," he shrugs.

"Michael, you're only sixty-two," I say. "You talk like you're eighty. A lot of men in your position are taking up with twenty-year-olds. Is sex still okay with you; do you function all right? Do you still have desire?"

"Yes, yes," he assures me. "That's not the issue. It's just that . . ." He pauses, searching for just the right word. "She's a *free spirit*," he says. I glance at Ashley and she turns away. To them both, I reflect, I must look pedestrian. Too middle-class to appreciate the nature of their refined connection.

"So, Michael, if it's all so all right with you, why do you think you're depressed?" I ask.

Again, he shrugs. "From the reading I've done," he replies, "I was under the impression that most professionals consider depression to be largely biological. Am I wrong in that?"

I start to feel like we're fencing, and I don't have the patience for it. "Then why are you seeing me and not someone who can prescribe medication?" I ask none too gently.

"I like your work on depression," he answers. "I thought you'd have something to say."

Ashley still isn't looking at either of us. Her presence doesn't feel harsh or even uninvolved; it feels spectral, ghostly.

"I do have something to say," I address them both. "What I have to say is that it's abuse to be with someone and give him the message that you're not sure he's really right for you, really quite good enough. I believe that kind of ambivalence has a very short shelf life before it begins to get toxic." Ashley begins to stir. "I believe it is an assault on someone's self-esteem to wake up and go to sleep each night with someone you're not sure you belong with. And I don't quite know how to help someone get over depression when he's in the middle of depressing circumstances."

Graceful and unhurried, Ashley gets up from her chair and, with a slight nod, bids Michael to do the same. As I rise, she smiles and shakes my hand. "Thank you *so much* for your time," she murmurs, her eyes soft, her voice warm and appreciative. Turning toward her husband, she says, "Michael, I think we're having this discussion with the wrong person, all right?"

Without a word, Michael heads toward the door. I know I should say something like "If I can be of help to you at some point, please don't hesitate . . . ," but the words just won't come out.

"I understand that we're responsible for the entire day," Ashley says, sweeping past me. "Please have your assistant send us an invoice." And then I'm alone.

Ashley is walled off and one-up.

If you are walled off and one-up, what are you being so high and mighty about? Who are you kidding? I want you to really *see* the way you walk around as if whomever you're with isn't good enough, isn't quite worth your while. I want you to let in just how mean you are being. Yes, covertly shaming and mean. You withdraw from real closeness like a ship steaming off under the full sail of your own magnificence. You act as though you possess untold riches that you'll happily bestow—on someone else. (I'm sorry, am I keeping you? You seem anxious to get to a much more important engagement.)

While the illusion of self-sufficiency in which you cloak yourself is powerful and convincing, you and I both know it's a sham. Actually you are a vulnerable, imperfect little human being just like the rest of us. Come down off your perch of irony and needlessness. Stand on the rich earth of humility. Let yourself get dirty, here in the disorderly mess of relationships. You can protect yourself and stand up for yourself without all this posing.

Lose the attitude and connect.

Breathe yourself down from your superiority and out from behind those walls. Come back into engagement. You were dying in there, in that empty fortress.

Let yourself feel that you've come to center. Let yourself have the pleasure of knowing that you can affect your own mental state. Congratulations!

Come to Center

I've included these vignettes to help you get a feeling for each of the four quadrants of the grid, to understand what it's like to predominantly inhabit each of them. Like the people in the vignettes, you may reside mostly in one quadrant, but you may not be that consistent. You may notice that you tend toward one quadrant in this relationship but that in a former relationship you were mostly in another. Or you may feel that you skip around quite a bit from day to day, or even from minute to minute.

Here's the deal on using the grid: Keep it simple.

If you are in a shame state, bring yourself up. If you're being grandiose, breathe yourself down. If you're boundaryless, pause and reset your boundary. If you're walled off, take a deep breath and get back into engagement. You will learn the techniques for doing all this in the practice section, but for now, simply understand that these are not complex skills with many facets that are hard to grasp. They are relatively straightforward skills that require tons and tons of practice.

Like being a beginner at anything, at first you will find this internal work stilted, arduous, and largely ineffective. Press on! Wait until the first time someone says something provocative to you and you feel it *boink* against your psychological boundary and bounce off. Or the first time you feel a hot wave of shame and, rather than feeling rotten for hours about it, you can breathe your way back into center in a matter of a few minutes. I look forward to your excitement the first time you don't just understand but have the palpable experience that this technology really does work—that you can directly and powerfully impact your own state of mind.

Nonviolent between yourself and others and nonviolent between your ears, connected and protected at the same time, neither better than nor lesser than anyone else on this earth, you are now intimacy ready. You have cleaned up your environment, and you have begun to gain clarity and solidity inside your own skin. Now you're prepared to turn toward your partner, roll up your sleeves, and tackle your relationship.

Chapter Five
Practice Section

LEARNING TO USE YOUR BOUNDARIES

This is a visualization exercise intended to give you a visceral sense of containment and protection without becoming walled off.

Step One: Containing Yourself

If you are right-handed, put your right hand flat just a few inches in front of your stomach, palm facing toward you, as if you had just stopped a few inches short of patting your tummy. This is how to imagine the containing part of your psychological boundary.

Push in toward your stomach with your right hand, as if you were compressing the air between your stomach and your hand. Don't actually touch your stomach, but imagine increased air pressure on it as you press. Pull the muscles of your gut in as you push inward. Feel the strength of the containing force against you, like an air girdle. This is the feeling of you reining in you—your thoughts, feelings, emotional energies, and impulses. Every time you feel moved to blurt out or act out, this is the force that will stop you. As you imagine it throughout your day, as in your mind's eye, and begin using it to stop some action or word, it will grow stronger.

Step Two: Protecting Yourself

Now, stretch your left arm straight out in front of you, parallel to the floor, and bend your hand back so that your fingers point up toward the ceiling, like a policeman signaling "Stop!" This is how to imagine the protective part of your psychological boundary. In your mind's eye, feel the strength of that force field represented by your powerful outstretched hand. Understand that nothing gets inside your emotional space unless you agree to let it enter. If you agree with something someone says about you, let your "Stop!" hand relax so that you "open up," with the hand now facing palm, toward the sky. You have let down your barrier and allowed something in. Immediately put your hand—and the barrier—back up, waiting for the next thing to evaluate. Keep your arm straight out and your hand straight up. I want you to feel the power in this gesture. You have the power to protect yourself, letting in nothing that is untrue or unkind.

Step Three: What Containing and Protecting Yourself Feels Like

Stand or sit with your arms in the positions I have described—the right one pressing on the air in front of your belly, the left straight out with your fingertips up (or the reverse if you are left-handed). Think, "Stop!—until I decide to let you in." Imagine anything coming at you going *splat* against that force field, hanging there against your perimeter until you've evaluated it. Then either lower your hand, as if opening a hatch, and let it in, or keep the hand vertical and closed, keeping it out. I'm going to say some things to you now and as I do, I want you to let your hand drop to the open horizontal position and let in what I say, or keep your hand vertical and strong, keeping it out. Remember to go back to the vertical, closed position immediately after you let something in. Ready?

I believe that you are reading this book out of a sincere desire to make your relationship better. (React.)
I believe that you have some doubts about whether your partner will be as thrilled with all this as you are. (React.)
I believe that you care about your partner (or a potential partner, if you're single) and are committed to making yourself healthy for both of your sakes. (React.)
I believe that you've always maintained a secret fetish for Labrador retrievers in black lingerie. (React.)
You stole your brother's rubber ducky and you know in your heart that he's never been the same. (React.)
You like cold peaches in summertime, but nothing beats ice cream. (React.)

Okay, got it? As you listen (or read), you're thinking, "Yes," "No," "Well, maybe a little," "Are you kidding me?" and so on, letting my points gain entrance or not as you choose.

Congratulations! You now possess a working psychological boundary. Now try taking it out into the world. When you wake up, imagine that force field surrounding you. Cloak yourself in it as you would clothing. You don't want to go out into the world emotionally nude, do you? I didn't think so. As you go through your day, remember to exercise your boundary whenever someone speaks to you. Do your best to hold yourself and the speakers respectfully even as you protect yourself from their possible projections.

SELF-ESTEEM

This is two-step exercise designed to introduce you to the practice of self-esteem.

Self-Esteem Step One: Monitoring Your Internal State

For ten days write in your journal, for about fifteen minutes each evening, about how and when your self-esteem fluctuated throughout the day. Make note of moments when you went one-up into grandiose judgment or entitlement, or one-down into toxic shame.

Reflect on your reactions, and in each case try to determine the following:

The trigger:

What happened just before you went up or down?

The sensations:

This is the most important thing to note and write about. What were the physical sensations related to being one-up or one-down? This is important because we each have our own particular set of physical sensations that are usually consistent whenever we go up or down. One workshop participant spoke of feeling that she was literally looking down her nose when she went into grandiosity. Another spoke of feeling his shoulders hunch up around his ears, like a little boy expecting to be cuffed, whenever he went into shame. What are your physical sensations? By learning them, you can come to recognize your state by its telltale physical signs.

Your thinking:

What was the thought, or thoughts, immediately connected to the trigger?

Your emotions:

What was the feeling, or feelings, connected to your thoughts?

Self-Esteem Step Two: Altering Your Internal State

Once you've had a while to become aware of your many self-esteem fluctuations, it is time to begin doing something about them. In moments throughout your day, as you notice yourself in either grandiosity or shame, you begin the practice of intervening:

If you feel grandiosity: In your mind's eye, reach up and pull your grandiose self down, then pull yourself back into your body, so that you come to look at whoever is in front of you from eye level, from same-as.

If you feel shame: Reach down and imagine pulling your shame-ridden self up so that you feel that you inhabit yourself fully, that you are looking straight ahead to meet the world straight on.

There are a few different affirmations you can use to help you stay focused while you attempt these exercises:

- Each person has inherent worth. No one is less than. No one is more than.
- I am enough, and I matter despite my human flaws and imperfections.

Or you can be more specific:

- I am enough, and I matter despite losing my temper with my child.
- I am enough, and I matter despite getting poor reviews on my last presentation.

Chapter Six

Get What You Want

EMPOWERING YOURSELF, EMPOWERING YOUR PARTNER

Summary

Chapter five introduced you to boundaries and self-esteem. You learned about *psychological boundaries*, both the *protective* (outer) part and the *containing* (inner) part. Two types of boundary dysfunction were defined: being *boundaryless* and being *behind walls*. You then turned to the topic of self-esteem, which is being *same-as*, neither superior to nor inferior to others. Having a false sense of superiority is the condition called *grandiosity*. Having a false sense of inferiority is the condition called *shame*, or, more precisely, *toxic shame*. Toxic shame was differentiated from healthy shame, which, along with guilt, is the force that empowers the containment. Grandiosity, a shameless state, erodes that capacity. Unlike shame, grandiosity feels good, but it impairs judgment.

You learned to use the relationship grid to help you *come to center*, the core practice of coming up from shame or down from grandiosity, growing boundaries where they are lacking, and softening walls. You have begun to realize your capacity to bring yourself into the healthy condition of same-as, neither above nor below, and into healthy engagement, being protected and connected at the same time. Clear and centered inside yourself, you now turn to face your relationship.

Five Winning Strategies

Early on, you were introduced to five losing strategies, strategies for navigating the crunch that will never succeed—not because they are ineffective in achieving their goals, but because the goals themselves have little to do with granting you satisfaction. You've identified your particular losing-strategy profile, and you've come to understand how your repertoire of failing moves only serves to reinforce your partner's, locking you both into the endless loop of your bad deal. Most important, through the development of second consciousness, you have begun to practice stepping away from your bad deal. The question now is: Stepping away from your bad deal toward *what*, exactly? Intimacy—yes, of course, that's the goal, the destination, but how do you reach it?

I have said that in order to succeed with one another, contemporary men and women must have a road map, a new rule book containing a set of skills capable of turning the twenty-first-century vision of truly intimate relationships into reality. There's no turning back. The new vision will not just fade away, and twentieth-century maps and skills won't get us there. Relationship empowerment is an approach that enables you to honor both your own and your partner's desires. It enables you to create a nonviolent life in which your wants and needs are asserted with an attitude of helpfulness rather than judgment. This model of full-respect living can well serve as our rule book; it is a new orientation befitting our new terrain. As for the new skills, the remainder of this book describes *five winning strategies*, strategies designed to translate the principle of relationship empowerment into an everyday practice.

The five winning strategies are:

1. Shifting from complaint to request
2. Speaking out with love and savvy
3. Responding with generosity
4. Empowering each other
5. Cherishing

These winning strategies equip you to succeed in the critical tasks of *getting, giving,* and *having.* The first two strategies, *shifting from complaint to request* and *speaking out with love and savvy,* help you get what you need. The second two strategies, *responding with generosity* and *empowering each other,* help you give everything that you can to your partner and to your relationship. The last winning strategy, *cherishing,* helps you grow, sustain, and honor all that you have.

Why Should You Become a Proactive Lover?

Learning and practicing these five winning strategies are the practical means by which we transform our relationships. Our culture's norm is to get whatever it is that we get from our partners and then react. But mastering the skills of relationship technology changes all that. By disrupting our usual knee-jerk reactions, the defaults we learned as kids from our families, second consciousness opens the door to a new world—a world in which we have options, in which we develop the ability to control our responses rather than being controlled by them. This isn't a matter of white-knuckled suppression, but rather, as your practice matures, the cultivation of artfulness. No longer the pawns of our own reactivity, we can think about how to intentionally shape our relationship, about what we want for ourselves and our partners and how best to get it.

The idea of deliberately shaping our relationships is in itself a significant departure from the old rules. As modern and sophisticated as we think we are, we still cling with surprising tenacity to the idea that a great romantic relationship should be *spontaneous.* You might be thinking, "Did Guinevere and Lancelot or Romeo and Juliet have to 'master a relationship technology'? Give me a break." Well, you're right about that. Like all great lovers, these couples moved on impulse, straight from the heart, all reason swept aside by their passions. But then again, Guinevere and Lancelot were adulterers, and Romeo and Juliet died. It's hard to get over the notion that self-consciously chosen behaviors in love are cold and calculated, stilted and cerebral—in a word, second-rate. Men don't want to work all that hard, and women still think that an ideal lover "would just know." I can't tell you how many women I've heard say, over the years, "If I have to tell him, it doesn't count." Well, I'd like you to take a look around and ask yourself how well spontaneity seems to be working. Of the countless people I've listened to in my practice and in workshops, only a tiny percentage proactively shape their relationships. Most people of either sex do not do the hard work of sitting down, clearly identifying their relational wants and needs, figuring out how best to ask for them, going after them, and then, if the first attempt fails, regrouping, rethinking, and trying again.

What both sexes seem to do equally and remarkably well is complain. In this chapter you will learn to speak up (without complaining), to ask for (and get) what you really want.

Winning Strategy 1: Shifting from Complaint to Request

You might assume that the revolution of individual empowerment that swept aside the traditional virtues of acquiescence would have taught women the first part of relationship empowerment—how to identify their desires and assert them. But you'd be wrong.

Instead of using assertion, both men and women seem to subscribe to the truly nutty idea that an effective strategy for getting more of what you want from your partner is to *complain about not getting it after the fact*. This has got to be about the worst behavioral-modification program I've ever encountered. It's like trying to train a performing dog a new, complex trick not by showing him how or by rewarding him when he gets it right, but exclusively by shocking him each time his movements don't match your requirements. In no time at all you'd have a terribly confused, frustrated, and profoundly unmotivated dog on your hands. Probably he'd learn way before you did that the best thing for him to do is lie still and lay low, a strategy adopted by a fair number of men.

Jenna and Ian: "You're a Loser, Honey."

Jenna is a feisty young art student who regularly rakes her boyfriend, Ian, over the coals for his thoroughgoing lack of commitment—to her or to much of anything else, in her estimation.

"I mean, you know I just *adore* you, Ian," she proclaims in one of our couple's sessions. "You *know* I do. But, like, who's kidding who? You know what I mean, baby? Ian, you are a *classic* slacker. You're a loser, honey. Living with you is like starring in my own dysfunctional reality show, understand? It's like, 'Oh m'god, oh m'god, that Ian! He is *so cute*! Do you think he's like ever going to get off that fabulous ass and, you know, actually *do something? Anything?*' " she yells at him. "*EVER?*"

"Jenna," I ask her. "This is your idea of how to help Ian feel more warmth and commitment?" She looks up at me, perky, expectant, as if to say, "And your point *is?*" I make the observation that Jenna would not treat her dog the way she was treating her boyfriend.

"Well, sure," she says, leaning forward with an adorable smile. "But my dog *learns*."

What Jenna at that moment seemed unwilling to grasp was her part of the equation. Their vicious cycle wasn't subtle or all that difficult to discern. The more Jenna beat Ian up for his lack of commitment, the more unsure of their relationship he became, and . . .

Here's the real deal on complaint. It is such an utterly contorted way of trying to get more of your needs met that I'm tempted to call it perverse. Complaint is *double negative thinking*. Instead of saying, "I'd be really happy if I could have *more* of this *positive* thing," you try to get more of something you want by saying, "I *would have been* happy if only you *hadn't engaged* in that *negative* thing." Just what do you expect your partner to do with *that*? He can apologize, I suppose: "Gee, I'm really sorry for making you unhappy with that bad thing I did. It was really a bad thing. I know that. I feel really bad." Well, I guess that counts for something. But while an apology might be a good first step, when I want something in my relationship, what I'd really like, above and beyond an apology, is to actually get what I want. Complaining won't get me that. Complaining masquerades as information, but it's actually nothing more than unbridled self-expression.

FROM NEGATIVE/PAST TO POSITIVE/FUTURE LANGUAGE

Instead of focusing on what your partner has done *wrong*, discipline yourself—and it does take discipline—to focus on what he *could* do now or later that would be *right*.

You shift from a *negative/past* focus to a *positive/future* focus. In simpler terms, remember this phrase:

Don't criticize, *ask*!

WHY DOES ASKING FOR WHAT YOU WANT FEEL SO UNCOMFORTABLE?

The answer to this question is critically important to understand, especially for women. As crazy as it might seem, complaining, arguing, and even getting downright nasty actually feel safer to most of us than simply and directly making a request. And not without reason! In fact there is not one, but three reasons why you may be squeamish about making requests:

1. You must own your right to *have* wants and needs
2. You risk possible disappointment or rejection
3. You risk shaking up your relationship

OWNING THE RIGHT TO WANT ANYTHING

This can be a particularly difficult issue for some women who, despite years of growth and enormous changes in our society, still feel the influence of their caretaker training. If the essence of traditional masculinity is invulnerability, the essence of traditional femininity is selfless service to others. The centuries-old harsh judgment branding pleasure and good self-care as immoral selfishness has, unfortunately, followed more women than one might imagine into the twenty-first century. For them, self-assertion can trigger feelings of shame and guilt. They must learn that pleasure and honest connection are gifts and birthrights.

RISKING DISAPPOINTMENT

When you complain about not getting what you want, you might look like you're being vulnerable, but actually you're not. Since you're not asking for anything, you can't be let down. Complaining in your relationship is a form of *pseudo-pursuit*. If you listen to the content of your complaint, it sounds as though you're trying to connect. But if you attend more closely, solution is rarely what's on your mind, while being right, control, unbridled self-expression, or retaliation are very much on your mind.

> Complaint is just the flip side of acquiescence. It is personal empowerment's clarion call. And it works no more effectively than acquiescence does.

SHAKING UP YOUR RELATIONSHIP

Judging from the women I've worked with over the years, by far the biggest reason women have been reluctant to bring their hard-won public assertiveness back home with them is fear. Complaint is *not assertiveness*. Just as complaint is a form of pseudo-pursuit, it is also a form of *pseudo-assertion*. Complaint certainly looks and sounds assertive, but slow down and think about it. The issue isn't whether or not your needs get aired; it's what happens if your partner doesn't comply. When people complain, no matter how vehemently, they tend to *blow up and back down*. That's not assertiveness; it's a meltdown.

People in general and men in particular are not unfamiliar with, nor all that upset by, someone (especially a woman) "pitching a fit." Most men are extremely adept at battening down the hatches, ducking under the wave, waiting for the storm to pass over, bobbing up on the other side, and then doing whatever they were going to do anyway. In a recent workshop an older man, Zack, called this move "turtle-ing." Zack claimed that instructions on handling irate women by "pulling head, tail, and limbs" into your shell came secretly stamped on the back of every blue ribbon, blue blanket, and blue toy handed out to male infants.

What people in general and men in particular are emphatically *not* used to, and are extremely discomfited by, is someone (especially a woman) who says what she wants moderately, respectfully—and with teeth.

Let me repeat something I said early on:

Traditional femininity taught women to shut up and eat it.
Feminism taught women to speak out and leave it.
Relationship empowerment wants women to stand firm and mean it.

DARING TO ROCK THE BOAT

Whether they admit it to themselves or not, women understand the difference between blowing off steam and standing up for something unflinchingly. My last-ditch intensive sessions tend to attract unusually desperate partners (most often women) married to unusually difficult mates (usually men). I can't tell you how many women have asked me to somehow "get" their immature or bullying partner to be more responsible while at the same time not "threatening" him. What they want is, of course, impossible. I tell such women, "Listen, if you're serious about changing your relationship, then I'm not going to make your partner uncomfortable — *you'll* have to. I'll go out on the limb *with* you. But I won't go out *for* you. It's not my fight; it's yours."

RULE: ONE OF THE GREAT PARADOXES OF INTIMACY IS THAT IN ORDER TO HAVE A HEALTHY, PASSIONATE RELATIONSHIP, YOU MUST BE WILLING TO RISK IT.

You cannot create an extraordinary relationship unless you're willing to do the hard work of identifying what it is that you want and pursuing it. You cannot sustain a great relationship without taking risks. Too many of us are afraid of rocking the boat. We're frightened of staying as truthfully engaged as we deserve to be because experience has shown us that asserting our wants and needs simply hasn't worked. And so we "compromise," trying to make peace with what we see as our partner's limitations. This common outcome woefully sells short both you and your partner. Your lack of success does *not* stem from deeply wired-in limitations in either of you, but from your lack of skill, because, as you've painfully learned, it isn't enough to simply assert yourself. You must assert yourself in a way that will work. The first winning strategy provides a clear illustration of why your ordinary approach gets you nowhere and what a skilled alternative looks like.

WHY IS THE SHIFT FROM COMPLAINT TO REQUEST SO IMPORTANT?

Because it's the only way you will ever get your needs met.

RULE: YOU HAVE NO RIGHT TO COMPLAIN ABOUT NOT GETTING WHAT YOU NEVER ASKED FOR.

By definition, behaving skillfully means behaving in ways that work, using strategies that get you more of what you want. So let's compare these two strategies, complaint and request:

Which would you prefer hearing?

Choice A:

"Honey, it's really important to me that you're home in time to help the kids with their homework. It is a big value of mine that we both stay involved in family life. Would you be willing to do that?"

or Choice B:

"You're never around when the kids need you at night. I'm stuck with all three of them. I can't answer all of their questions, and I certainly can't answer them all at once. It's overwhelming, John. I don't know why you're having so much trouble hearing this. What's so difficult about showing up for your kids now and then?"

Which do you think would better enable your partner to give you what you want?

Choice A:

"Listen, I want to hear what you have to say. For that to happen, could you just take a minute and calm down, honey? Speak in a way I can hear, okay? Would you do that?"

or Choice B:

"I can't *stand* it when you get like this, John. Do you really expect me to just stand here and be spoken to like that? Where do you get off treating me like that, treating *anyone* like that?"

You may be thinking about now, "Oh, but the answers behind 'Door A' sound so artificial. Real people don't ever talk like that." To which I say, "They do if they want to be effective." Even if you can't see yourself sounding quite that composed, isn't it possible that with practice and support you could learn to manage a less polished version? A shift from negative/past to positive/future? A shift, for example, from "I just hate it when you talk to me like that!" to "I'm not speaking disrespectfully to you. Would you please do the same?"

I'll bet you could if you put your mind to it.

WHAT'S SO TERRIBLE ABOUT COMPLAINING?

Nothing at all, if your goal is self-expression. But as a strategy for helping your partner change, it doesn't work.

RULE: CRITICIZING WHAT YOUR PARTNER HAS DONE WRONG RARELY ENGENDERS AN ATTITUDE OF INCREASED GENEROSITY.

Complaint doesn't:

- Identify what it is that you want
- Express what you want in a way that your partner can understand
- Help break down your request into actionable behaviors that your partner can accomplish
- Appreciate his willingness to listen and try
- Reassure him that sincere attempts, even if imperfect, will be valued
- Motivate him
- Make talking to you about your relationship something he'll look forward to

The fact that most men freak out every time a woman tells him she has something to say about their relationship is a well-recognized phenomenon; such aversion is legendary. But has anyone ever taken the time to ask guys *why* they'd generally prefer a root canal? Well, I've heard all about it over the years, and let's just say that most men don't expect this particular discussion to be either constructive or a whole lot of fun. What they anticipate, and not without reason, is that they'll find themselves on the receiving end of an extended, overheated, one-sided ration of . . . complaint.

The shift from complaint to request illustrates a change I believe in so strongly, particularly for women, that if I were allowed to offer only one piece of advice, this would be the one new rule I would choose:

RULE: GREAT RELATIONSHIPS MEAN *MORE ASSERTION UP FRONT* AND *LESS RESENTMENT ON THE BACK END.*

You may well think, "Assertion? No problem." But let me give you an example of what I mean. What follows is a situation so common it has become a virtual cliché:

Lucy starts talking about feelings she's having concerning a troubling issue at work. Her boyfriend, Hal, asks if she's tried such-and-such a strategy. Lucy says, "Yes, it didn't work," and goes on to elaborate how absolutely horrible she's been feeling about it all. Hal asks, "Well, have you tried *this*?" Lucy says that she hasn't, brushing his suggestion aside, and then shares that she's not only feeling *horrible*, she's actually found herself beginning to get *frightened*. She's not sure, exactly, what she's so scared about, but all sorts of raw feelings have come up for her. Hal says, "Well, wait a second. If you haven't tried such-and-such, then why not? What's stopping you?" "Oh, I don't know," Lucy pouts. "The whole situation is just so *overwhelming*." Hal says, "Well, maybe it wouldn't *be* so overwhelming if you were willing to *do* something about it." To which Lucy replies that if she'd *known* Hal was just going to criticize her like this, she wouldn't have brought the matter up to begin with.

By about this time, no matter what Lucy and Hal may be *saying*, at least a part of them is *thinking*, "Strangulation? Strangulation might be satisfying. And that big, fat kitchen knife over there is starting to have some appeal."

Before anyone reaches for the cutlery, I'd like to explain what just went wrong here and also how easily this heated transaction can be fixed. Watching these two well-intentioned people reminds me of the O. Henry short story about a desperately poor young couple at Christmas. Out of love, the wife sells her beautiful hair to buy an elegant chain fob for her husband's prized watch, only to find out that he's pawned the watch in order to buy lovely combs for her hair. There's absolutely nothing wrong with what either Lucy or Hal is doing—individually. The problem, of course, is that they're at cross-purposes. And they find themselves in this quarrel because *Lucy did not assert her needs up front.*

Let's give Lucy the benefit of the doubt and assume that she *requested* Hal to listen to her. That's excellent as far as it goes; it's certainly better than not asking and then grousing about not getting the attention later. But the transaction still fails because Lucy has not specified what *kind* of listener she'd like Hal to be.

There are three kinds of listeners:

Empathic listeners:
> "Oh gosh! That sounds awful."

Problem-solving listeners:
> "Well, have you thought about this?"

Sharing listeners:
> "You know, the same thing happened with my son, Tim."

As outside observers, we can see fairly quickly that Lucy wants an *empathic* listener, while poor Hal launches into *problem-solving* mode. "Typical guy/gal stuff," you might say. Well, in this instance, yes. But the issue isn't that guys *naturally* do this while gals do that. Don't book your flights to Mars and Venus just yet. The issue is not primarily about gender, but about *learning to become specific about what you want.* The same problem could just as easily have occurred between two women— between Lucy and her mother, for example, as in:

> "Mom, I can't believe the tongue-lashing my boss gave me today in front of the whole office. I was so humiliated!"

"You know, that same thing happened to me when I was just about your age. I had a job at this little place in New York . . ."

"Ma, this is about *me*."

If you'd like to see what accomplished requesting looks like, I know just the right person to show you:

Harry and Denise

As part of their forty-fifth anniversary present from their kids, Harry and Denise received a gift certificate for two days' worth of therapy. Their children hoped that they might finally learn to stop bickering. Denise was sometimes painfully slow and deliberate as she took in each new relationship skill, but once she "got it," she seemed to know just how to put it to use. In a follow-up workshop a few months later, Denise offered a rendition of herself as she put to use what she'd learned by reminding Harry one night about how to be an empathic listener:

"So, I say: 'Harry. Between my sister and my arthritis, I had a rotten day today. Can I vent and you listen just for ten, fifteen minutes? Yeah. That's sweet, honey, thanks. Now, remember, what I'm looking for here is *empathic* listening, you remember that? I don't want you to give me advice or make any suggestions. Nothing like that, okay? Just hear me out . . . No, Harry, thanks, I know you're trying to help, but remember? What *I* need is—here, put your arm around me, that's good. Now, I want you to say like what one of my girlfriends would say. Like say, "Aw Denise, that really *sucks*." You know what I mean, Harry?' "

Actually, Harry *did* get the picture of what Denise meant. It wasn't that hard, because Harry happens to have married a relationship-empowerment quick study. Denise has now gone way past resenting how unfair it is that she has to work so hard to help Harry. Why is she willing to break down the skill of empathic listening into teeny little baby steps to teach him? Because she's married to him, that's why. She loves her husband and she'd like him to learn. What makes Denise's coaching so effective is that after forty-five years together, she knows her husband. Just as she knew exactly which buttons to push in their old bickering days, she now knows what he'll need from her to understand what she's asking of him. Denise is willing to put her ego aside and help her husband. *She wants him to win.*

And while Harry might have been relationally ill-informed, he was by no means stupid. Nor was he devoid of an interest in satisfying his wife. "Hey, I figure, 'What the hell?'" he tells me toward the end of our second workshop together. "Listen, in all these years with my wife, one thing I've learned. If Denise is happy, then everyone's happy."

"And if Denise isn't happy?" I ask, needling him, just a little.

"Nah, nah," Harry dismisses me. "We don't want to talk about that."

Harry's enlightened view sums up the crux of relationship empowerment. If you want to be happy, then do whatever you reasonably can to keep your partner happy. And if you want something more or different in your relationship, do what you reasonably can to facilitate that happening; get down off of your high horse and help out.

Of all the rules in the practice of relationship empowerment, the one that sums up the essence of this new orientation comes in the form of a question.

RULE: "WHAT DO YOU NEED FROM ME SO THAT I CAN HELP YOU GIVE ME WHAT I WANT?"

WHAT IF REQUESTS AREN'T ENOUGH?

No matter how good a job you do at anticipating your needs in advance, like Denise, or how hard your partner tries to meet them, like Harry, during the course of a long-term relationship there will be innumerable times when you find yourself in the crunch—dissatisfied, hurt, and angry, not merely wishing for something to happen but wishing that something hadn't already happened.

Positive, future-focused requests help keep your relationship steady. But how do you get back on track after you've already veered off?

For that you need a *process of repair*.

WHAT IS REPAIR AND WHY IS IT IMPORTANT?

The process of repair is the means by which we move from the crunch to satisfaction. It is a couple's *mechanism of correction*. Repair, just as the name implies, is how partners come together to fix what's wrong—how they get back on course. A couple with little or no capacity for repair is like a car without a steering wheel. The steering wheel is your car's main mechanism of correction. As you drive down the highway, your car drifts a bit to the left, so you pull lightly to the right. When it drifts a bit to the right, you nudge it back. A vehicle in motion that suddenly loses its steering will swerve back and forth in ever-widening arcs until it crashes into something that stops it. Unfortunately, much the same can be said for some of the couples I've worked with.

ORDINARY REPAIR

RULE: THE ESSENTIAL DYNAMIC OF ALL RELATIONSHIPS IS A DANCE OF HARMONY, DISHARMONY, AND REPAIR.

Like walking, the rhythm of relationship is an endless loop of balance, imbalance, and the restoration of balance—closeness, disruption, and a return to closeness.

Only a tiny fraction of repair incidents ever even register in our consciousness. You walk into a room occupied by a few of your friends, interrupting their conversation. Everyone experiences an awkward moment. And then someone includes you ("John was just saying . . ."), or pulls out a chair for you, or cracks a joke ("Hey, Charlie's here. The fun can begin."). Closeness, disruption, and restoration. I call these tiny incidents *ordinary moments of repair*. Their scope is so small, and they seem so natural, that we hardly notice.

The relational sensitivity commonly called good manners always casts a keen eye on this dance, ever sensitive to the prospect of disharmony, quick and clever about repair:

Elizabeth

Elizabeth, a young southern woman hailing from, as she put it, "modest means," recalled her first formal dinner with the old Boston society family who were soon to become her in-laws. To her utter shame, Elizabeth spilled a few drops of red wine on the immaculate antique tablecloth. "I could hardly speak, I was so embarrassed," she confessed in a recent therapy session. Not ten minutes later, her soon-to-be mother-in-law, in an animated moment, knocked over her own glass of wine. "Elizabeth has an *excuse* to be nervous, Mother," Elizabeth's fiancé teased, leading off a round of unabashed wisecracks from his siblings. "I think I started breathing right about then," Elizabeth told me. "That old matriarch? I swear she gave me the tiniest little hint of a smile. Blink and you would have missed it. But I knew what she'd done. And I knew we were going to be just fine, she and I. And we were, too. We still are."

WHAT HAPPENS WHEN ORDINARY REPAIR ISN'T ENOUGH?

While it is true that so many small instances of repair occur that most go unnoticed, it is also true that not all prospective mothers-in-law are as sensitive as Elizabeth's and not all experiences of disharmony resolve themselves so genteelly. While waiting around hoping that "things will work themselves out" may be just the right thing for a while, in my experience such a passive approach has a very short shelf life before it starts to turn sour. If you're in a state of *disrepair,* acutely experiencing the discrepancy between what you want and what you've got, I'd advise you to stop waiting and get to work. Sit down and figure out what would help you feel better. And then go after it—skillfully. This is the essence of the second winning strategy: speaking out with love and savvy.

Winning Strategy 2: Speaking Out with Love and Savvy

The repair process begins with the second winning strategy, *speaking out with love and savvy*. But perhaps the most important part of this strategy occurs before you open your mouth. If you're unhappy, before reaching out to your partner to initiate the repair process, take a minute to recall your goal. And take a minute to recall that the person you are about to speak to is not a monster, nor even an enemy. He is someone you love. Someone you've pledged your life to. At the very least, recall that he's the person that you have to live with.

This powerful internal strategy is *remembering love*.

Mark and Jan: Who Could Blame Her?

In a recent workshop, Jan, a lovely twenty-six-year-old from Ohio, confronts her wayward husband about the lingering effects of a brief affair he'd had a couple of years ago. Just a few days before the workshop, Mark had gone off on a business trip, an infrequent occurrence since the affair. Mark was with a few of his co-workers, men who had either turned a blind eye or who had, themselves, indulged in similar behavior. While Jan's hurt and her fury toward her husband had subsided over time, the thought of Mark traveling with these men she had once thought of as friends set something off in her. And when she tried to talk it out with Mark, she felt that he had just "shut her down." " 'Oh c'mon now,' " Jan imitates her husband. " 'Not this *again*! We've been over it and *over* it.' "

"Who could blame her?" I think to myself as I listen. Who could possibly blame this woman for her pain and rage?

"Mark, I just don't understand." Jan is so overcome with emotion that she visibly shakes. *"You're* the one who cheated on *me*, remember?" Her voice rises. "Has that slipped your mind? *You* are not the victim, here,

Mark, *okay*? *You* didn't drop thirty pounds in a month. *You* didn't lay awake every night, crying. I *know* this must be a big f—ing *drag* for you, a real *bummer*, to have a wife who just won't *snap out* of it. But, you know what? You know what, Mark?"

"Hold it there, Jan," I stop her. She looks up at me, startled and annoyed.

"Hey, I just want to say . . ."

"I can pretty much guess where you're headed," I cut her off again. She considers me for a moment.

"You know where I'm *headed*?" she quotes. "Don't you consider that a little presumptuous?"

"No," I tell her.

"And your certainty comes from . . . ?"

"It's your tone," I reply.

"My tone?"

"Yes," I tell her.

"You mean that I'm *angry*?" she asks, rhetorically, "I can't believe this! You don't think . . ."

"That you have a right to be angry?" I finish the sentence for her. "Sure, of course. Of course you do. I can't imagine the pain you have endured, Jan. But can I ask you something?" She waits, not answering. "What do you want?" I ask her. "What do you really want right now?"

"I want Mark to understand," she says.

"Why?" I ask.

"I don't mean just about his affair, but also about his insensitivity to me. His whole 'hurry up and get over it' attitude."

"I understand," I say. "You want him to see both the affair and his selfishness now. I get that, but why?"

She looks genuinely bewildered. "Why?" she repeats. "I don't know. So he'll get what he did."

"Okay, and then?"

"Well, feel bad about it, I guess."

"So, you want him to suffer?" I ask. "It's about punishment?"

"No," Jan raises her voice, frustrated with me. "I don't . . . It's not about hurting him so much. I just want him to *understand,* to be *accountable.*"

"So that?" I prompt.

"So he'll *get* what he did, what he *does.* So he'll *treat* me better," she says, wailing a bit, as if all this stating of the obvious is taxing her beyond patience.

"So you want him to get it, to be accountable, and treat you better?"

"Yes."

"Treat you responsibly enough that you might trust him again?"

"Yes."

"Because you want to get back to that?" I more state than ask.

"Of course," she says.

"Of course," I repeat. "Of course. Because, despite it all, you still love him?"

"Yes I do," she states unequivocally as, for the first time in our encounter, she looks at her husband sitting beside her. "I do. Still. Very much."

"I can see that," I say, "as you look at him now. I can feel that, Jan. Can you feel some of that emotion now, as you say this? Some of that warmth for him?"

"Yes," she says, her voice softer. "I think I can."

"Okay, great," I say. "What I'd like you to do is to close your eyes for a moment. Would you do that?" She nods and then does so. "I want you to feel that, that love-despite-everything feeling. I want you to remember that the person you're speaking to is the man that you love."

"I know that."

"I know you know that," I tell her. "But I want you to really feel it. Get grounded in that remembering: 'I am talking to the man I love in order to help him understand some of the things he does. So he can do them better. So we can be better. Maybe we won't be all that joyful right now with all this pain from the affair and everything, but at least we can be loving again, tender.' " I face her. "Isn't that what you really want?" I ask. She nods, her face relaxed. She seems as vulnerable and as sweet as a girl. "So now," I say, after a moment, "from this tender place, Jan. Tell him. Say what you need him to hear."

She cries a little as she opens her eyes and turns to him. "Just be patient, Mark," she tells him. "Be a little patient with me, will you? I don't *mean* to be still . . . I *want* to be over this, believe me. I just . . ."

Mark, standing beside her silently until now, scoops her up in his arms. "I'm sorry," he says. "I'm sorry for all of it. And I'm sorry for my stupid, selfish impatience," he says. "I just can't stand it sometimes." His eyes slick over with moisture.

"Say it," I urge him. "Let those tears in your eyes speak."

"I just shut you up sometimes because I can't stand how much I've hurt you," he chokes out, not giving in to his feelings and yet barely able to speak.

"Go on and hold her," I tell him. "Take your time."

And they do; they hold on tight, as grief washes over them and they remember love.

HOW DO I SPEAK IN A WAY THAT EMPOWERS MY PARTNER?

Remembering love, the internal prelude to repair, means getting straight about your goal. As such it is really just a particularly focused moment of second consciousness. As your relationship practice matures, you'll find yourself glancing at the compass of your goals before you do much of anything with your partner. You'll ask yourself two key questions virtually every time you're about to speak:

1. What do I want here; what's my goal?
2. Is what I'm about to say going to lead me closer to or further away from my goal?

RULE: IF, BEFORE YOU SPEAK, YOU REALIZE THAT YOUR GOAL IS
UNCONSTRUCTIVE (USUALLY ONE OF THE FIVE LOSING
STRATEGIES), *QUESTION IT.* IS IT YOUR REAL GOAL, YOUR
DEEPEST GOAL? IF YOUR GOAL IS CONSTRUCTIVE AND IT'S
CLEAR THAT WHAT YOU'RE ABOUT TO SAY WON'T HELP YOU
ACHIEVE IT, *SHUT UP.*

Successful repair entails more than just "being heard." It means that you actually get enough of what you want to feel satisfied. The only person who can grant that to you is your partner—the person you're asking.

In order to effect true repair you must, along with asserting yourself, do your best to support your partner's ability to listen and to respond as you'd like. Approaching your partner in such times of distress with a sincere desire to be of help to him is a profoundly uncommon attitude. But the most challenging moments are also the ones that demand the most maturity. We turn to the skills of repair only in discordant times, so that's when we must learn to use them.

So here you are in the midst of some upset—feeling alone, perhaps hurt and angry. And my suggestion is for you to think of yourself as *dedicated to helping empower your partner.* Sounds a little daft, doesn't it? Until you recall that what you are trying to help your partner do is to give you what you want. How can you best do that? Here's a simple guideline to keep in mind:

RULE: *FUNCTIONAL* WORDS OR ACTIONS ON YOUR PART *ENABLE*
YOUR PARTNER TO DO SOMETHING. DYSFUNCTIONAL WORDS
OR ACTIONS *RENDER YOUR PARTNER HELPLESS.* THE MORE
A MOVE ENGENDERS HELPLESSNESS, THE DIRTIER AND
NASTIER IT IS.

An appreciation of the negative effects of helplessness is what drives our shift in focus from complaint to request. We want the people we're asking things of to know what we're asking for, and we want them to feel confident that they can succeed. Perhaps because we've become so thoughtful about our parenting these days, most of the adults I've worked with do a better job of this with their children than they do with one another. Whenever you call a child to account for some failure or misdeed, you must always be sure to allow him a way to redeem his wrong, some avenue by which he can regain his good standing in the group. A healthy parent doesn't just nail a child and then leave it at that.

But we sometimes fail to extend the same courtesy to our mates.

Let me illustrate. Imagine that you were to say to me:

"Terry, you left the milk out of the fridge and now it's turned. There's no milk for tomorrow. What are you going to do about it?" (Negative past/potentially positive future)

There's a lot that I can do with that. I can apologize for being such a dunderhead. I can run to the store to get milk for tomorrow. I might even address my chronic issues of absentmindedness.

Now let's imagine that I hear:

"Terry, you left the milk out and it's gone bad. I really feel put upon when you act like a child. I had to go out, tired as I was, and get more milk. I just *wish* you'd be more responsible." (Negative past/wishful-thinking future)

Well, all that may be true. But because it's now in the past, there's less that I can do about it. I can say I'm sorry. I can admit to my chronic issues about it. I can empathize with your feelings. I can do my best to reassure you. But my options are *weaker* than they were in the first example.

Now, imagine that you were to say:

"Terry, you've left the milk out again. You *always* do this kind of thing. I don't know what it will take to get you to wake up. Do you think this is okay? Well, it's not okay. You're not a bachelor anymore. You have children. And what you don't take care of falls to me. Why do you do these things? What is *wrong* with you?" (Negative past/negative future)

It's fairly obvious that here I have even less opportunity for repair than I did in the previous example. It's not clear, actually, what the speaker even wants of me, or what actions, if any, would help her feel better.

The first example gave me opportunities to make things right. The second, by focusing more on an unchangeable past than a changeable future, left me little to do beyond apologizing. In the third example, the speaker has moved to *you always* statements. It's no longer about *this* particular carton of milk. This milk has now become a *symbol*, an emblem of all the milk cartons I have ever left out, and more than that, of all the irresponsible acts I have ever committed, and presumably will continue to commit. The speaker has moved into *trend talk*. And, of course, there is now very little room for repair. I might be able to do something about *this* milk carton, but it's hard to imagine what might help with every milk carton ever.

Now, imagine this:

"Terry, you've left the milk out again. You just refuse to care about anyone other than yourself. You're not just a slob; you're a *selfish* slob. Your father acted like this, and now your sons are picking it up too. Does that make you happy? Are you proud of the way you're preparing them for the world? I'll bet you are. I'll bet you see absolutely nothing wrong with the messes you make. Someone else will just clean it up, right?" (Negative past, present, and future!)

Oh dear. By now, most red-blooded men would be roaring with indignation. This speaker is abusive. She is sarcastic and name-calling; she tells me what I am thinking and feeling and what my motives are, and she is shaming—internal boundary violations all. But let's take a closer look for a moment. Sarcasm is one-up behavior. So are a lot of other things. But why does cutting sarcasm always feel so particularly vile? Because, as I've been saying, there's nothing anyone can do with it. Sarcasm is the *indirect expression of anger*: "Oh, sure. Go ahead. *Be* like that."

If my hypothetical partner had said, "Terry, I'm angry at the way you model bad behavior for the kids," I would have been able to address it. But how could one ever functionally respond to "I hope you're proud of yourself?"? The same is true for the speaker's *character ascriptions*. Sloppy *behavior* can change. But *being* a slob? Years of psychoanalysis, perhaps?

In these examples, the speaker escalates, moving through:

- A bad situation I can correct
- A bad situation in the past that's too late to correct
- A bad situation that is emblematic of the kind of things I always do
- A bad situation that exemplifies my selfish, irresponsible character

The speaker has moved from the present, to the past, to trend talk, to character assassination. *Each increase in nastiness represents an increase in helplessness—and an increased likelihood that your partner's response will be either fury or withdrawal.* Often a partner's withdrawal is preceded by a sense of "It won't do any good anyway. Why bother?" And so much of the rage that flames through a couple's fighting is *helpless rage.* Whether your partner goes into withdrawal or attack, into shame or grandiosity, the chances of successful repair will always decrease in proportion to the sense of helplessness he feels. Why are we willing to help empower our partners? Because, on the most selfish level, it is in our own interests.

RULE: A DISEMPOWERED PARTNER IS SELDOM GENEROUS.

All right, then, when you're angry and hurt, how *should* you best approach your partner? Well, don't just pound him into the ground, much as he might deserve it. Reach into the hole he's dug himself into and help him climb out.

Here's how:

USING THE FEEDBACK WHEEL

For years, I have taught couples how to speak effectively in difficult moments by using the *feedback wheel*, which was first devised by Janet Hurley. The wheel is the simplest and most structured formula for speaking that I've encountered and the least likely to get you into trouble. It was initially presented as a circle. I've changed the format—it's not really a wheel anymore—but I've kept the name in deference to its creator. The feedback wheel wonderfully embodies many of the rules of relationship empowerment. Using it forces you to:

- Keep to your side of the line by speaking strictly from the "I"
- Take full responsibility for your thoughts and feelings without blame
- Stay focused on a particular incident without going into "you always"
- Stay focused on behavior rather than attitude or character
- Offer your partner clear achievable behaviors that would help you feel better

That's a lot for a format to accomplish, and while the steps of the wheel aren't complex, in order for them to keep you on a straight path, you must adhere to them faithfully.

Before launching into using the wheel you must first *ask your partner if he's willing to listen*. Remember, contracts protect you as well as your partner. When you ask for your partner's consent, you show him respect and at the same time make it clear that, since he has a choice to say no, he is not being forced. Once your partner agrees to listen before you speak, you must *remember love*. If you are angry, or driven by a losing strategy, breathe yourself into a more moderate state. Recall that the person you're speaking to is the partner you care about and that your goal is to make things better. Once you're clear and focused, use the four steps of the wheel. Finally, having spoken your mind by using the wheel, you must *let go of the outcome*. Your partner will answer or not, as he wishes.

But whether you are happy or unhappy with his answer, you know that you have done your job well, and that is all you can directly control.

The Feedback Wheel

 A. Ask your partner if he is willing to listen.

 B. Remember that your motivation is that you love him.

 C. Take the four steps of the Feedback Wheel. Tell him

  1. what you saw/heard about one particular event.

  2. what you have made up about it.

  3. how you feel about it.

  4. what you would like to have happen in the future.

 D. Let go of the outcome.

Step One: "What I Saw or Heard": Reporting Observable Behaviors

Step one is the most concrete of the four steps. You recount the behavior(s) that troubled you. The behaviors you describe must be *particular* and *specific*—never "you always." And they must be *observable.* Your goal is to give your partner clear data about what happened as you recollect it. You will have the opportunity to say how you interpreted his behaviors in the next step, so be reassured that there is room for that later. This is the time for your version of "the facts and nothing but the facts."

Here's a hint: Before speaking, ask yourself if what you're about to describe is something that a video camera could record. If the answer is no, then you've drifted into intangibles like your partner's attitude, emotions, or motivations.

You want to share information about what triggered you as a way to assist your partner's understanding of what happened *to you,* what *you* experienced that was disturbing. Along with helping him see you more clearly, your naming specific difficult behaviors of his might help him to see himself more clearly. Behaviors that lead to a state of disruption are almost always more thoughtless and careless than your partner's usual behaviors. The odds of getting what you want from him will dramatically increase if he "gets it," if he sees the behaviors for what they really are.

Julia and Larry: From "Why Can't You Just Deal with Your Anger?" to "Last Night You Came Home and Yelled at the Children."

When I ask thirty-three-year-old Julia, a workshop participant, why she volunteered to "demo" the feedback wheel for the group, she answers that she's been "trying to get through" to her husband, Larry, about "his anger issues" for years. "Why can't you just deal with your anger?" she asks him, not expecting an answer. Larry, a high-powered lawyer, replies that aggression is just part of his nature. It's one of the reasons for his success.

In the past, Julia often complained only to back off eventually. But within the last year, she has begun to see Larry "starting up" with their children. She vows that she will not back down this time.

I ask Julia to think of a recent example. She smiles. "How about just yesterday?" she asks. We begin the first step. She turns to her husband and says:

> "Last night you were so disrespectful to the children."

I stop her. This description of her partner's *attitude* lies outside the wheel's parameters. Whether or not Larry was disrespectful is a matter of opinion. Julia tries again:

> "Last night you stormed into the house, absolutely furious and taking it out on everyone. The kids were petrified."

I stop her again. This description of Larry's *emotional state* also lies outside the wheel's parameters. Telling Larry what he felt is not only an internal boundary violation; it's also "cruising for a bruising." Informing someone about what he feels is a marvelously effective invitation to fight. ("Furious? I wasn't even *angry*. I was just a little stressed, that's all. It was just something from work.")

I suggest that Julia ask herself the video question: Would a camcorder record "disrespectful"? Would it record "furious"? What were Larry's *observable* behaviors?

On her third try, Julia gets it right:

> "Last night you came home and yelled at the children. You told Tom that his work was sloppy and lazy. I heard you then say to Billy, in a voice all of us could hear, 'And you're almost as bad as your brother!' "

Julia's third attempt was more than merely better than the others; it was perfect. So, does her perfect form mean that Larry will "get it"? No one knows. As you go through each of these steps, it's important to remind yourself that you cannot control your partner's reaction. It's a lot harder for Larry to deny saying the specific words Julia reports than it would be to deny the less precise "being angry" or "disrespectful." Citing Larry's specific behavior increases the chance that he will see it, but it doesn't guarantee this. I've had people argue over things as concrete as whether they went out to dinner last night or the night before. Remember, one of the benefits of "speaking from the 'I' " is that no one can argue with you, even about "facts." Your response to such a challenge is not to argue back but just to stick to your (subjective) guns. "This is my recollection of what happened," you answer. "You may recall it differently, but this is how I remember it."

Step Two: "What I Made Up About That Was"— Saying What You Think

Step two provides you with the opportunity to share your interpretation of the behaviors you've reported, what the behaviors meant to you. Pia Mellody added this step to the wheel, and I like her suggested introductory phrase, "What I made up about that," as artificial-sounding as it may seem, because it so clearly acknowledges your own role in how you construe things. From a relationship-empowerment perspective, people's behaviors are just raw data. They have no meaning until you assign meaning to them. The story you create about the interactions you observe may not jibe with that of the person standing next to you. We've all had that experience: You think that something your partner said was outrageous, but the friend you confide in thinks that you're being silly. One of the many great things that come from unburdening yourself of the myth of objectivity is how much wear and tear it saves. Just think of the minutes and hours you've squandered throughout the years in such utterly fruitless endeavors as trying to set the record straight, correcting someone's faulty recollection, pointing out the distortions in someone's thinking, arguing for your point of view, or trying to reach agreement. If you want to sit around with vehement friends and solve the world's problems, go have fun. But if you have real feelings and real issues on the line, then forget it. For all the good it will do, you'd better off walking the dog.

RULE: INTERPERSONAL CONFLICTS ARE NOT RESOLVED BY ERADICATING DIFFERENCES, BUT BY LEARNING HOW TO MANAGE THEM.

Julia and Larry

Julia has said:

> "Last night you came home and yelled at the children. You told Tom that his work was sloppy and lazy. I heard you then say to Billy, in a voice all of us could hear, 'And you're almost as bad as your brother!' "

Now she continues, telling him what she "made up" about what happened:

> "So, what that told me was that you were obviously in a rage about something and . . ."

I stop her. Julia has made a common beginner's mistake. While she knows enough not to speak with outright authority about what went on, she says, in effect, "this is what your behavior (objectively) indicates."

I wonder if Larry would so readily agree with her description. Julia has just moved objective reality back a bit. She no longer *knows* it; instead she *infers* it.

The wonderful thing about step two is that, once you've been careful to own the meaning of an event as *your* meaning rather than *the* meaning, this is the moment when you get to say all the mean, nasty things you've made up. Because you are sharing only *your own mad thoughts*, right or wrong, and not descriptions of your partner, you have *stayed on your side of the line* so that no matter what horrid nightmare you've imagined, it's explicit that it's *your* nightmare; the process stays clean.

Julia tries again:

> "What I made up about that is that this one incident is an example of a long-standing problem that you have with anger, that you came from an abusive family and that, while you're a million times better than what you grew up with, you are still abusive. But you don't or won't see it and you keep refusing to deal with it . . ."

I stop her. "Julia," I say. "I think that's enough." I turn to Larry. "Well," I ask him. "How did she do?"

Larry looks at his wife and smiles. "Clean as a whistle," he says, still looking at her. I nod agreement. "And clear as a bell," Larry adds. Julia grins. "I guess you got bells and whistles, baby," Larry says, apparently unable to stop himself. I glance at him. As a kindred spirit, I can spot another geek jokester when I see one. His wife responds with a gratifying look of disgust—the same look, I imagine, that he coaxes out of his kids when he's not mad and they're horsing around.

Julia and Larry

"Okay," I tell Julia. "Why don't you take it from the top."

"You want the whole thing?" she asks, and I nod. She takes a minute to get settled, and then says, "Larry, last night I observed you come home and yell at the children. You had a scowling look on your face from the second you walked in. You told Tom he was lazy and you told Billy that he was as bad as his brother . . . in *front* of his brother . . ."

" 'What I made up about that,' " I prompt.

"What I imagined then, and *still* imagine," she says, "is that you have a long-standing problem with anger, and that because you have so much more control over it than you experienced growing up in your family, you think it's in the range of normal. And that you're simply wrong. What I made up is that you need treatment, possibly some medication . . ."

"Okay, okay," I say, stopping her. "That's fine. Leave it there." We both pause for a moment. "Good," I say, pushing on. "And 'about that I feel,' " I say, "or 'I made myself feel.' "

"What I felt was that, like you so often do, you were taking out your . . ." When I stop her this time, she laughs. "I can't even get through *a sentence*?" she mock whines. "What did I *do*?"

"Everyone does this," I assure her.

I prompted Julia to stop once I heard her say, "What I felt was that *you* . . ." Here's why I stopped her:

In step three you state, with as much simplicity as you can, the emotions that got kicked up in you. In order to do that, you need to be able to identify what your feelings are, which is a task some people, particularly men, can have trouble with. Most people, however, find this step the easiest of the four—once they get clear on what they need to leave out. All this step is asking you to share is an unadorned list of the feelings you experienced during the incident under discussion. When people have trouble with this step it's because, either along with or instead of their emotions, they throw in everything under the sun. I can't number how many times someone in my office has said, "I just need to get my feelings out," only to launch into lambasting his partner up one side and down the other. After a few minutes of that, I usually interrupt by saying, "Excuse me. Can you tell me when the feeling part comes in? That's what I've been waiting for, and I haven't heard one feeling yet." How many of us are guilty of this one? "I want to share my feelings with you: *You* . . . And then *you* . . . , and furthermore *you* . . ." This hardly counts as keeping to your side of the line.

Another common mistake is mixing up feelings and beliefs. That's where Julia was headed when I stopped her. "I feel like you don't respect me anymore since that time I forgot your dog's birthday." This isn't an emotion; it's a theory. In common speech, we often use the word "feeling" to mean having a sense of something. We say "I feel," as a way of saying "I have an intuition that." That's usually no problem, but, when using the feedback wheel, don't use "I feel" for "I believe." The phrase "I feel," should always be followed by an actual emotion.

As I discussed earlier, just as with primary colors, a small number of irreducible feelings can combine to produce a seemingly infinite array of shades and hues. While a general consensus exists about the concept of primary feelings, there are slight variations in different researchers' proposed lists. Over the years, I have adapted one first proposed by Pia Mellody, and the people I've worked with have found it useful:

Seven Primary Feelings

Joy
Pain
Anger
Fear
Shame
Guilt
Love

These primaries can have variations. Pain can be felt as sadness, loneliness, or helplessness. Shame is an acute sense of embarrassment triggered by the exposure of some imperfection or of behavior that is culturally disapproved of, such as getting caught in a lie or while picking your nose. Guilt, a close relative of shame, is the feeling you get when you have gone outside the bounds of your own value system. You "feel bad" about not putting some money into the charity box passed around at your church, although no one else noticed your moment of selfishness.

Julia tries it again:

"Larry, when you yelled at the kids that way, I hypothesized that you have an untreated anger problem. And what I made myself feel about that was . . . and *is* . . . well, I feel lonely . . . very lonely actually. And sad. And quite helpless." She considers the list for a few beats. "I feel some shame," she continues, "and also guilt, a lot of guilt to be honest, about letting this all go on so long. I'm frustrated that you won't listen to me about this, and frightened. I'm really scared, Larry, that it will all get worse as the children get older. It will escalate as they get more of their own will." She stops there. I wait a moment, and then look at her.

"Done?" I ask.

She nods. "Think so," she answers. Another pause.

"That was extraordinary," I enthuse. "Just wonderful! Can I ask you, though, any anger?"

She looks a bit crestfallen for a second and I wonder if she's feeling criticized. "Well, I did say I was frustrated," she answers.

"Right," I agree with her. "You did. That's true. But . . ." I hesitate. She nods me on. "Julia, how angry *are* you, really?"

With that, Julia looks up into my face and, with no change whatsoever in her expression, two tracks of tears appear on her cheeks. "How angry do you want me to be?" she asks, her eyes like lasers trained on me.

"I don't understand," I tell her.

"How *angry* do you want me to be?" she repeats. "How *angry* . . . ?" she doesn't finish the sentence. Her voice has not risen, but she looks as though she despises me. I just gape at her for a moment, totally confused. "Angry enough to pack my bag?" she continues. "Is that what you want? Take the kids? I *said* I would do that, didn't I? Didn't I already say that?"

Looking at her, feeling the heat she was radiating, after a miserable few seconds, Larry tries to explain. "Her mother," he tells me, looking awkward and uncomfortable. "Her parents separated when Julia was, what . . . ten, I believe." He doesn't dare ask his wife. "Her mother thought it best if the girls, Julia's sisters . . . if there was no contact. I don't think she even saw him until she was an adult."

"I see," I tell Larry. "Julia?" I turn to her. She has her face buried in a pile of tissues.

"He had a problem," Larry goes on, utterly ill at ease but compelled to tell me anyway. "Evidently . . ." his voice trails off; he's stalled out.

"He had a temper," I guess. Larry nods. "He was a rager. Julia?" I turn back to her. She also nods. "Julia, your anger?"

"At who?" she asks, blowing her nose. "My mother? My dad? Everyone?"

"Larry?" I ask.

She looks hard at her husband. "Oh, he knows," she says finally. "He knows, this time. He knows how angry I am." She looks into his eyes until he turns away.

I don't respond, but inside I think, "Good for you, Julia. Good for you."

Here's a final bit of coaching on the use of step three. I'd like you to name all the emotions you are feeling, certainly, but I invite you to be especially interested in the emotions that are *not* the ones you customarily experience and express. What feeling or set of feelings comes most easily to you when you're in a state of disrepair? Fear, perhaps? Anger? Loneliness? Or even guilt? Whichever emotion comes most automatically, the strongest and quickest, the one you most often express—that is the emotion I am *least* interested in. Instead, I want you to express—and more important, to deeply feel—the other, less familiar emotions. And I'd like you to pay special attention to the feelings that seem in a way the *opposite* of your usual set. If you are used to leading with anger, shine the spotlight of your attention on the quieter feelings of hurt or fear. If your strongest response to disharmony is shame or desperation, open yourself to your denied anger, as Julia did that afternoon in the workshop.

I'm not advising you to act on your feelings by shifting from withdrawal to attack, or vice versa; remember, we're talking about feelings, not behaviors. But I am saying that if you are accustomed to leading with vulnerable feelings, try leading with emotions of assertion and power. And if you are used to leading with strong, assertive feelings, try moving into increased vulnerability. In short, *access and express the unusual.*

RULE: MORE OF THE SAME EMOTION MOST OFTEN BRINGS MORE
OF THE SAME INTERACTION. LEAD WITH THE UNACCUSTOMED
AND SEE WHAT HAPPENS.

Step Four: "What I'd Like Now": Inviting Healing

Step four drives us into the heart of the repair process. It *forces* the speaker to give up a negative/past focus and to move beyond his or her usual set of losing strategies to a positive/future mode. In step four, you tell your partner what he could do to help you feel better and move back toward harmony—in other words, what he can do to help heal the disruption. Perhaps the most potent aspect of step four occurs before any content is even shared. The sheer act of saying "You could do *this* to help me feel better" conveys a willingness to *let* things get better. This in itself positions both partners as having the ability to end the discord if they want to. For many people, the negotiations that flesh out the terms of peace aren't nearly as difficult to complete as is the process of bringing themselves to a desire for peace to begin with.

This last step, in its way, mirrors the first step in that, having ventured out into the world of thinking and feeling, you are returned to the specificity of behaviors. You cannot legislate what your partner thinks or feels. If you ask him to understand something, "get" something, or change an attitude, you must follow that up with things he might practically say or do that would indicate those changes or his intentions, his willingness to change. "I'd like you to reassure me that . . ." is a phrase that often seems helpful: "I'd like you to reassure me that you understand, you care, you too see this as a problem, you will follow through this time."

RULE: WHEN MAKING A REQUEST, YOU CAN START WITH INTANGIBLES
   LIKE CHANGES IN ATTITUDE. BUT THEN YOU MUST TRANSLATE
   THE CHANGES YOU'RE ASKING FOR INTO CLEAR, ACTIONABLE
   BEHAVIORS.

Julia and Larry

Julia has done well up to this point. She has shared how she saw and heard Larry behave, her theory about it, and her feelings. Now it's time for the bottom line, what she wants Larry to do:

"What I'd like now," Julia tells her husband, "is some reassurance that you'll believe me when I tell you your anger is over the line. Whether you see it or not."

"And?" I ask, nudging her a little.

"That would be earth-shattering," Julia says. I am about to speak, but she rushes in to beat me to the punch. "*And*," she enunciates emphatically, "I want you to get help for it. *Commit* to do what it takes already. Get it done, Larry. Get that . . . crap out of our house."

HOW LONG SHOULD THIS BE?

The work I did with Julia does *not* represent a typical wheel. It was far too wordy. The work with Julia is more representative of what teaching someone how to use the wheel for the first time tends to look like. Once you understand the basic working principles of the feedback wheel—as you now do!—the steps should each be *no more than a sentence or two*.

Janet Hurley, the wheel's creator, saw the task of hearing someone describe the ways that he's made himself miserable about his partner's behavior as about the most challenging kind of listening there is. She believed most human beings have a four-sentence-long attention span for that sort of listening and not much more. She used to say, "If you haven't pared it down to four clear sentences, you're not ready to use it yet." I'm not as strict as Janet was, but I do recommend that you keep it very short.

Here's how Julia's feedback to Larry sounded when she was all done:

"Larry, last night *I saw* you walk in the door with a scowl on your face. Then you yelled at Tim and humiliated both kids by telling Billy he wasn't much better than his brother.

"What *I made up about that* is that something happened to set you off and that, once again, you felt entitled to spew your anger around even if it meant hurting our family.

"*The meaning I gave to your behavior* was that it is a symptom of a long-standing anger problem you have so far refused to deal with.

"*I feel* hurt, frustrated, sad, guilty, frightened, and angry, Larry. I feel very angry.

"And *what I'd like* is for you to stand up and fight for the health of the people you love by tackling this thing, get the help you need, and stop arguing with me about it."

Julia and Larry: A Postscript

After Julia had worked so hard to get it said right, Larry, who had for the most part stood quietly beside her the whole time, turned to me and asked, "Well, what would be the best way to respond to all this?"

Standing, as we were, in front of the group of workshop participants, I shared what was on my mind with Larry and gave him an option. "You can go for the whole thing after lunch, or you could do the short-short version right now. What would you like?" He shuffled around for a moment and chose the short version. "You're sure?" I asked. Larry nodded. "Well, the very short answer to your question as I see it just sounds like this: 'Julia, you're right. I'm sorry I've been so stubborn. I'd cut off my hand before I'd hurt you or the kids. And I swear to you in front of these people that I will get treatment and I won't stop until both of us are satisfied.' That's what I'd say, Larry."

Larry looked at me for a minute, nodding to himself as if to say, "That's about what I'd expected." Then he turned to Julia and, in his own way, told her point for point just about everything I'd suggested. And as I listened in, I had little doubt that he'd be true to his word.

Chapter Six
Practice Section

EXPERIMENT WITH A COMPLAINT-FREE TEN DAYS

Hold a ten-day moratorium on all complaints, large and small. Do your best to deal with issues as they come up by *focusing exclusively on what you'd like to see happen*. See if you can say what you need to without resorting to the past—even the past two minutes.

Here's a tip: To *yourself*, say it first the way you normally might. Then rephrase it in your head until you feel ready to try it out loud.

EXPERIMENT WITH APPRECIATION AND REQUESTS

For one week, work with two of your wants. The two things you're after, such as more talking or greater punctuality, should be fairly bite-sized, not the biggest issues you face. See if and how well you can grow more of the behaviors you'd like using *only* these two practices:

- Appreciating anything your partner does, or has ever done in the past, that gives or gave some of what you're after.
- Making requests.

Here's a tip: Make your requests as *specific* and as *behavioral* as you can. If your partner responds at all positively, go back to step one.

THE FEEDBACK WHEEL

A. Ask your partner if he is willing to listen.

B. Remember that your motivation is that you love him.

C. Take the four steps of the Feedback Wheel. Tell him

1. What I saw or heard
2. What I made up about it
3. How I feel about it
4. What I'd like

D. Let go of the outcome.

Step one is a journaling exercise. Step two is optional.

Step One:

Write about a recent incident in which you tried to communicate to your partner your thoughts, feelings, or wishes about something that troubled you. Pick an incident in which you weren't wonderfully skillful, the kind of incident you might choose if you were asking me for some relationship coaching.

As best you can remember or re-create, write out the exchange you had with your partner. As much as possible, write out the important phrases you spoke to each other. If you feel ambitious, you might even create a dramatic vignette, a small play.

Now, imagine and then write out as dialogue what you would have said if you had skillfully used the feedback wheel.

Step Two:

Tell your partner that you are working on a new relationship skill designed to help you be less of a _____. *(Use your own language: hot-head, pain, witch, etc.)* Ask him to help you by participating in a dramatic re-creation of your recent conflict. Tell him you want to improve your interaction by using a new skill called the feedback wheel. Sit him down and go through the steps. Accept whatever he says by way of response, barring abusiveness, and be warmly appreciative of his help and cooperation.

Chapter Seven

Give What You Can

EMPOWERING EACH OTHER

Summary

Chapter six began your introduction to the five winning strategies that make up the core practices of relationship empowerment. These winning strategies are:

1. Shifting from complaint to request
2. Speaking out with love and savvy
3. Responding with generosity
4. Empowering each other
5. Cherishing

The last chapter focused on the first two winning strategies, requesting and speaking out, both of which help you to proactively shape your relationship, to go after and get what you're looking for. The cardinal rule you learned is *More assertion up front and less resentment on the back end.* But you were also reminded that the critical task of getting occurs within a relational context. Whom are you getting from? Your partner, of course. And what does he need from you to help him deliver? You were asked to recall the central question of relationship empowerment: *What can I give you to help you give me what I'm asking for?*

While the first winning strategy, *shifting from complaint to request*, may be effective on many occasions, even with the most responsible of partners things sometimes go awry. The second winning strategy, *speaking out with love and savvy*, is the first step in the *process of repair*, getting the relationship back on track, moving from disharmony back into harmony. Perhaps the most important part of speaking out happens before you actually speak. Prior to inviting your partner into the repair process, you must *remember love.* What is your goal? Why are you doing this? Before speaking, you remind yourself that the person you are about to address is not the enemy but the partner you love, and that your purpose in speaking is to feel close to your partner again. You were introduced to the *feedback wheel*, a powerful guiding formula for speaking that keeps you on track and out of the clutches of losing strategies. Following the wheel's four steps, you learned to say what happened, the meaning you gave to it, the emotions you felt, and what you'd like from your partner. Now, we turn to the other side of the process, giving—responding with a generous heart.

Winning Strategy 3: Responding with Generosity

Before learning how best to respond, we must first know how to listen. Every couple that has trouble with repair, that does not possess a functioning *mechanism of correction*—one of the most basic and essential skills of healthy relationships—is a couple that has foundered on the issue of *listening.* And virtually *every* failed effort to listen, every "breakdown in communication," happens because the listener does not appreciate one seemingly obvious fact:

RULE: WHEN SOMEONE INITIATES REPAIR, *THE SPEAKER ROLE AND THE LISTENER ROLE ARE TWO DIFFERENT ROLES.*

Overwhelmingly, our common approach to problems is to have a dialogue: *You tell me your side and then I'll tell you mine, and then we'll thrash it out together.* There are, indeed, many times when heads are cool enough and misunderstandings clear enough that the mutual dialogue process works just fine. However, remember that repetitive fight you and your partner seem destined to have for the next forty years? Remember what happens once CNI meets CNI? How well is dialogue serving you there?

For most couples, any intensely charged issue quickly reveals that the *that's your side, here's my side* approach carries a high risk of increasing rather than decreasing tensions because *neither* side feels sufficiently heard or understood. In a great relationship both you and your partner can, if you must, air your upset about an issue. *But not at the same time.*

RULE: THE REPAIR PROCESS IS *UNILATERAL,* NOT MUTUAL. ONE PARTNER ASKS FOR AND RECEIVES HELP FROM THE OTHER IN ORDER TO MOVE OUT OF A STATE OF ACUTE DISCONTENT (DISHARMONY) BACK INTO THE EXPERIENCE OF CLOSENESS AND CONNECTION (HARMONY). *THE LISTENER MUST PUT HIS OR HER OWN NEEDS ASIDE.*

Here is a tough but necessary pill to swallow:

While he may be too polite to say it, someone experiencing distress, even if he's intent on making things right, isn't really interested in your thoughts, your feelings, or your reasons or explanations. In those first raw moments of reconnection, the upset partner doesn't care all that much about you one way or another. *What he needs to know is whether or not you care about him.* Once you have demonstrated your care and sincerity, once you have addressed his concerns, then he might have an interest in you. But before that occurs, a distressed partner will inevitably perceive any bid on your part to focus on your experience as a deflection. And though you may have nothing but the best of intentions, he will see your behavior as defensive, ungiving, selfish, or evasive. And, by the way, he'd be right!

RULE: IN THE REPAIR PROCESS, THE LISTENER HAS ONLY ONE GOAL:
   TO HELP THE SPEAKER MOVE BACK INTO HARMONY, TO HELP
   HIM OR HER FEEL BETTER. THE LISTENER'S ATTITUDE IS:
   "I AM AT YOUR SERVICE. HOW CAN I HELP?" ANYTHING ELSE
   WILL BE PERCEIVED AS AT BEST EXTRANEOUS AND AT WORST
   INFURIATING.

WHAT DOES "BEING AT YOUR SERVICE" MEAN HERE?

Being at your partner's service is the listener's way of remembering love, and it is perhaps the most challenging example of "You can be right or you can be married; what's more important to you?" As a listener, resisting the temptation to surrender your true goal of repair to the first losing agenda of being right can feel almost impossible. You might ask, "How can you expect me to just sit there and listen to things that are clearly inaccurate without saying something about it?" You *will* have your chance to air your opinion, I promise, but not yet.

The second losing agenda that may pull you away from skilled listening is unbridled self-expression. This is most evident when couples, under the guise of "communicating," go tit-for-tat: "Oh yeah? Well, if you're disturbed about this, let me tell you, I am really upset about *that!*" Whenever you shift attention away from your partner's concerns over to your own, you create a situation in which there are *two speakers and no listeners.* And that is precisely how most of us do it, how we try, and fail, to effect change.

Scot and Alyssa: Is Anyone Listening?

No one seemed to disagree that Scot had been verbally and psychologically abusive to Alyssa for much of their twenty-four years together. For her part, Alyssa had retaliated with at least one, if not several, affairs. Scot horribly shamed her, while Alyssa manipulated and lied.

In their hometown of Seattle, Scot and Alyssa were seen as the quintessential power couple, at the center of art, business, and regional politics. And yet their pattern of escalating brutality consumed any joy either might have found in their accomplished lives. Scot cloaked his raw pain in sheer nastiness, and Alyssa paid him back with betrayal. But then Alyssa found her way to a clinician courageous enough to confront her double life as both shameless and lonely. Alyssa came to realize that she deserved more than a marriage united by retaliation. She told Scot she was filing for a divorce. That's when Scot first called me.

When I initially met Scot, alone, only a few days after Alyssa's announcement, he looked like a humbled man, a tragic king undone by his own fatal pride. By the time they both came to Boston, however, only a week or so later, Scot's arrogance had returned in full measure.

In our session, I ask Alyssa to articulate what changes she would need to see in order to reconsider her plans for divorce. Her list is substantial, mostly centering on Scot's obnoxious behaviors. When I ask her for an example, she speaks, not without difficulty, about feeling pressured for sex: "For years, Scot was the one who rejected me. I was supposed to just accept it. But now our roles seem to have reversed. Only Scot isn't as gracious as I was. There's always a comment, 'Well, another great night for us!' or, 'Some men have sex lives,' or, 'It's a shame we're so young. Your next husband should be seventy and impotent; that would suit you.'"

As Scot listens, the indignation radiating from him grows palpable. "And what did *you* say after I told you that?" he demands of his wife.

"Why?" Alyssa responds. "Why are you even asking me that question?"

"Just tell me," he insists. "How did you answer me?"

"I don't remember," she dismisses him.

"You don't *remember*," Scot repeats, doubtful, disgusted.

"I don't care . . ."

"You *said*," he overtalks her, "'And you should get yourself one of those blow-up dolls with a hole you can just stick it in anytime you want.' Does that bring it back?"

"I already told you. I don't care."

"And anyway, how long ago was all this, Alyssa?" he continues with infuriating calmness.

"What does it . . . ?"

"Well, I mean two months ago, five months, a *year*, three years? In fact, when was the last time I said *anything* to you about your rejections?" he asks, his voice measured and hostile. "*Anything*?" he repeats.

"Scot," I turn to him, "would you mind if I interrupted this for just a second or two and asked you a question?"

He lifts his face toward me, bland and pleasant. "I don't mind at all," he grants me permission, magnanimously, regally. I glance at him for a moment as he sits all puffed up in his chair, looking just like the fool he is being.

"What in the *hell* are you doing?" I ask him. The question stops him for barely a second.

"Well, I just . . . Look, if we're going to get things straight around here we have to be honest in the way we . . ."

"Oh," I cut him off. "So, you think you're here to straighten things out. Now I get it."

"I don't see . . ."

"We're not here to straighten things out, Scot. We're not here to be brutally honest. We're here in a last-ditch attempt to salvage your relationship."

"Well, sure. But how are we going to . . ."

"Your wife," I go on, "has about one and three quarters feet out the door; you do realize that, don't you?"

The indignation that Scot has barely held in check ripples over him. "Look, Terry, I'm just tired of . . ."

"*You're* tired," I say.

"Damn straight. And if you think that I'm sitting here like a good little boy while she . . ."

"If I think *what*?" I ask in mock confusion. "You're not going to sit there and *what*?" We just look at each other for a minute. "Scot," I continue, "for some reason I, frankly, can't fathom, you seem to be under the impression that what's important here is what *you're* aggravated about, what *you're* tired of, what *you* won't stand." I lean back and turn to Alyssa. "He doesn't seem like a man desperate to save his marriage to me," I tell her. "Does he to you?"

"Welcome to *my* world," she replies, tapping her feet, restless, impatient, confirmed in her conviction that this meeting is a waste of her time.

"Look, Scot," she begins, her glance falling on the door.

"Alyssa, hold it a second, would you?" I try heading her off. "Let me do it." Before she can answer, I turn to her husband.

"Scot," I say, "you're a very bright man. Would you characterize your behavior in this office so far as particularly *attractive*?" Scot takes a moment to think and then, unexpectedly, he laughs.

"I'm fighting with the hangman," he says, smiling, showing me— finally—some of the charisma I assumed a man this successful possessed.

"Pardon?" I ask. He chuckles again.

"It's a phrase I use in business," he tells me. "It's when you take a position you're absolutely in no position to take."

"There you go!" I reply. "I knew it was in there somewhere."

He turns to Alyssa, who only half looks at him. "You know it's bullshit," he tells her. "My bluster. It's all front . . ."

"And underneath?" I try, but he ignores me.

"It's exactly this kind of bullshit that got me into this mess to begin with, Alyssa," he admits. Neither of them seems able to come up with anything more to say.

I look inquiringly at Alyssa, who remains quiet, unmoving, offering neither encouragement nor resistance. Then I turn to her husband. "Want to try it again?" I ask.

"Yes," he agrees, glancing over at his wife's closed face, all the air suddenly let out of him. "If I could have another chance," he says softly, "I'd be grateful."

AND YOU CALL THIS LISTENING?

What was bizarre about Scot's behavior was his total disregard for the reality of his situation. He acted exactly like someone storming out of a marriage, not someone desperate to win it back.

Because Scot's disconnect is so profound, it's easy to see how foolish he's being. But before you judge him too harshly, you should realize that Scot's behavior is just an exaggerated version of how most of us operate. The truth is that when most of us engage in so-called listening, we have a hot nanosecond's worth of attention span before we're off and running. And just what are we off and running to?

Rebuttal.

"Geez, *that's* not right," we might say, or "Hey, *I* never said that. That is *such* an exaggeration." Or, if you're a psychologically sophisticated couple, you might sound something like this: "Honey, that's *your* projection." "No, dear, it's *your* denial."

Some partners start protesting almost immediately. Others who are more restrained manage to keep their mouths shut, but don't be fooled: They're saying exactly the same things; they just keep the debate in their minds. What does all this mean? When we cast a cool eye over the so-called listening most of us claim to do, it turns out that we're most often not listening at all. Whether it's out on the table or locked in our heads, what most of us do, sentence by sentence and point by point, is *argue*. Then we have the gall to get "frustrated" by mates who are being "difficult," when in fact we haven't really appreciated a word they've said. Finally, we answer most of their concerns by either discounting them altogether or by replacing those concerns with our own.

Here's the challenge: When you listen, *listen*; put your ego aside. Remember that what you're doing is making things better, or, more precisely, making things better *for your dissatisfied partner*. You won't be able to fix anything without listening enough to know what's wrong. *That* is the point—not judging the correctness of your partner's experience but simply understanding it. Attend to the distressed partner who has approached you for help, not to *yourself*. Focus on him rather than on some imagined yardstick of validity. Remember, the relational answer to the question "Who's right and who's wrong?" is "Who cares?"

RULE: LISTENING EQUALS UNDERSTANDING.

DO YOU USE YOUR INTERNAL BOUNDARY?

You cannot really listen *without* a functioning boundary. But using a boundary is not the same as being *primarily* concerned with accuracy. As you listen, not only do I want you to do the exercise of judging "true" or "not true," I want you to take particular notice of what doesn't jibe. You're going to put that information to good use in short order. But even as you note what does and does not coincide with your perception, remember two things:

First, unlike Scot in the above example, have some humility. You are judging what your partner shares, not against an objective measure of *the* reality, but the subjective measure of *your* reality.

Second, think of this process of judging, "true, not true," as something you do *in passing*, as if you were offhandedly tagging the points that don't jibe with your perception as they fly by. The main focus of your attention should be on your partner. You are trying your best to get inside his shoes, to understand how he sees things. You note discrepancies, but they don't occupy you. What matters is getting inside his head.

IF YOU UNDERSTAND LISTENING IN PRINCIPLE, NOW WHAT DO YOU ACTUALLY *DO*?

I've said a lot about what *not* to do—don't argue, don't focus on yourself, don't worry about "the truth"—so what *do* you do? Your job as a listener is done when you can say to the speaker, "Okay. I think I have it. What you're saying is . . ." and the speaker replies, "Yes. You do have it. That's right." The best way to get that understanding is to go through the same four steps of the feedback wheel that your partner used: "So, this is what you remember. And the story you told yourself about it was this. The feelings it evoked were these. And what you'd like now is this." Seems easy, doesn't it? And it would be a snap if all that was required of you were to parrot back what you'd heard. But your aim is higher: to truly understand what you've heard, and even to let yourself feel it as your partner did.

Step 1: What I Saw or Heard

Understanding your partner's version of observable events shouldn't present much of a challenge—once you're willing to put your version aside. I'd like to focus now on the two steps that come next.

Step 2: What I Made Up About It: Find the Story's Internal Logic

Your task here is to figure out the *internal logic* of your partner's construction.

RULE: NO ONE IS IRRATIONAL TO HIMSELF.

As wildly different as someone's perceptions may be from your own, thoughts rarely seem nonsensical to the thinker; it's just that others may not understand the sense. To someone suffering from paranoid delusions it's perfectly obvious that you too would be cowering under your chair, as he is, if you only knew, as he does, that terrorists had unleashed a deadly toxin in the ventilation system. *The challenge lies in letting go of your story enough to enter into your partner's.* Don't reference his story to yours, and don't reference it to "objective measures." No matter how it might seem to you, you can trust that your partner's story makes perfect sense to *him.* Pretend you're one of those FBI profilers so popular on television, an empathy expert brought into a tough case with the task of getting inside a *very* strange mind—your partner's. See if you can see things as he does. This is called "understanding."

Step 3: How I Feel About It: Feel the Emotions in the Story

Your job here is to grasp the emotional feel of the incident as experienced by your partner. Make the connection between the meaning he gave the events and the feelings that flowed from that. You're making headway when you can say to yourself, "Yes, I can see how, if I saw it the way he did, I might feel the way he did." If you can move *your* feelings aside, this should be a relatively easy step, because *feelings come naturally from the meaning we give to things.*

RULE: EMOTIONS FOLLOW COGNITION. THE WAY YOU PERCEIVE AN EVENT WILL DETERMINE HOW YOU FEEL ABOUT IT.

For instance, on Tuesday your partner blew a kiss your way as he left in the morning, saying, "Have a good day, honey." You felt warm and tender. On Wednesday you went to bed angry at each other, and this morning's breakfast was tense. You receive the same kiss and the same wish from your mate, but this time you think that he's being sarcastic. Where are those warm feelings now?

What you think about a situation will determine how you feel about it. If you think that you're in danger, you'll be frightened. If you think someone's taking liberties with you, you'll get angry. Seeing a change in his circumstances as freeing will leave one person joyful, while seeing the very same change in circumstances as a great loss will leave someone else feeling sad. The most responsible way to express an emotion is to take explicit ownership of your own process. You'd say, "I made myself feel," which sounds more stilted in the abstract than it does in real usage, as in *I drove myself crazy. I scared myself. I worked myself up and got really mad.* The important thing when you speak is to not take a victim position, as in *it made me feel*, or the absolute worst: *you made me feel*.

RULE: DELETE THE PHRASE "MADE ME" FROM YOUR VOCABULARY.

Short of outright abuse, no one *makes* anyone feel anything. Our feelings are our own.

The importance of all this when you listen is that *if you can see something the way your partner sees it, you will understand his feelings about it.*

WHY IS UNDERSTANDING SO IMPORTANT?

RULE: UNDERSTANDING BUILDS EMPATHY, EMPATHY BUILDS
COMPASSION, AND COMPASSION ENDS COMBAT.

To be compassionate means that you are sensitive to, feel the pain of, someone else's suffering. Compassion comes from empathy, your ability to put yourself in someone else's shoes. The more you can understand someone, the more able—and the more willing—you will be to, in an act of imagination, *become* that person for a moment, feeling as he does. Conversely, the more alien someone seems to you, the more difficult empathy will be and the less you'll be interested in trying to empathize. This is why stereotypes and derogatory caricatures abound during wartime. You don't want to know too much about the enemy; you need him to remain *other*—a *Jap*, a *Gook*, a *Cockroach*. With familiarity comes understanding, which opens the door to empathy and compassion. And these make it harder to kill someone. It is this same principle that leads experts to advise hostages to talk about themselves to their captors. The more a captive shares, the more real he becomes as a person, the more difficult it will be to harm him.

The reason it is not helpful to empathize with an enemy is precisely the reason it *is* helpful in the close engagement of long-term relationships. The more you can understand and empathize with your partner, the easier it will be to remember to whom you're really talking. In troubled relationships, a partner may be someone you need to stand up to, perhaps even someone who must either grow up or get out. But, short of outright abuse, he is still not an enemy. If you honestly feel otherwise, you probably should leave. But if, in your sane mind, you know better, then you must work to hold the thread of that knowing even in times of disrepair. Remember your core negative image? Your CNI is your personal version of a derogatory caricature, your very own, "*Jap*," "*Gook*," or "*Cockroach*." Your CNI represents, at its core, the fear and despair that comes over you when you view your mate as unalterably "other."

I said earlier that speaking to repair, both the preparatory work of remembering love and the formula of the wheel force you to stay on track, and away from losing agendas. Learning to listen with generosity does much the same thing.

Understanding, empathy, and compassion are powerful CNI-busters.

RULE: PARTNERS RARELY ENGAGE IN TOXIC COMBAT WITH EACH OTHER; *THEY COMBAT EACH OTHER'S CNIs.* **WHEN THE** *REAL* **PERSON EMERGES FROM THE CARICATURE, COMBAT SUBSIDES.**

WHAT IF I GENUINELY DON'T UNDERSTAND MY PARTNER'S STORY?

First of all, you should not expect to understand everything about your partner's perspective right off the bat. If your views were that intelligible to each other, you probably wouldn't need to repair. So, in practical terms, how do you bridge such a gulf? By turning what had been your biggest obstacle into your most helpful instrument. Earlier I asked you to take note of each element of your partner's perception that contrasted with your own. I promised that we would put these to good use at some point. Well, now is the time.

RULE: WHEN LISTENING WITH A GENEROUS HEART, *POINTS OF CONTENTION BECOME POINTS OF CURIOSITY.*

Rather than seeing points of contention as further indications of your partner's lunacy—or, said differently, as confirming your CNI of him—I want you to turn this issue on its head and think of each point of "disagreement" as *an opportunity to further your understanding.*

Carla and Thomas: But Why Would You Ever Think That?

In a recent workshop, two volunteers offered to demonstrate listening with a generous heart. Carla and Thomas, an impressive African

American couple only in their late twenties, have already accomplished a great deal. Living in D.C., they seem to thrive in the buzz of Washington politics and beyond. They are both recognized innovators in designing health-care systems for large underserved countries. Indeed, they first met in a graduate course on international health-care policy.

With little help needed from me, Carla begins using the feedback wheel about an incident they'd been incapable of even mentioning without triggering a terrible fight. I ask Carla to remember her purpose and, when she felt ready, to invite Thomas into the repair process.

"Thomas," she begins, "about two weeks ago, I saw you flirting . . ."

"Hold it," I stop her, but she's already caught herself drifting beyond observable behavior.

"A few weeks ago," she tries again, "at the big kickoff party for the W.H.O. project . . ."

"The one at Georgetown, I know," Thomas volunteers until a look at me stops him. "Oh, yeah. Sorry," he says. "Go on. I'll listen."

"At that party," she continues, "I saw you speaking for quite a while," she glances at me, "with that really cute grad student, what's her name?" She looks at Thomas, who remains resolutely mute. "Anyway, you know the one. She kept leaning in close to you and whispering to you and you were both laughing. Then, you strolled on out with her onto the balcony."

"Great, Carla," I say. "So far so good. Keep going."

"What I made up about that is that you had very little regard for our conversation going into the party in which I asked you to stay close to me because Boyd—an old boyfriend," she explains in an aside, "Boyd was going to be there and I didn't want to deal with him. I made up that it was far more important to you to flirt with this girl right in front of my eyes than honor your commitment. It made me realize . . ." I start to correct, but she beats me to it. "I *told* myself that you were still such a boy. I'm not sure if you're ready for a real relationship, Thomas."

" 'And about all that I felt,' " I prompt.

"What I *made* myself feel," Carla says, ever the A student, "is hurt, angry, sad, lonely, disgusted, a little bit ashamed, you know, from being rejected. And *afraid* that if I stayed with you I might wind up getting *really hurt.*" Now her tears come, and she is suddenly no longer one of the best and brightest, but just a vulnerable young woman.

" 'And what I'd like now,' " I urge her on. "Can you keep going, Carla?" She nods, takes a minute.

"What I'd like now is some explanation of how you could do that after what we've been through. Like, what was going on in your *head*? I was standing right *there*, Thomas. And I also want to know what you plan to do about your immaturity, getting into therapy or whatever to deal with why you *do* things like this." Tears come again. "Or you're gonna lose me, Thomas. You really . . ."

"Okay," I stop her. "Okay, you did great."

A few minutes later, Thomas says he's ready to find out more. As a way of getting started, I propose that he answer Carla the way he normally would and then I could coach him. But he shakes his head.

"I'm going to tell you right now," he says, "I will not answer here the way I do there because it's just too . . . Hey, look; I don't need to get into all of this *negativity*. Why don't I just jump in and try to do it right the first time?" Thomas sits back in his chair and then inches closer to his wife, with his long arms draped over his knees and his face drawn in concentration. "Carla," he starts, "what just makes no sense at all is . . ."

" 'What *I* don't understand,' " I rephrase, coaching him. " 'What *I'm* confused about . . .' "

"What I can't figure is . . . This girl is *not* a graduate student. Well, she will be I guess for another month or so, but I mean, she's part of the project. You know that. She's part of the team going out. So, this is her first field job; it's her first job, period. And her new boss is standing an inch away from us . . . You know, Carla, you made it out like we were alone, she and I, but there must have been *twenty* of us standing together. So, in front of her teachers . . . her *colleagues*, her *boss*, she's going to move in on a married man, with, as you say, his wife standing right over there *looking* at them? I don't even get how you could make that *up*. You think she's *suicidal*? You think she's just *stupid*?"

"Okay," I say, "stay moderate. Take a breath." He does. "All right, good work. 'And so, Carla, could you help me understand how you see this?' " I say, modeling for him.

"Help me put this together," Thomas says. "Because, to tell you the truth, I just don't see . . ."

"Okay, okay," I stop him.

Carla looks at him for a minute and then says, "Well, I do know all that about her being out in front of everyone. And I thought she walked right up to the line. You think I was the only one checking out how all over you she was? But she played it just cool enough to pass as innocent."

"Jesus, Carla!" Thomas breaks in. "You really believe that?"

"Hey," she says, sternly. "You asked me, right? Do you not want to hear the answer?" Thomas nods, sheepish. "That is what I thought, Thomas. That's what I *made up* all that whispering was about. I don't know what she was busy whispering, but it sure didn't look like anything meant for anyone but you. Not to me it didn't."

"But, honey," he pleads. "She was just making fun of some of the people on the team."

"Good manners, too." Carla sniffs. I figure that they're only a few seconds short of derailing.

"Thomas," I cut in. "What's your goal right now?" He shakes his head, equal parts sheepish and disgruntled. "Is this about defending that girl? Scoring points?" I press. The head shake. "Straightening Carla out?"

"No," he drags out. "I don't even get to defend myself, right?" he asks.

"Defend against what?" I respond. "The nutty things Carla dreams up? Thomas, we don't *care* what that girl was really saying. What matters is that Carla is driving herself bonkers about it. You can decide to not get involved if you want and just let her deal with it; that's a respectable choice. If you can bear the consequences. You can choose to help her out with it; that's another respectable choice. Or you could just fight about it, which is where you usually go. And where you're headed right now, by the way. So, which would you like?"

He doesn't even look at me. "Carla," he says, "so you think that all those people around us were just a big smoke screen?"

"You could put it that way," she answers.

"And," he asks, "when we all moved out onto the terrace, that was just a smoke screen as well?"

"I'm not sure. Could have been. I'm not saying it was you who suggested it," she replies.

"So, the whole thing was just . . ."

"Listen," she snaps at him, clear and angry. "I don't appreciate you sitting there acting like I'm such a fool for making up a bunch of *paranoid* stories, okay? I don't know about this or that specific, okay? I'm saying that it looked like . . ."

" 'What I imagined,' " I say.

"What *came* to me about it was that the whole thing looked innocent—*sort of*. And to tell the truth, I didn't . . ." She starts to cry. Like Thomas, I find myself wondering why this small incident unleashes so much feeling. Then I find out. "It isn't like it would be the *first* time, Thomas," Carla blurts out. "I don't know why you're so 'confused.' You *did* try to pick up Elaine's sister right out on *my* own front lawn. That *was* you, wasn't it?" Thomas's eyes drop to the floor. "So, here on a night that I thought you'd be with me, that you'd help me out, that's the night you chose to mess around with another young student right in front of my face?"

"But honey," he starts as she glares at him. Then Thomas stops himself, stops the momentum pushing them both toward conflict. In a much different voice than the one he'd been using, he muses aloud, "So, it doesn't even matter, really, what that girl said. Just being there like that with her at all . . ."

"You think I catch you setting up to cheat on me and then you say you're sorry and it just all goes away?" she asks, crying. "You think I don't feel insecure? It *hurts*, Thomas . . ." and then the dam breaks; crying shakes her as she bends over the tissues in her hands.

"Oh honey." He comes to her. "I never would have called Elaine's sister. I was just being an idiot. I was just playing stupid games with myself. I'm so sorry. I'm so sorry." He touches her gingerly and she doesn't resist. Then he folds her in his arms. "It's only you, baby." He kisses her forehead as she cries. "It's only you."

By the time Thomas ran through his four-part restatement of Carla's wheel, the exercise was strictly pro forma. He had already demonstrated his understanding when he realized, without being told, that even without flirting, the act of deserting Carla and allowing such a scene was in itself caddish behavior given their recent history. As Thomas shows us, the point of this exercise is not the cultivation of flawless technique, but a shift in the listener's comprehension, in his consciousness. A highly structured form, like disciplined listening, or the feedback wheel, is only a tool to help you get where you need to go. It's where you arrive, not the instruments, that matters.

RESPONDING WITH A GENEROUS HEART

You have listened well to your partner, and he has agreed that you understand what he said. But hearing is not enough; you must respond with the same generosity and compassion with which you received. It is time to move into action. Unlike many couple's therapies, relationship empowerment does not see one partner's empathic reflection of what that partner has heard from the other as, in itself, a major change agent. In fact, as Thomas illustrated, listening with generosity primarily affects the psychological state of the *listener*. Whatever joy or sense of connectedness it brings to the speaker as well is icing on the cake. So, you needn't be overly fussy about telling your partner what you've heard; there's no need for exquisite reflecting. Getting the gist of what your partner shares is serviceable enough for our purposes.

Once you and your partner agree that you understand what has been said, it is time to respond. Here again, your generosity holds the key to success.

WHAT ARE THE GUIDELINES FOR RESPONDING?

RULE: A GREAT RESPONSE IS DRIVEN BY ONE SIMPLE IMPERATIVE: GIVE.

If you want to help move your partner toward reconnection, then give him whatever you reasonably can. To thoroughly respond, you will:

- Clarify
- Acknowledge
- Give

Step 4: What I'd Like Now Is
The link that connects the activities of listening and responding is the fourth step of the feedback wheel: *what your partner wants*. Once the listener repeats what he's heard, he *returns* to that critical piece of information and *clarifies*, as in:

> "You said that what you'd like now is for me to explain what was going on with that young woman, and to commit to some process, like therapy, to work on the ways I can be immature. Have I got it? Okay. Is there more, or anything else you think I need to understand about what you'd like?"

Once you are both clear about the speaker's requests, it is your time, as the listener, to show what you're made of. "Breathe deep," I tell listeners I work with. "This is going to be difficult." Your first active step in effecting repair is to let your partner know that you understand his experience at a deeper level than before—and not just that you understand, but that you're mature enough to take responsibility for yourself. You do this by *acknowledging whatever you can about the truth of what you've just heard*, as in:

> "Carla, you're right. It was stupid of me to do anything that even looked like flirting in front of you and in a public place like that,

too. I had zero sensitivity to how humiliating that might feel to you, particularly after what I'd done before. And that was a terrible thing that I did, hitting on Elaine's sister like that. I was just trying to prove to myself that I still had the stuff, or something like that. Getting used to not being single, if you know what I mean. But it was ridiculous and humiliating and I am so sorry I hurt you. I didn't mean to. You're right, honey. We both know there are ways that I can be boyish, and some of them work but a lot of them don't. I want you to be my lover, Carla, not my mother. I already have a mother."

RULE: WHEN YOUR PARTNER CONFRONTS YOU ABOUT SOME
        BEHAVIOR OR CHARACTER FLAW, DO A ONE-EIGHTY ON
        DEFENSIVENESS. *RATHER THAN DENY WHATEVER YOU
        CAN, ADMIT WHATEVER YOU CAN.*

TRANSFORM ARGUMENT INTO ACKNOWLEDGMENT

RULE: IN THE WAKE OF DIFFICULT BEHAVIOR, THE MOST REASSURING
        THING YOU CAN DO IS TO SHOW ACCOUNTABILITY. IF YOU
        REFUSE TO "OWN" WHAT YOU'VE DONE, YOUR PARTNER WILL
        THINK THAT YOU EITHER DON'T UNDERSTAND OR DON'T
        CARE. IN EITHER CASE, *THERE'S NO REASON YOU
        WOULD NOT REPEAT THE BEHAVIOR.* IN OTHER WORDS,
        YOU ARE DANGEROUS.

Acknowledging whatever you can is generally so reassuring—and not acknowledging your contribution is generally so alarming—that I routinely advise listeners to scour their souls for *something* in what their partner has shared to admit to, as in:

"Carla, I'm so sorry you went through all that that night at the party. But, honey, remember? I was in Geneva that night. I wasn't there. You took my evil twin, Alfred, to the party instead of me, remember? But, you know what? I can *see* how you might be so sensitive about it because I did pull that awful stunt with Elaine's sister. That was one of the stupidest things I ever did and I . . ."

Or let's even imagine that Carla's concerns are completely unfounded, that not only was Thomas absent from the party, but that he'd never made a pass at anyone. His response *even then* might sound like:

"Carla, I can understand how—even though I wasn't there and it's my evil twin, Alfred, that you saw—you might be insecure about this issue. I am only twenty-six. I travel a lot without you. We both know guys in that circumstance who cheat. And there are lots of other ways I've been immature. So I want to acknowledge that your concerns don't come out of thin air. I think it is hard, at our age, to think about being faithful. I can see how you might be nervous about it."

How many of us would possess the generosity and presence of mind to forgo the utterly natural response of "Are you out of your mind? I wasn't even *at* the party! I wasn't even in the country!"? How many of us would replace our "justified" indignation with the extraordinarily unstinting response above? If you want an extraordinary relationship, you're going to have to behave extraordinarily in it. But let's be clear about the nature of what's being asked of you. The discipline here concerns *consciousness*, being aware of what you're doing and the effects your choices will most likely have. Furthermore—and this is the really tough part—it concerns *humility*. "Pride goeth before a fall," the saying goes. But here is the splendid part of *transforming argument into acknowledgment*: Other than sheer pride, what does it cost you? Even in this last, silly, example, what does it cost our imagined Thomas to admit to being young, a traveler, and at times immature? I'm not suggesting that you lie; that's never called for. But where is the heavy price for choosing *these* particular true things to acknowledge instead of others? I can't imagine any.

While, by contrast, the cost of *not* acknowledging them isn't hard to envision at all. You can "stand up for yourself," or you can reassure your partner and have a nice evening. It's strictly your choice. Ask yourself. What is your priority?

AFTER ACKNOWLEDGMENT, THEN WHAT?

After clarifying your partner's story and acknowledging all that you can, the third part of responding is to *give* as much as you can. *You want to grant as many of your partner's requests as are feasible.* By feasible, I mean that performing the request isn't so difficult that you feel that you've overextended yourself, or that the nature of the request doesn't seem to you so extreme that fulfilling it would compromise your sense of integrity.

Secure in knowing that you have an absolute right to turn down any request, consider a few things. First, in healthy relationships no one has much to prove. While I don't want you to debase yourself, I do want you to be generous. Requests can be too extreme to be healthfully granted, for example: "I'm germphobic, so could you please wash your hands and also the children's hands every time someone comes in?" But if you *can* find a way to be beneficent, then stretch a bit and do it, as in: "Even though I'm on antibiotics and the doctor said I was no longer contagious, for another day or two I'll act as if I still am to help you feel less stressed about it."

Since full-respect living means respecting your own reasonable limits as well as your partner's needs, it is inevitable that some—perhaps even many—of your partner's requests will go beyond your comfort level, even when you are being generous. There's absolutely nothing wrong with that. In fact, it's healthy for both you and the relationship. But, please do yourself and your partner a favor and *front-load your response with all the terrific things you are willing to give rather than all the things that you're not.*

I said earlier that most men and women act with more relational skill in their work settings than in their homes. *Leading with an argument* during a time of repair is a good illustration of what I mean. No one would be at all surprised to hear Thomas, for example, answer Carla's request with something like "Now, honey. You and I both know that I am not going to see some therapist." Some of us might even have the temerity to call such an answer *negotiating*. "Thomas is just being clear about what he's willing and not willing to do," such an observer might claim. But consider this: What negotiator in his right mind leads off his response to a good-faith proposal by emphasizing everything he *won't* do? Of *course* a professional negotiator would lead off with at least some of what he's willing to grant. Why? Because he wants to succeed, that's why. He wants the war to end, the teachers to go back to work, the deal to close. And I'd wager that if you were in a work setting, rather than at home, you'd do the same. "Well, I'm just a plain-speaking person," you might be thinking. "I don't like building up someone's expectations. I want to be clear and forthright." Well, perhaps, but then again, just because something is honest doesn't necessarily mean that it isn't also stupid. *Even if you cannot find one single action to agree to, emphasize your good intentions and find something to give to your partner*, as in:

"Carla, I take this issue of my being irresponsible very seriously. I'm going do some hard thinking about it; let's talk more about it. I'm going to ask my friend William what he thinks about it too. Let me get on top of this thing and, if I can't, we'll deal with it."

We anticipate that our partners will respond to anything short of total agreement by harping on what we don't offer. Indeed, that does sometimes happen, and later on I'll describe some strategies you might use when it does. But if you try being generous, and also try being your own advocate by diplomatically emphasizing your generosity, you might be pleasantly surprised. Your partner may be so taken aback by what you do offer that he's distracted from what you do not; your unexpected good-will might leave him temporarily disarmed. And one never knows. While your partner is off guard, some gratitude might even sneak through his defenses.

Winning Strategy 4: Empowering Each Other

The first two phases of the repair process have now been completed. The speaking partner, for example, the wife, initiated the process by using the feedback wheel—speaking out with love and savvy. The responding partner, her husband, has listened until he has understood; he has acknowledged whatever he could about his own behavior; and he has given as much as he could of what has been requested of him; he has responded with generosity. In the final phase of the repair process, *empowering each other*, the tables turn; it is now time for the speaking partner to be of service to the listener. In this instance, the wife begins with *appreciation* of everything her husband has been willing to give. She then asks him what she might do to *help* him follow through on his commitments. In this moment the speaking partner puts into practice the Golden Rule, the core principle, of relationship empowerment: *How can I help you give me what I want?*

This question exemplifies full-respect living any number of ways. The question at once asserts the wants of the speaker while at the same time respecting the listener. It takes as a given the listener's goodwill, honors the relationship between them, and offers, with humility and sincerity, to act like part of a team. I'd like you to take a moment to appreciate how very different all this is from the five losing strategies. It isn't hard to see how the misguided agendas of proving yourself right, control, self-expression, retaliation, and withdrawal all pull both speaker and listener far away from the actual issues at hand, whatever they may be.

In contrast, nothing could more directly optimize the possibility of success than this combination of clarity in asserting your wants mixed with goodwill and a genuine willingness to help. The question "How can I help you give me what I want?" represents an attitude toward your partner that conveys a number of positive messages:

- I believe that you care enough about me to want to please me.
- I believe that you are sophisticated enough about relationships to understand that neither of us will be happy if one of us is unhappy.

- I trust in your goodness and your competence. I know you can do this.
- I am truly and humbly at your disposal. Tell me what I can do to help and I will.
- I trust that you understand that I will do the same for you.
- I *want* you to succeed. While there may be many neurotic reasons to want you to fail (self-protectiveness, mistrust, anger), I have no interest in indulging them. I would rather get what I want and be happy.
- I will support you in your efforts and treasure the results, appreciating what you give instead of carping about what you do not.

At the point when the speaker commits to *helping his or her partner succeed*, the tables turn and an abbreviated version of the whole repair process occurs in reverse. The listener now speaks up, and the one who has spoken now listens. In this instance, the husband, if he chooses, requests changes in his wife's behavior that he thinks would help him make good on his intentions. And the wife gives as much as she can to help him.

Time after time, when couples reach this juncture, I have seen the inspired and the unexpected. Maybe it's because the listener has shown so much compassion and generosity. Maybe it's because the communication occurs in the context of helping the speaker get what he or she wants. Whatever the reason, at this tender, often awkward moment when the roles reverse, things are said and things are heard in ways that might have seemed unimaginable just moments before.

Dora and Jack: "Why Can't You Just Do the Dishes?"

Dora and Jack, a couple in their late forties, respond to my request for a "bite-sized" problem to illustrate repair. Dora and Jack both look strong, their bodies broad-backed and solid. Dora works in an insurance office and Jack troubleshoots for the local phone company. They have three teenage boys, all taller than their dad and at least as dense with muscle. All the boys, according to Dora, share their father's "rock jaw and stubborn disposition," an announcement that Jack greets with appreciative laughter. Their problem, Dora tells me, concerns getting the dinner dishes done. "Ah," I say, clever gender expert that I am. "It must be hell getting these men to clean up after themselves." "Well actually," Dora gingerly replies, "I'm the one with the problem. You see, Jack is a gourmet cook and he prepares all the meals in the family." I glance over at Jack, who speaks not a word but shoots me a look that says "Gotcha!"

"Well, well, well," I muse, looking anew at this slab of a guy.

"I'm part chick," Jack modestly demurs in a voice about four octaves below sea level, much to the delight of the crowd.

It isn't difficult to help Jack move quickly through the feedback wheel. "Dora," he says, "last night, and several nights a week, you fail to follow through on your promise to clean up, and the boys and I wind up picking up the slack. About that I make up that you're too busy off somewhere talking to your girlfriends or your mother and sisters to be a part of your own family. And about that I feel," he pauses, thinking hard, because I've asked him to connect with something other than his usual anger, "well, I guess I feel *lonely*," he says. "Like, where are ya?"

" 'And what I'd like now . . .' " I try keeping him on track. Jack goes on to ask for an explanation and a commitment for follow-through. Dora jumps right in to acknowledge her culpability. "I was just shirking my responsibility," she admits. And she dutifully promises to "clean up my act." It seems like we're cruising toward a soft landing as Jack thanks Dora and asks what he might do to help. Dora turns to her husband, about to speak, and I watch her eyes widen in astonishment as at first nothing comes out, followed by what amounts to a scream. "You can stop yelling at me all the time, Jack!" The words sound ripped out of her, as she collapses in fierce sobbing. "You can stop going after the boys." She looks up at her husband, her worn face a mess, seized with grief and anger. "Do you know what I'm doing instead of cleaning up after you all? Do you want to know what I'm really doing? I'm hiding from you, Jack. Just getting through dinner . . . I can't take all the yelling and fighting, Jack. I've tried to tell you so many times . . ." She bends down low over her lap. I can't tell whether she's crying or hiding. Jack looks on in silence, but his countenance is soft as he watches her. I fight an urge to step in. Finally, with painful awkwardness, Jack reaches over to touch Dora's arm. She covers his hand with her own and looks into his face. "Jack," she says, "no one could love you more than I have. But you've got to *do* something about your temper. Please, *please*, listen to me this time." Jack looks for a while at Dora's lowered head, looks at her hand over his on her forearm. His face betrays no emotion. What seems like a long time passes.

"What would you like me to do?" he finally speaks. "Dora? What do you think I should do?"

LIVING LOVE

I have said several times that we will achieve twenty-first-century relationships only once we have designed a matching set of twenty-first-century skills. The new ideal of love demands new rules for its implementation, practices that help us remember and act in accordance with the simple fact that we are partners in this together. We must help each other. Neither acquiescence nor blind assertion will get us what we most deeply want, because what we most deeply want is each other.

While the daily practice of a great relationship is comprised of many skills—working within healthy boundaries, pulling oneself up from shame and down from grandiosity, staying on one's side of the line, time-outs, and dead-stop contracts, to name just a few—the *repair process* most directly translates into action the twenty-first-century road map of mutual empowerment. Repair demands that both partners ask: *What can we do to work as a team? How can we face the challenges life throws at us and the challenges we present to each other in a practical way? Isn't it in our own best interest to assist each other? What do you want from me in order to help you feel loved and fulfilled? How can I help you give me the things I would like to feel loved and fulfilled? How are we going to make our lives together as rich and trusting, as joy-filled as we can?*

The process of repair may seem daunting at first, because each step is spelled out so specifically. But try to remember that the instructions are there only to help keep you on track. It is so easy, as you begin this practice, to take your eyes off your goal. Let me again reassure you. Becoming proficient in the art of great relating is about on a par with acquiring any other complex and rewarding skill, such as mastering a new language, instrument, or sport. You may begin self-consciously; your first runs may seem inefficient and not terribly graceful. But as you practice, more and more, the artifice drops away, the craft recedes, and a space is cleared for the gift of inspiration, the influx of grace.

Chapter Seven
Practice Section

Responding with Generosity and Empowering Each Other

The following exercises are designed to help you begin practicing your new skills of listening, responding, and empowering.

LISTENING WITH GENEROSITY

Invite your partner or a friend to participate with you in an experiment. Ask him to address with you some relatively minor issue that could use some understanding and repair. A friend might bring up, for example, a time you kept him waiting a few weeks earlier. If your friend is willing, teach him how to use the feedback wheel and invite him to try it out by using this small incident. Remember, this is for practice, so try to keep the issue small and manageable. Tell your friend or partner that you intend to listen in two different ways and that you will ask for feedback about how each of them felt to him when the exercise ends.

First: As your friend gives you feedback, do not attempt to use your new skills but deliberately answer as you might have responded before acquiring them. Feel free to interrupt, explain, or correct—all the things you're used to doing. Have fun!

Second: As you listen to the same material the second time, practice using your internal boundary, noting areas of discrepancy between the speaker's recollection, meaning, feelings, or wishes and your own. Use those points of divergence as points of curiosity until you believe you have the gist of what the speaker is saying and some grasp of how he might feel as he does, given his perception. Feed that back to the speaker, allowing him to correct you until you have it reasonably well.

Ask your friend to share with you his experience of each interaction.

RESPONDING WITH GENEROSITY

This is an alternating-day exercise.

During the next ten days, invite people you trust to help you practice a new communication skill you're working on by bringing up some relatively bite-sized issue they have with you. Between spontaneous opportunities with people you encounter throughout your day and the opportunities you've requested, you should find yourself facing someone's feedback about you several times a day.

During this ten-day period, you alternate between "magic" and ordinary days. On ordinary days, you *must* respond just as you typically would at home, work, or school. On "magic days," however, you are fully enabled to respond for repair. As a master of relationship practice, you know to first *clarify*, making certain you understand the nature of the speaker's discomfort. More important, you attempt to clarify the speaker's request of you: What could you do to help the speaker feel better right now? Someone unused to relationship empowerment might not even have a request in mind. All the better the challenge, then! Next, you *acknowledge* anything that you can about the truth of what the speaker has been saying. And, finally, you *give* as much of what he requests as you can.

Journal at the end of each day about what you've learned from the juxtaposition of these two approaches.

Chapter Eight

Cherish What You Have

FULL-RESPECT LIVING:
A NEW RULE
FOR LIFE

Summary

The last two chapters led you through the repair process, the mechanism of correction that turns the principles of relationship empowerment into a living, practical method of getting and giving everything you can in your relationship. You have learned to understand and use the first four winning strategies. You can:

1. Shift from negative/past-focused complaints to positive/future-focused requests
2. Speak your truth with love and savvy
3. Respond with a generous heart
4. Help empower each other

In the last chapter, you learned to listen with enough generosity to lay aside your version of what happened in order to understand your partner's thoughts and feelings. You committed to the discipline of opening your heart to understanding, turning points of contention into points of curiosity and clearing a path for empathy and compassion. This is the listener's version of remembering love. You learned that repair requires more of us than simple understanding and empathy, no matter how exquisite. The next step you began to master was how to respond, which was comprised of three parts:

1. *Clarify* your partner's wishes
2. *Acknowledge* all that you can about what's been said
3. *Give all* that you can of what's been asked for

Once you've given your partner all these wonderful things, your partner acknowledges you and asks you the quintessential question of relationship empowerment: *What can I do to help you deliver?* And then the tables turn. You tell your partner your truth with skill, and it is his turn to understand, acknowledge, and give. You are now working as a team to realize the fourth winning strategy: helping empower each other.

Winning Strategy 5: Cherishing

The first four winning strategies focus on setting things right, on optimizing your and your partner's satisfaction in the relationship. They are about getting and giving. The final winning strategy, *cherishing*, focuses on what to do with what you want after it's been given to you. It's about *having*. At first it might seem odd to think of having as a skill that you must acquire. And yet, while it requires no skill to simply have something, it requires great skill to *cherish having it and keep it well*.

You may be thinking at this point, "Well, I certainly don't have that problem," but I would challenge you to roll back that quick answer and consider it again, more slowly. It may indeed be true that you don't have an issue with cherishing. But if it is, I must tell you that you are a fortunate and rare individual, because nearly every person I work with has something to learn about cherishing.

Virtually all of the couples I meet, both in clinical work and in workshops and seminars, are *appreciation deficient* and learn to become *appreciation proficient*. Partners seldom let each other know how much they appreciate the effort or the good qualities they enjoy in each other; they often don't even let themselves feel how much they treasure the many wonderful aspects of their partners, or the richness of their lives—until, through age, illness, or some other life circumstance, they face the possibility of their loss. I don't want you to wait for an impending crisis in order to cherish your life's abundance.

The last winning strategy you must cultivate is your capacity to *enjoy*. Why does a healthy relationship demand pleasure? Because not taking pleasure in what we have is a form of ingratitude. It is, by definition, unappreciative. At bottom, failure to enjoy the fruits of good fortune and of our own efforts is mean-spirited and perverse. It's like responding to someone who has cooked you a fabulous meal by not eating it, or like laboring for years to produce an exciting piece of art only to store it where no one will see it.

RULE: FAILURE TO TAKE PLEASURE IN THE GOOD THINGS IN YOUR LIFE DISHONORS THE GIFTS OR ACCOMPLISHMENTS THAT DESERVE APPRECIATION. IT ALSO DISHONORS YOUR RIGHT TO BE HAPPY.

"But why are we even discussing this?" you might be thinking. "Of *course* I will enjoy the fruits of this work. Why wouldn't I enjoy finally getting more of what I've been after all this time?"

It seems only logical, doesn't it? It's only sensible that we would receive our partners' increased closeness with open arms, and sometimes we do embrace their efforts. But often we do not. *There is a world of difference between the ease of complaining about not having something and the challenge of actually getting it.*

Philippe and Anna: Refusing to Take "Yes" for an Answer

"I don't know how I could have made more of a mess of things," Philippe confesses to me in our first session, crossing his long legs. Dressed in a pearl-gray linen suit over a pale blue sport shirt and woven sandals, he is elegant from head to toe. Sitting beside him, with thick black hair and arresting green eyes, Anna is rougher cut, more avant-garde. And she is even more attractive than her handsome husband. It's clear within the first few minutes that they have loved each other passionately through-out close to twenty years together. How baffling to them both was Philippe's monstrously irresponsible behavior! For close to a year, Philippe had carried on an affair with the wife of a couple they were friends with, Sarah, who was also the mother of their daughter's best friend. Sarah, who in hindsight had obviously used Philippe to blow up her own un-happy marriage, who seemed to relish public scenes—the louder and more scandalous, the better—in front of the children, in front of the girls' classmates! What a sucker he'd been! How much carnage lay in the wake of his heedless appetite!

Their marriage, Anna explains later on in the session, had already been stretched to the breaking point. Philippe was "in bed with his fa-ther," as she put it. Father and son together ran a lucrative real-estate de-velopment company not far from Miami. Philippe Senior was as socially gifted as his son was clever, and together they had parlayed the small amount of money they'd been able to carry from their native Cuba into considerable holdings. But "Pappi Phil," as he insisted on being called, was a brute in private, and particularly cruel to his son. Philippe's unwill-ingness to stand up to his father created endless, bitter fights between him and Anna. But Philippe, for his part, was far from happy about Anna's relationship to her mother, Elena, and her two older sisters—all of whom, he complained, formed a cadre that ran his own family. "Every decision made about my daughter," Philippe tells me while staring at Anna, "her school, her teachers, her *therapist*, for Christ's sake, is made by my mother- and sisters-in-law, and then—*maybe*—I'm informed."

"But you're never around," Anna protests, without much conviction.

Philippe turns a baleful eye upon her. "That's not true and you know it, Anna," he says, his voice filled with restrained anger and hurt. "You don't *want* me."

"Because you are *so irresponsible*, Philippe!" Anna cries back at him. "You were such a great father? You were so deeply concerned about our daughter's welfare when you . . . ?" But she can't even finish the sentence. Instead, she slumps back in her chair, head bent, hand on her forehead. "I don't know," she mutters. "I don't even know why we're here."

"You're here to save your marriage," I remind her. After the affair, they'd blown through three couple's therapies, one lasting close to a year, with no real results. "Your next stop after this is a lawyer," I add.

She looks up at me, head still bent, hair over her eyes, looking beautiful and utterly contemptuous. "I'm aware of that," she says, acidly.

"Good," I respond, not yielding. "I would hope so."

After listening to Philippe for a time, his diagnosis seemed clear enough to me: He was a boy. And I told him so. "I believe that for most of us, monogamy is unnatural and yet open marriage generally doesn't work, so pick your poison," I tell him. "It takes effort to maintain fidelity," I explain. "I don't think you *had* this affair, particularly. It seems more like you just lacked the oomph to *not* have it."

"Like he lacks the oomph to stand up to his father," Anna chimes in.

I turn to her. "Do you think I need a co-therapist, Anna?" I ask. She shakes her head, sheepish. "And, yes," I agree, turning back to Philippe, "you do need spine . . ." He nods, compliant. "With your mistress . . ."

"That's *over*," he interjects quickly.

". . . with your father . . ."

"That's *not!*" Anna blurts, unable to stop herself.

"And with you, Anna," I conclude.

That gets her attention. Again, she glares at me through the thick strands of her hair, doubtless aware of her beauty's disconcerting effects. "I've . . ." she stammers, "I've *always* said . . ."

"Just be careful," I interrupt. "Be careful, Anna, what you wish for."

Philippe proved to be as clever in therapy as he was in his business, and, in short order, he came to understand the consequences of his ongoing resentful acquiescence. "I just wanted to keep everyone happy," he sighs sadly during one session.

"You did a great job at that one," I tell him.

Philippe was a hero child, the "good one" growing up, used to abdicating his own needs for the benefit of all. But, as he came to see, every time we overextend there's payback. That's the underbelly of martyrdom—retaliation. Over the years, he could have had any number of discreet sexual encounters far away from his family. He'd chosen not to. The ugly truth was that the mess he'd made was his disowned declaration of independence, a hearty "screw you" to all and sundry. His traumatized daughter was merely collateral damage.

With support, Philippe stood up to his father's exploitation and formed his own company. Their parting was every bit as bloody as he'd feared it would be. He made amends to his daughter, cut back his work hours, and "showed up" at home in ways Anna had been asking him to for years. One might think that Anna would be overjoyed, but no one was all that surprised when she wasn't. In fact, the more Philippe made strides toward closeness, the more horribly Anna treated him.

"Is this *it*?" she cries out rhetorically in one session, speaking to me although keeping her eyes fixed on her husband. "He throws me and our daughter a few *sops* after all these years and I'm just supposed to . . ."

"Supposed to what?" I say, taking her on. "Supposed to *appreciate* the changes he's making? Be *thankful*?"

Her outrage only increases. "So *what*?" She turns to her husband. "So you just *fuck* this . . . ?"

"Anna," he pleads.

"Oh, I'm *sorry*," she goes on, dripping sarcasm. "You '*make love to*,' is that better? You have an *affair* with? Get *entangled* in? *Find* yourself?"

"Honey, *please* . . ."

"And it all just goes away? Just like *that!*" She snaps her fingers. "You act like a good boy for . . ."

"Anna," I stop her. "You're not listening to a word he's saying. You're behind a wall of indignation."

She snorts. "Perhaps he'd be better served with rose petals."

"And your fury and sarcasm didn't start with this affair, I'd bet. Did they?" I ask and then turn to Philippe. "Did they?" I press.

"No," he shakes his head, looking tired.

"In fact, you've been enraged on and off with Philippe for . . . ?" I look at him. He hesitates, and then takes the plunge.

"For years," he admits, "for decades. As long as I've . . ."

I can feel the rising heat of Anna's rage, like a gathering physical force.

"You do understand, don't you, Philippe," I ask softly, "that you married your father?"

"How *dare* you!" Anna explodes. But almost instantly she regains control of herself. She retreats to the icy-hot mask of her sarcasm, and smiles. "So, now, I suppose *I* am the one responsible for his affair? Is that it? I *drove* him into the arms of another with my . . . ?"

"Oh, Anna," I say. "Why don't you just knock it off?"

"*Excuse me?*" she answers, losing all composure. Her hands tremble as she scrambles to gather her things.

"Anna," I try as she stands up.

"I *can't*," she says to herself, distressed almost beyond coherency. "I simply . . ." She heads toward the door.

"That's okay," I try again. "Take a few minutes to cool off and . . ."

"*You* are out of your *mind*," she informs me.

"Anna," Philippe calls to her.

"Anna, listen," I speak quickly, before she takes off. "If you care about your marriage . . ."

"Not with *you*," she spits back at me. "Not if *this* is what it takes. I simply . . ." She reaches for the door.

"Anna." Philippe stands up as well. "*Anna!*" he shouts. "COME

BACK AND SIT DOWN!" We all freeze as the room reverberates. It feels exactly as though a pistol has gone off. Philippe's breathing is heavy and raw. No one moves. Anna slowly looks into her husband's eyes and recognizes, I think as I watch her, the same quality that I now see in them. Sometimes even the most stubborn boys stumble their way into manhood.

"All right," she says, at last slipping back into her place on the couch, her light summer coat still drawn around her. "All right, Philippe. You have me. Now, what do you want from me?"

He faces her. "Everything you've said about me is true, Anna," he begins, moving close beside her. "I don't deny any of it. I am only now . . . I'm only now learning to love you." She says nothing. We wait. "But now, it's your turn, honey," he resumes at last. "It's your turn to learn *how to love me back.*"

Anna remains still and makes no sound, although tears streak her face. "So you believe, Philippe," she asks softly, "you *truly* believe, after all this, that I must now *learn* how to love you?"

Philippe breathes deeply. "Yes," he answers courageously. "Yes, I do. I believe you must learn, Anna. Just as I must. I have been selfish and you have been angry. Neither of us has loved like we should." Anna takes time to reflect on all this and then, finally, sighs.

"So," she says to him. "Make me understand, Philippe. Tell me just how unloving I have been to you, then," she says, "over these many years, long, tortuous years."

I smile. "Why don't you try that again, Anna," I suggest.

Without looking at me, she purses her lips, equal parts sober, vexed, and impish. But when she shifts toward her husband, everything falls away. The face she turns toward him is plain and unguarded. She stretches out her hand to touch him. "I will learn," she says simply, nodding once softly as if to further reassure. "As you say, Philippe. I promise. I will learn to love you back."

"Thank you, darling," he answers. Bending, he kisses her on the forehead as she cries. "You are so precious . . . so precious to me."

"Do you want him to hold you?" I ask Anna. She nods and lets Philippe encircle her in his arms.

"It's all right," he whispers through the tangle of her hair, her soundless tears. "It's okay. We're okay, now, Anna," he repeats. "We're okay."

It took a lot for Philippe to stand up. It took just as much for Anna to let him. Sometimes, having is harder than getting, more painful and more frightening.

Why Is This Usually Such an Uncomfortable Moment for Women?

When men actually do, in their imperfect way, take seriously what their partners are asking for and start trying to give it to them, do you think that most women swoon in their spouse's arms and say, "Thank you, dear!"? They do not. Just like Anna, most women greet their partners' progress with some form of *disqualification*. It's too little too late. Or, it's not quite right. He doesn't really mean it. Or—my personal favorite—he's only doing it because she's told him to. Anna and Philippe may be on the far side of the bell curve, but they illustrate something we all go through as we transition toward a great relationship.

RULE: CONTRARY TO WHAT ONE MIGHT EXPECT, PROGRESS IS A SOURCE OF *BOTH* JOY *AND* DISTURBANCE. A SHIFT TOWARD INCREASED LEVELS OF INTIMACY IN ONE PARTNER IMPLICITLY DEMANDS INCREASED LEVELS OF VULNERABILITY IN THE OTHER, LEVELS OF VULNERABILITY THAT MAY NOT BE COMFORTABLE.

Why Is Saying "Yes" to Your Partner So Difficult?

Your experience of progress in the relationship, of your partner's actually giving you more of what you want, can be unsettling for two reasons:

- Your mistrust of the relationship
- Your mistrust of *all* relationships

THE MARITAL WOUND

In relationships in which dissatisfaction has been long-standing, the complaining partner is usually behind a wall of mistrust. You may be loath to give up the protection of your wall for fear of being disappointed. After so many rounds of hope and frustration, you may feel that you'd be an absolute sucker were you to let down your guard once again. But at this juncture you have to make a decision. If you truly believe that your mate is hopeless, then you should probably end the relationship. But if you say that you want to make things better, then come out from behind the wall—as understandable as it might be to want to stay back there—and lend a hand.

It has to be one or the other.

You cannot ask your partner to change so fundamentally, and then stand back with your arms folded and not support him in the effort. It's not fair, if that matters. More important, it won't work. Your partner will not keep laboring to please you if you give him nothing in return.

DEEPER WOUNDS

The second reason saying yes to your partner's progress may be difficult is because it throws down the gauntlet of increased intimacy. It calls your bluff. A friend of mine once quipped that everyone is either blatant or latent. In most of the couples I encounter, there is one partner who seems to be the soul of relational health but who is thwarted by a mate who behaves in ways that are so blatantly off-putting that no one could be close to him. It's a great cover if ever there was one. Anna, for example, was the daughter of a man who deserted the family. That is part of the reason she is so close to her mother and sisters. There was always a sense in Anna's family that men were not to be trusted. In her marriage, Anna didn't have to own up to her extreme discomfort with healthy dependency all the while that Philippe, obligingly, proved himself to be so thoroughly undependable. But what happens when Philippe turns around and starts to become the responsible partner Anna has always claimed she wanted? What happens to Anna's walled-off anti-dependency then? As Philippe rises to the occasion, Anna's first instinct is to maintain stability by undercutting the very changes in his behavior for which she's ostensibly been longing. She repeats the old dance steps even though the music has changed. Why is Anna having so much more trouble being intimate since Philippe's behaviors have improved? *She isn't. She's having the same amount of difficulty being intimate that she's always had.* But until now, her subtler intimacy issues looked like an understandable reaction to his more obvious ones—that is, until the smoke screen of his difficult behaviors began dissipating.

I often tell the couples who face this moment the old joke about the guy who has an accident and asks his doctor if he'll be able to play the violin. When the doctor assures him that he will, the guy answers, "Funny. I couldn't play it before the accident." Why can't Anna depend upon Philippe now that he's become dependable? Why would she be able to when she's been incapable of healthy dependency all along?

Why Is Cherishing Your Partner's Progress So Important?

Cherishing progress, learning to take yes for an answer, is a fundamental principle in all healing. It's your capacity to *let healing work*. At the most practical level, it turns out that *the single most effective means of eliciting more of something is by cherishing it when it appears.*

RULE: SET LIMITS WHENEVER YOU MUST. REWARD WHENEVER YOU CAN.

A common tenet in family therapy is the principle that says *Whenever you want to engender more of something in a system, simply pay a lot of attention to it.* You want your kid to keep getting into trouble? Turn it into a family obsession. You want your husband to fudge on telling you the whole truth? Then keep interrogating him like he's Jack the Ripper. These are *negative amplifications.* Fortunately, the same principle holds true for *positive* amplifications as well. You want your spouse to come home when he says he will next time, the way he did tonight? Let him know how wonderful you feel about what he did. Celebrate the success.

**RULE: DARING TO ROCK THE BOAT IS AN APPROPRIATE STRATEGY
TO HELP YOUR PARTNER TAKE YOU SERIOUSLY. BUT ONCE
INSTANCES OF CHANGE BEGIN TO OCCUR, YOU NEED TO
AMPLIFY HIS PROGRESS. CONTINUING TO ROCK THE BOAT
ONCE YOUR PARTNER "GETS IT" IS THE RELATIONSHIP
EQUIVALENT OF *SELLING PAST THE SALE.***

Are You Fully Open to Pleasure?

Are you and your partner appreciation deficient? A lack of appreciation is sad, because it deprives each of you of pleasure—the pleasure of feeling appreciated, obviously, but in some ways even more perniciously, the pleasure to enjoy what you have.

In our culture, pleasure remains highly suspect. Like connection itself, pleasure is fine in measured, "appropriate" doses, so long as it doesn't interfere with the *real* work of production and caretaking. But the enforcers of social order have always understood that pleasure is not a very docile or obedient force. Pleasure is hard to corral and hard to resist. What would happen if our young men, like Ferdinand the bull in the famous children's story, suddenly cared more about smelling the flowers than about donning their suits and briefcases to enter the ring? What if our young women were to care more about exploring variations of sexual pleasure than about marriage, fidelity, and children? Western society has always understood that pleasure is by its nature insurrectionary.

We don't take pleasure in one another and we don't give pleasure to one another nearly as much as we could because, as a culture, *we simply don't much value it.* As a couple's therapist for close to thirty years, I cannot overemphasize how stupid I believe that is. Our government can spend millions of dollars trying to understand and reduce the high rate of divorce, coming up with dizzyingly complex analyses, but I'd like to keep it simple. I want to talk about the profound, underutilized powers of joy, appreciation, cherishing, and fun. Dutifully going through the motions of trying to make your relationship better might have been sufficient in the twentieth century, but it won't work anymore. Cherishing, pleasure, and joy are what make a relationship worth fighting for these days. The sense of being cherished, and of being able to cherish—this is the very core of positive intimacy. It's what gives us the strength to withstand troubled times; it's what gives us the motivation to stretch and grow. If you're in a relationship in which you feel that fundamentally either you are not cherished or your partner will not let you be cherishing, by twenty-first-century standards you are not in a living relationship; you're in a shell.

And yet, as central as this issue is, we often don't take the time or effort to cherish one another. We don't stop for a moment and let *ourselves* have the pleasure of enjoying deeply the wonderful things that keep us bound to one another. In large measure we don't cherish simply because we're given the message in all sorts of ways that our desire to either receive or bestow the nurture of cherishing is somehow frivolous, sappy, or unnecessary. Earlier I claimed that today's women want more from their relationships than most men have been raised to deliver. Cherishing provides a good illustration. I'd like you to remember that the twentieth century's Breadwinner/Caretaker Deal had a purpose. It was in the whole family's best interest for women to take care of whatever they could in order to keep their breadwinning husbands as uncluttered and as competitive as possible. Women were—and in most marriages still are—the social hub and coordinator, and for at least a century we have instilled in our daughters all the skills needed to create and sustain social connection. As a rule, women are significantly more interested in and better equipped for the many measures, large and small, that maintain connectedness. Women generally understand that positive feedback, compliments, and attention are like the water that keeps a plant growing. Most women understand that cherishing is not merely something to feel, but something to do.

One of the casualties of personal empowerment has been a decreased desire on women's part to give their men many of the small, thoughtful rewards that now seem to belong to quieter and simpler times. Men, on the other hand, didn't have much ground to lose in the cherishing department to begin with. For most men, unless they're courting, cherishing has always meant something you have in your heart rather than something you do.

When men tell me that they don't understand why their wives need to be *told* that they love them—after all, they *know* that they do—I usually point to a plant in the corner of my office. "How do you think that plant would fare if you were to tell it, 'I don't really need to *actually water you*. After all, we both understand that I want nothing more for you than to be nourished and well.'?"

Why Is Cherishing a Winning Strategy?

When you lose sight of cherishing, the cost to you, as an individual, is the madness of not being able to relish what you've worked so hard to attain. The cost to you as a partner in a relationship is that you fail to utilize what is perhaps the most effective winning strategy at your disposal. *I believe that the constructive power of cherishing is so great that it equals all of the preceding strategies combined.* All of the other strategies focus on eliciting new behaviors that you want, but cherishing has the power to *amplify* those new behaviors once they appear. It's as if everything you've learned so far results in a tiny green shoot of new growth, and now cherishing will take you from that tiny first shoot to a strong, healthy plant.

Why? Because cherishing *means* growing. Webster's dictionary defines cherishing as holding something dear and nurturing it.

How Can You Best Amplify Progress?

There are two great reinforcements that encourage your partner's positive efforts:

- Acknowledge and cherish his efforts
- Demonstrate, through your actions, an increased desire to be pleasing in return

As simple as positive reinforcement is, I cannot tell you how stingy many partners are with it. A fear people sometimes express is that, having finally made some progress, their partners will just backslide once they "get comfortable" again. Having finally learned how to wield a stick effectively, these partners are loath to trade it in for a carrot too quickly. Their fear usually stems from years of cycling through the exact pattern they describe. They kick up a fuss and their mates shape up for a time; the fuss dies down and the old behaviors return.

I want you to remember that the phrase isn't carrot *or* stick; it's carrot *and* stick. People tend to think that you can be either tough or nice, strong or sensitive. But the smart money is on being both at the same time.

Here's the bottom line. So much of what you've needed to learn so far—developing second consciousness, staying on your side of the line, giving up losing strategies—is work that can be truly demanding. How nice to know, then, that all you need to do once these techniques start to bear fruit is to cherish the tender new growth. Be gentle, as you would be with any new growth. Don't flood it and don't ignore it. Just receive it with the joy and the care it deserves.

Cherishing Your Relationship

Now that we've spoken about cherishing your partner's progress, I want to speak about the power of cherishing in your relationship practice and in your life. What are you doing to cherish your relationship? And what are you doing to live a cherishing life in the world?

If you're like most of the couples I know, nurturing your own relationship comes about dead last when it comes to allocating your time. After work, the kids, family and friends, a dash of hurried self-care at the gym or a yoga class, what you mostly are by the end of the day is beat. I agree with coach Cheryl Richardson that when it comes to understanding what we really value in our lives, all we need to do is look at where we're putting our time and energy. *When it comes to our values, we vote with our feet.* You may *say* you value all sorts of things, but let's take an honest look at how you spend your resources. There are 168 hours in a week. How many of those do you give directly, specifically, and purposefully to your relationship? I'm thinking of long walks on the beach holding hands, cell phones off, kids ensconced elsewhere, your work concerns merely a door that you closed once you got home, plenty of time for talk and for sensuality. If you want a sustained great relationship, you must understand that your attempts to realize that dream occur in a hostile environment in which the phone is ringing, the kids are screaming, and the boss wants more of your time.

We live in a society in which intimacy is idealized in principle and devalued in fact. The demands of work, family, friends, community, and self-care are dizzying in today's world. More than ever before, we seem hell-bent on improving our lot in life, which is fine so long as we stay rooted in what is most dear—which is one another.

Why You Should Hate Your Children

There is yet another force that shapes, and often misshapes, our couple-hood, a force at least as potent and as historically novel as the brand-new vision of intimate marriage: our child-centered wish to be perfect parents.

Around the midpoint of the twentieth century, one of the great pioneers of the burgeoning field of child development, the pediatrician-turned-psychoanalyst D. W. Winnicott, wrote a startling and, for its time, quite radical academic piece that detailed "ten reasons young mothers should hate their infants." Winnicott's reasons included such complexities as the fact that infants usually puke on you, keep you up at all hours, scream as loudly as they can in your ear, and bite your nipples. It was an enormously liberating piece that unearthed, normalized, and showed compassion for those quite natural maternal feelings that didn't fit in with Hallmark cards or Norman Rockwell fantasies.

In that spirit, I would like to spill the beans on one of the great elephants in the middle of the room, one of the largest open secrets kept about modern family life:

Having children eviscerates romance.

No one can prepare you for the experience of having your first child. No matter how much you read or how many people you talk to, the altered consciousness that comes at the time of your first child's birth can't really be grasped until you've been through it. Nothing can prepare you for the onslaught of a love so unalloyed, so encompassing and sudden, that you really would sacrifice your life for this tiny being. In modern Western families, and most particularly in the United States, the couple's relationship that was once the whole of your experience now takes an abrupt and emphatic backseat to the task at hand.

You are no longer a couple; you are now a family.

What happens to your couple's relationship? In most of the families I have encountered, during the child-raising years—which is quite a stretch by any account—the couple's relationship is, candidly, largely sacrificed. The unacknowledged truth that everyone knows and few name aloud is that for many, many couples, having children just rips the guts out of romance. And by romance, I don't just mean sex, as important as that is. I mean all of the many ways couples *cherish their connection*, all the ways you treated each other when you first fell in love. Why does this happen? Well, for many reasons, some of which can be ameliorated and some of which probably shouldn't be.

What's Wrong with Being a Sexual Parent?

While sex isn't the whole of romance, it's easy to track. There may be ambiguity about whether or not you've been considerate, but there isn't much ambiguity about whether or not you've been sexual. So let's start there. Why is parenthood at odds with romance? I must confess that as an American raised in a country with Puritan roots, the very phrase *sexual parent* gives me the creeps. And while Americans may be unusually uncomfortable with it, the tension between one's sexuality and one's parenting is by no means strictly confined to the United States, or even to the West. One of the few prohibitions found in virtually every human society is the incest taboo. And using the containing part of our internal boundary to shield our children from our own sexual and aggressive impulses is a fundamental responsibility. But we Westerners, with roots in the Germanic and British traditions, do seem to have a particularly hard time allowing healthy sexuality or even robust sensuality to be a normal part of family life.

In her book *The Erotic Silence of the American Housewife,* and then again in *Marriage Shock,* sociologist Dalma Heyn interviewed women from all over the United States who spoke openly about feeling, often to their own surprise, a sense of sexual "shutdown" after marriage. These women revealed to Heyn a current in our culture's belief system that disassociates eroticism from the role of being a "good wife," a current powerful enough to significantly alter their feelings and behaviors. From the vantage point of a therapist who has listened closely to women for quite a while, I'd like to say that if the message that "good wives" should not be sexual can be envisioned as a covert steady stream, then the message that mothers should not be sexual would look like a massive tidal wave. The centuries-old Madonna/Whore split seems to be still very much alive and with us, whether we choose to acknowledge it or not.

While many women, and some men as well, do seem to sexually shut down upon the advent of parenthood, there is no rational, healthy reason for it. There's a difference between shielding our children from whatever sexual impulses might arise toward them and needing to blot out the fact that, as adults, we are sexual beings.

Not all of this is about inhibition. How many young mothers—after both the sensual stimulation and the physical depletion of a day spent being crawled over, grabbed at, spit up on, and sucked by their infants and young children—put the kids to sleep and are then just dying to don their latest Frederick's of Hollywood gear for a wild night of abandon? Not many.

Muriel

"Okay," Muriel, a workshop participant in her mid-forties, shares with a small group. "The first years were horrible. Breast-feeding, sleep deprivation; first we had Brian and then Michael right after him. Sex? Forget it. Don't touch me. Just, yech, leave me alone! Then, we had about five great years when they were both settled in school, ages eight through fourteen, maybe. But now, it's worse than it ever was. We live in a regular old front-entrance colonial, with everyone's bedroom on the same floor. So, I want to know how other people manage this. Brian's eighteen and Michael's fifteen. They're both well over six feet. *And they never go to sleep anymore!* We try waiting them out, but I just can't crank it up at midnight on a weekday. Jeff calls them 'The Things That Won't Go Away.' Jeff and I start something and the next thing I hear are these hulking, clunking *Things* just outside our door. I know they won't come in, but even so. It's like we're making love whispering. We're the teenagers hiding from our parents. Once Jeff actually put his hand over my mouth. This is not a turn-on!"

———

Just as sexuality shifts from center stage to an also-ran, so too does most everything else that nurtured you—not as a family, but specifically as a couple. We have never been so intent, as a culture, on giving our children every advantage that we can. So now both parents feel overwhelmed. Between school, camps, sports, tutoring, lessons, playdates . . . on and on, we worry over, work for, and put more effort and energy into our kids than any generation before. Some psychologists worry that we are entirely too gratifying to our children; they are concerned that we are actually disempowering them by giving too much. Others disagree. But while the benefit to our children may be a matter of debate, the cost to our relationships is inarguable. We have only so much to give; there are only so many hours in the day. We can all remember, fondly and longingly, if perhaps dimly, the ways we used to nurture each other. But for most of us, between the twin tasks of doing well for our families out there in the work world and doing well for our children back here at home, an enormous amount of the nurture we used to give to each other goes elsewhere.

We must do better than this. And we can.

**RULE: YOU CANNOT SUSTAIN THE INTIMACY YOU ENJOYED IN THE
EARLY STAGE OF YOUR RELATIONSHIP UNLESS YOU ARE
WILLING TO CHERISH EACH OTHER IN SOME OF THE WAYS
THAT YOU DID AT THAT TIME. YOU WILL NOT FEEL LIKE
LOVERS UNLESS YOU ARE WILLING TO BEHAVE LIKE LOVERS.**

How Can You Have Lover's Energy?

One way to describe the new vision of twenty-first-century marriage is that we have grafted onto the companionship marriage of the previous century the expectations and mores of a lover relationship—the kind of passion, attention, and emotional closeness that we most commonly associate with youth, and with the early stages of a relationship. The common thread running through both of these times is that the couple is principally concerned with itself. I call this *nose-to-nose* energy. But sooner or later—and certainly with the advent of those things that won't go away—healthy couples turn to *side-by-side* energy. No longer principally wrapped up in each other, the partners stand in harness together shoulder to shoulder, facing out toward the life they are building. What I'm calling romantic or lover's energy comes from the experience of facing each other, attending to your partner and to the relationship itself. It is the exciting, warming, and erotic experience of *being available to each other in the present*. This is always what the "other woman" or "other man" offers in an affair—interest and attention. This is what wooed you when you first fell in love. And this is the experience that dries up when we fail to nurture the relationship.

Here is a description of five tactics for cultivating lover's energy in your long-term relationship:

1. Reclaim romantic space
2. Tell the truth
3. Cultivate sharing
4. Cherish your partner
5. Become partners-in-health

TACTIC 1: RECLAIM ROMANTIC SPACE

In order to be romantic, you have to push back the demands of everyday life enough to create a space to be romantic in. You need time, a place, and energy. The simplest way to clear that space is by going away. Send the kids to your mother's, or bring in a trusted sitter, but take a few days for yourselves. If your kids are a bit older, take a week or more by yourselves. Your children will manage to live without you for a short interval, and *you need the time to reconnect with each other*. Consider it a capital investment. It will do your children no good if you run your relationship on empty only to then expose them to your depression or anger with each other, or, at worst, to risk rotting the relationship altogether.

Send your kids away—to a summer camp, if you can afford it, or to a relative or good friend. If you have more than one child, do your best to synchronize their programs so you have some time alone.

Taking off and physically leaving is a macro-level tactic. Smaller, micro-level tactics focus on reclaiming space in your everyday lives. Think of the demands of the world as encroaching on your couple's time, and think of yourselves as needing to deliberately push back. I can't tell you how many couples I tell to schedule sex. ("Here: Thursday nights. Put it in your PDA.") Or, if that feels too pressured, then schedule "sensual time" together, which may or may not become sexual. Couples regularly schedule *date nights* every week or couple of weeks, time that's just for the two of you. One of my favorite things to do is to go out for dinner and a movie with my wife. Nothing fancy. Sometimes it's just jeans and a pizza. But no kids, no friends (as much as I love them), no responsibilities for one evening, no homework to check, forms to fill out, or family to call. Just walking down the street holding hands, or saying over a drink, "Hey, how are you doing?" What a treat!

TACTIC 2: TELL THE TRUTH

Face-to-face time is a treat only if you're not worrying about having a lousy experience with each other. A great many partners, whether they admit it or not, don't want that much nose-to-nose time because it's rarely a great success when they get it. And that is precisely the trajectory of degeneration. Because repair doesn't happen, issues don't get dealt with; resentment builds up while sharing gets thinner and thinner.

Twenty-six-year-old Erin says of her boyfriend of four years: "When we go out, we're one of those couples that sit across from each other and hardly talk. Isn't that sad at our age? But it isn't that there's nothing to talk about. It's that there's too much to talk about but we don't know how to handle it."

As Erin and her boyfriend back away from "hot issues," they back

away from other forms of sharing as well. And the stimulation and nour-
ishment that keeps a relationship alive and juicy begins drying up.

It may be odd to think of telling the truth as a means of keeping your
relationship passionate, but a central belief in relationship empowerment is that not telling the truth shuts passion down. Full-respect living
means that you can *afford* to remain fully open to each other. Not
because your relationship is completely "safe." It isn't that you idealize
your love, as our culture invites you to; quite the contrary. You are very
realistic about your partner's imperfections, as well as your own. There
certainly will be times when you will be hurt. But while you don't put
your faith in fairy tales of perfection, what you do trust is your accountability as a couple—and your relationship skills. And so you stay *engaged*
with each other. There is no aphrodisiac stronger than authentic connection. And there are few passion killers more effective than withdrawal.

TACTIC 3: CULTIVATE SHARING

Sharing—intellectually, emotionally, physically, sexually, and spiritually—
is what intimacy is; it is the stuff of intimacy itself. Sharing occurs in so
many aspects of our lives together: sharing a physical activity, such as
hiking or tennis, or the love of a place, like the mountains or the ocean;
sharing a project or a cause, or church, or an important value; sharing
books, friends, and ideas. Toward the very beginning of this process, you
assessed your and your partner's ability to give and receive in these domains. I'd like you look at pages 26–28 now. Where are you strong?
Where are you weak? And what would you like to do about it?

TACTIC 4: CHERISH YOUR PARTNER

In order to feel like a lover, you have to act like a lover. Cherishing our
partner is what we do as lovers and start not doing in long-term relationships. We say that we get busy, but what we really get is lazy. Under the

banner of being "familial" and able to "relax," we stop observing many of the simplest niceties that we offer to co-workers, subordinates . . . hell, even to strangers on the street. Everywhere you look, current styles seem to grow more and more casual. In some ways, that's freeing and more authentic. But I like to remind the people I work with that while it's fine to relax the form, the content of good manners is sensitivity. We need to be more considerate of others in our family.

When in Doubt, Be Nice

Good manners, even in your own living room, pay off. Make an effort to treat your partner graciously. I'd like you to try to be at least a little more like you were when you wooed each other—in other words, on good behavior. Smile. Show your partner you're happy to see him. Offer your partner the same warmth you'd offer a valued colleague or friend.

Whenever a couple asks for advice about how best to behave between sessions, I almost always tell them this story: Beginning when our kids were little, Belinda and I made a habit of sharing, in a very general way, some of the cases we were working on. And we'd often ask our kids for their thoughts or advice. Of course, they loved being invited into such a grown-up role and always had a lot to say. Justin usually came at it from some quirky angle that at first seemed like childish nonsense but that, as he continued, was often original. Little Alexander, who must not have been more than four or five at the time, resolutely came up with the same piece of advice for every occasion, each time offering it with utmost seriousness after a great deal of thought, as if he'd never suggested it before. His unvarying prescription? "You should tell these people that they need to be *nice to each other!*" It took me several years to appreciate that in most instances, Alexander was right on the money. Use Alexander's rule: *When in doubt, be nicer to your partner.* Treat him with warmth, or at least common courtesy.

Appreciate Each Other

When I speak of cherishing, I do not mean just feeling warm and fuzzy inside; I mean actually *doing* something to let your partner know what you appreciate. As you communicate to your partner, I'd like you to become aware of *the proportion of positive to negative feedback you're giving him.* This ratio is so important that researcher John Gottman claims to be able to predict, with 90 percent accuracy, which couples will divorce within three years based on this one factor alone. Gottman's research also showed that the ideal of low-conflict couples, couples who "always get along," was not a good predictor of happiness. There were many relatively satisfied partners who, it turned out, fought like cats and dogs. But as tough as their negative communications could be, their positive communications so far outweighed them that the couples seemed quite fine with it all.

How can you increase the positives in your relationship and in your partner? You can start by simply acknowledging them.

RULE: APPRECIATE EACH OTHER AT LEAST ONCE A DAY.

At the end of the day, tell your partner *three things you appreciate,* either about something current or something more long-standing. "I really appreciate your listening to me earlier this evening" is one example. But so is "You have always had the most beautiful eyes." Remember saying things like that? You'd be saying them again if you were dating; I guarantee it. So why not say appreciative things *now* and decrease the possibility that you will be dating again? Appreciate little things; they don't have to be earthshaking. Write notes telling your partner something positive about him or his behavior that matters to you. Leave a message or an e-mail. Every single partner who enters therapy with me feels underappreciated.

RULE: WHILE IT IS IMPORTANT TO TELL YOUR PARTNER THE DIFFICULT TRUTHS ABOUT YOUR EXPERIENCE OF HIM, IT IS NO LESS IMPORTANT TO SHARE THE PLEASURABLE ONES.

One of the greatest change experts in modern history, Mahatma Gandhi, once stated a principle so pertinent to relationship empowerment that at our Institute we now include it as one of our rules.

RULE: "WE MUST BECOME THE CHANGE WE WISH FOR IN THE WORLD."—M. GANDHI

The discipline of cherishing your partner calls to mind this profound spiritual truth. In terms of your relationship, the pragmatic action plan stemming from Gandhi's principle is this: If you want to evoke more of something in your relationship, *give it*. If you want to be cherished more, be more cherishing. If you want more laughter, joke around. If you want more respect, be more respectful.

Guerrilla Cherishing: Develop Smart Generosity

I can't fix how overburdened we all seem to be with the pressures of daily living, but I can help you lighten the load a tiny bit. Let me teach you the art of *guerrilla cherishing*. What does that mean? It means finding *particularly effective acts* of cherishing that have a big impact while not demanding a great deal of time. How do you do that? By *being thoughtful*. Women in our culture tend to be much better conditioned to know how to do this than men. That doesn't mean that they do it any more often than men do. However, if they remember to do it, they generally need less coaching about how. So, men, listen up to these examples of *smart generosity*:

Give your partner something you know she'd like.
Don't just buy a CD; buy the new CD of an artist you remember her being interested in. And don't choose the easy gift that you always get. In-

stead, try listening for something she mentions wanting. The "buck" you have to pay is the time it takes to make the purchase. The "bang" comes from showing that you listened and took notice.

Take initiative.

Like it or not, most women, particularly those of my generation, feel like their partners will do things for them only when given instructions. Chances are that your partner will love it if you show initiative about something, such as setting up an evening or a weekend together. You work out the babysitting and other logistics. Give her the present of feeling taken care of.

On a more everyday level, show attention to the domestic big picture. How many women expect to hear from their male partner a comment like "I've noticed that our linens are getting kind of old. Let's take a look at something new"? Or, "We haven't talked in a while. How are you feeling?" After you pick her up off the floor, things should go pretty well.

Step out of the rut.

Break routine. Arrange to go skydiving or skinny-dipping. Think like you did when you first met. Be adventurous.

Help out.

Women make passes at men who wash glasses. Or, said differently: *Get off the couch.*

Now, for both of you: **Be more romantic at the micro-level.**

For men: Tell her how great she looks, or rub her neck, or just hold her without sexual pressure.

————

For women: Here's a tip that couples have found extremely useful:

One of the things that many women stop doing when they transition from being lovers to being long-term partners is *demonstrating erotic interest*. For men, usually the most arousing thing you can do is to be aroused. Men get turned on by your being turned on. If you don't believe me, look at the faces of women in sexy magazines or even in advertising these days. Many of them look like they're three seconds away from an orgasm. You needn't go to that extreme, but you will get incredible mileage by keeping a little erotic energy in play throughout your day or evening together. It may take some effort, but extremely small gestures now and then on a regular basis will simply win him. Remember teasing? Ask yourself, when did you stop teasing? How nice it was to play around with the power of your desirability! It's one of the great gifts women have. Don't give it up just because you've been together for a while. Take a few seconds to breathe in your mate's ear, or kiss him passionately; touch him erotically or say something wild. That should help keep the juices flowing. It's a very specific means of cherishing his sexuality and yours, and it's good for you both. My only caveat is that in order for this to be useful, *you must have healthy sexual boundaries.* If you're afraid to be stimulating because he can't hear "no," then deal with that issue first. On the other side, the same advice applies to approaching a partner who's behind walls and sexually withholding. But, once you have reasonably healthy boundaries, *act like a lover.* It should cost you no more than a few minutes a day.

Now that you're brimming over with new thoughts and techniques, let's move on to the last tactic for cherishing your relationship.

TACTIC 5: BECOME PARTNERS-IN-HEALTH

What I mean when I speak of being partners-in-health is that both of you share a commitment to relational practice. You have gone beyond the ideal of "spontaneous" relationships, and you have agreed to learn about and use relationship technology. Sharing relationship practice is really one example of *sharing*, and, strictly speaking, it should go under that category. But it is sharing something so significant that I've assigned it a special place. What is it like, to share this practice together? In a word, it means that you have a partner you can thoroughly count on.

No one is perfect and no couple is perfect. I care less about how bad things get when you "lose it" than I care about the strength of your practice in making such instances *less frequent, less severe,* and *faster to recover from.* Never losing it is not the goal. Unbroken happiness, even unbroken connection, is a fairy tale. In real relationships the key questions are: Do you have a working frame surrounding such instances? How well do you both handle issues that you simply disagree about, or the inevitable times of conflict, even conflict that can get ugly upon occasion?

As partners-in-health, you are committed to developing your capacity to hold the frame of connection-in-the-face-of-disconnection so that you are able to access your second consciousness, to repair instead of destroy. You are accountable to each other and you share the goal of non-violent, full-respect living, not just with each other, but with everyone.

Sharing relationship practice also means that you subscribe to a common vision. You have both learned to see things systemically, relationally, so that, for example, you understand that playing the game for winners and losers won't really benefit either of you. While you recognize your interconnectedness, you also understand boundaries. Neither of you blames the other for "making" you distressed, and neither of you tries to "get" the other to think or behave as you'd wish. Along with a shared vision, you also both have an arsenal of skills to draw upon.

Accountability, vision, skills. Each of these elements, let alone all of them taken together, places you and your partner at an uncommon level of sophistication. Own it and enjoy it. You've earned it. No one gets this practice handed to him.

Finally, becoming partners-in-health means that you share the process of learning about and mastering a challenging discipline. At its most spiritual, it is like sharing a church, or a meditation practice. Politically, it's sharing a common cause—to go beyond twentieth-century roles for men and women, boys and girls, and to go beyond patriarchal rules to a relational approach that befits our new century. On a less lofty plane, being partners-in-health is like sharing a hobby, or learning a new sport or art form together. You go to lectures or workshops together, listen to tapes, turn each other on to a new book or author. It's fun.

What If Your Partner Isn't Onboard?

For many readers, this has been a concern since page one. As you might imagine, the answer depends on what "onboard" means. Let me briefly run through the spectrum of situations, from mild to grave.

Situation 1: You're in a basically good relationship, but your partner has no interest in learning relationship skills.

Your best shot is a combination of carrot and stick, with a predominance of carrot. Initially, at least, his participation is at your request; that is, you understand that it's not something he would want but you request it as something very important to you. Then do whatever you can to expose him to a speaker or to material that you know will be good. It will be hard enough to get him to attend a workshop or listen to a tape, so don't take risks with the opportunity. Expose him to people or materials that have a shot at knocking his socks off. By the way, let me be clear that this need not be relationship empowerment work. While I obviously believe in this approach, there are many programs out there for relationship skill building. Following any program that's effective will qualify you as partners-in-health.

One way of piquing his interest that you might try is to ask him for information about *you*. For example, you could set him up to write out his CNI of you and then compare it to what you guessed it would be. And you could do the same thing for most of the concepts you've learned: your losing-strategy profile, your boundary profile, where you are on the grid, or your role in your bad deal. If you're not too heavy-handed about it, he might get drawn in. It's a rare partner who can resist an invitation to discuss *your* imperfections. The beauty in this is that in order to fulfill his assignments, your partner will have to have some understanding of what you're talking about, such as what CNIs mean and what the relationship grid looks like.

Finally, just because your partner doesn't use this material doesn't mean that you can't. Just do it. Get your kids into it. Teach your kids about good boundaries. Show your mate some positive changes in you that are a result of this work. In all likelihood you will get a positive reaction.

Situation 2: Your partner is nice enough but you need more connection.
There are three different, though related, circumstances that might set this up:

1. Despite getting along well enough and enjoying each other, there's no working mechanism of correction beyond your partner's intrinsic civility and compassion, which, though good, isn't quite good enough. This means that issues get left on the table, unresolved, and that needs don't get fully met for either of you. The result is an undramatic but stultifying distance.
2. Another possibility is that your partner operates behind walls. For instance, he may have a wall between himself and his own heart, his emotions. When he speaks he'll be boring, even though the content may be highly emotional. It's hard for you to be present because *he's* not present.
3. The third possibility is that your partner can be present and can also work through issues well enough, but he's too selfish, or too immature, or simply too unsophisticated to be very cherishing.

In each of these instances, your sense that the connection is thin has less to do with something wrong than with the absence of what would be right. What you need to do depends entirely on how satisfied you feel. If, given the whole of the relationship, you don't feel that this is a big problem, then use the same strategies I spelled out above. If, on the other hand, you feel pretty lonely and stunted, then you need to let him know more clearly how dissatisfied you are. In other words, you're going to need to rock the boat. How big a deal you'll need to make of it depends on what it takes to command his attention. If he "gets it" that you're serious, you can then choose to:

- Teach him about relationship practice, or at least what you need more of from him.
- Expose him to seminars and workshops that could teach him.
- Insist on couple's therapy.

How do you know when to get professional help?

For some reason, people expect this issue to be very tricky, when in fact, it's really quite simple and straightforward. You need to seek professional help when you've tried very hard on your end of the seesaw—you've used your skills, rocked the boat, been clear about what you want, been willing to reward and appreciate—and nothing has worked all that well. This is not a complicated matter. You need to seek professional help when you can't do what you need to do on your own. The difficult part, as I see it, isn't knowing when you need help, but dealing with your partner's—and maybe your own—resistance to getting the help that you know you need. How to deal with resistance? That brings us to the next level down on the spectrum of "not being onboard."

Situation 3: Your partner is mostly okay but unaccountable whenever he isn't okay.

This is a personal judgment call that depends on the answers to a few questions:

- How bad is "not okay" when it happens?
- How frequently does it happen?
- How big an impact is it having on your life together?
- When he's being unaccountable, what is he doing?

- How much of your wants and needs are being met otherwise in the relationship?

As with the previous situation, your response to your partner should be governed by the severity of the problem and how much you are getting out of the relationship. Here's your choice: If you do not take on the issue of your partner's unaccountability, the odds are that what you see is what you're going to get. There may be better periods and worse, but you should probably assume that there will be no substantial change. If the downside isn't too bad and the upside is worth it, do your best with a little stick and a little carrot. But if either the downside is pretty bad and/or the upside isn't really all that great, ask yourself if you're ready to risk rocking the boat. If so, just know that you're most likely going to have a serious fight on your hands, and you may lose the relationship if he refuses to become more accountable. Personally, I'd find it hard to think of spending my life with an unaccountable partner. But I'm not in your situation, and it would be utterly presumptuous for anyone to make this decision but you.

Situation 4: Your partner is highly difficult and also unaccountable.
You are with someone who is shameless and who rides in the one-up position. You are not in a good relationship. Again, it's a question of severity, but it's hard to imagine a good reason to stay. I'd draw the line. Your partner can choose to continue to behave badly, take little or no responsibility for his behavior, and show no real motivation for change. If that's his choice, then I'd advise you to choose a healthier relationship.

What's Best for Your Children?

We are living in very conservative times, and a lot of emphasis has been put on preserving families at all cost. That's simply unreasonable. Yes, children are damaged by divorce. There's no question about that. The real question is, how damaged are they by staying in miserable homes?

Many researchers believe that the fault line concerns how obvious the marital difficulties are. As bad as divorce is, a child would be better off without the exposure to yelling and fighting and a blatantly disturbed environment. Few people argue that point. So now the question ratchets down to this: How damaged do children get in homes with a miserable marriage that is more contained? Many would argue that children are better off in such environments than with divorced parents. As a family therapist, I must say that I'm skeptical. Here's why:

First, over many years of working with families, I am astounded at how transparent we are to our children. Even very young children, when given a safe avenue to express themselves, will engage in role-play, draw pictures, write poems, and provide commentary that details with often remarkable specificity what's going on between family members. The perspicacity of children has so impressed us that it is a virtual cliché among family therapists to say, "If you want to know what's *really* going on in a family, turn to the children." It's not at all clear to me that the so-called contained or hidden misery in nonexplosive bad marriages is really as hidden as we might like to think.

Second, even if you were to convince me that children in such homes were less damaged in general, I will nevertheless guarantee you that they will sustain considerable damage when it comes to having healthy relationships of their own in the future. Almost every troubled relationship I have ever worked with was a replay of some aspect of the troubled relationship each partner grew up with. The only exceptions involve persons with a biological vulnerability to an emotional disorder or an addiction. Are children better or worse off going through the injury of divorce in order to see either or both of their parents in a stable, fulfilling relationship? I think the only honest answer—stripped of ideology or prejudice—is that we simply don't know.

Finally, even if it were proven somehow that children are more damaged through divorce than through remaining in homes with unhappy marriages, it is not at all clear to me that the moral imperative is for adults to sacrifice living healthy lives for the sake of their children. I have helped unhappy couples break up; I also have helped them stay together precisely for the sake of their children, and I admire the nobility of their sacrifice. In addition, I have helped a great many couples stay "a bit longer," until the kids were older or even out of the house.

If a couple can be brought into health, that is obviously the best outcome for everyone. In extreme circumstances, the choice seems clear. In less blatant situations I mistrust anyone, frankly, who claims to be able to tell you what's best for your children, or for you either for that matter. You must decide. Think long and hard; talk it out with those you trust, and listen to what you feel. In the end, most of the people I've encountered over the years who have been through this decision rarely speak about what they *should* have done, one way or another. They speak about what they felt they had to do.

When Should You Pull the Plug?

If there are no children involved, whenever you feel, despite the pain and turmoil that will ensue, that you have no interest in your partner and won't have any no matter what he does, then it's unfair not to set him free to go find someone else who will cherish him. If there are children involved, you should part when you feel you really have no other option.

In either case, the time to consider the question is after everything you've done has failed and after several attempts at professional help have also failed. It serves no one's interests to preserve endlessly toxic interactions. Addicts and abusive partners can be helped, and the first step should always be an ultimatum: *Get treatment or else!* But if someone simply refuses, or if he won't allow his treatment to be effective, I don't think there's much choice.

I firmly believe that any two partners who love each other and who are willing to do the work can transform even a terrible relationship into a good one, and even into a great one over time. *Once both partners are at the table in good faith*, anything *can be worked out. The one thing that cannot be worked out, however, is getting both partners to the table.* They have to take their places themselves. That doesn't mean that pressure can't be exerted. On the contrary, it absolutely should, and depending on how bad things are, as much pressure as is reasonably possible. Almost all the couples who see me for the last-chance two-day intensive sessions I hold are there because one of the partners has offered the other an ultimatum. And, in cases of addiction or of severe verbal abuse, I have often helped families and friends do an "intervention" with a plan for a rehab program in someone's back pocket, and with sometimes quite severe consequences should the addict or abuser refuse. But the bottom line is that, try as we might, we are merely humans and not gods. We cannot control the destiny or the choices of other human beings.

I always tell the people I work with that our goal is not preserving the relationship. No therapist can promise that. My goal is to do all I can to increase your capacity for intimacy. If the two of you can take your increased ability to be healthy and utilize it with each other, that is my wish, particularly when kids are involved. But you cannot control your mate's choices. If the worst happens and you must leave the relationship, the work you have done is far from meaningless. Your new vision and skills, particularly your commitment to full-respect living, will maximize the possibility of ending the relationship cleanly, of standing up for yourself in nonviolent ways during the transition, of maintaining as healthy a co-parenting relationship as you can, and, finally, of bringing your new health and skills into your next relationship, which will be with a better choice for a partner. While you may not have been able to salvage this relationship, you are on much better footing in your life and in your prospects for happiness in the future.

Cherishing Your World

RULE: NO ONE LEARNS HOW TO BE RELATIONAL BY HIMSELF.

The last topic we turn to is how to live a cherishing life in the world. We'll discuss how to keep up your relationship practice; how to realize, own, and use whatever talents or gifts you've been given; and how to give back to the world some of the goodness and wisdom you have begun to embrace.

HOW CAN YOU CHERISH YOUR RELATIONSHIP PRACTICE?

Here's the critical piece. No matter how smart you are, the best way to keep your relationship practice growing and strong is with other people, by letting yourself be inspired, encouraged, and informed by their journeys. And while relationship practice means bringing second consciousness into play, there will be times when you just won't be up to the task. You'll be confused, off-center, or simply deluded. *An important part of sustaining your practice is letting in help.*

When I'm upset or confused, I'm blessed with a number of people I can call who will support me and who will also be very frank about what they see. We all need that. Ideally, we can turn to a few trusted individuals and also a group setting or two. *Feed your practice.* Men's groups, women's groups, church groups, twelve-step programs, seminars, lectures, retreats—if you can't find what you want, then create it. But you need company. And company that will support your *relationship* empowerment, not just personal empowerment. People who will "support" you with "I wouldn't put up with that! What a jerk!" are a dime a dozen. I want you to find—or create—a community of individuals who are comfortable saying, "Now, let's take a look at your part in this."

This may not be as hard as you might first think. Remember the ideal of shaping your relationships instead of being passive? More assertion up front and less resentment on the back end? This is a great opportunity. I'll bet that you already have people in your life who will support relationship empowerment if you just take the time to spell it out for them: "Hey look, I don't want you to just side with me against my husband, okay? I already know he's a jerk. I want you to support our relationship even while you support me, know what I mean?" For a dear friend, that may be all that's needed.

CAN YOU RAISE TWENTY-FIRST-CENTURY BOYS AND GIRLS?

Absolutely. While supporting girls to step out of the traditional mold has been going on for some time now, our sons have had far less support. As you think about issues of gender, it's important to remain clear. Often the conversation will be couched as if a boy can be either tough or sensitive, a girl either competent or feminine. This nonsense sends me over the bend. I'm not talking about sissifying boys or masculinizing girls, but about raising all children to be whole: strong, big-hearted boys and competent, feminine girls. This isn't about teaching our children to be more this and less that, but teaching them to cherish and use all of the wonderful qualities they possess.

Both for your couple's relationship and for your family, I'd invite you to take steps toward building a relationship-cherishing subculture to surround you. Connect with other like-minded families. Form a committee or a study group in your child's school to look into how we can best support girls and, more especially, boys. I think that the more we can support boys right now the better, because I see them as "getting it" from both ends. Those holding on to the traditional early-twentieth-century model of masculinity will punish them if they're too sensitive or vulnerable, and those holding on to the feminist model of the late twentieth century will punish them for being too aggressive and overpowering. So the same boy may be heartily disliked by an old-school feminist-oriented teacher in class for displaying a "boyish" behavior, and then go to football practice an hour later, where he's demeaned by a coach for not displaying the same behavior enough! What people want from boys is very confused (and confusing) during this time of transition. That's why it's so important that you remain clear.

My attention to boys is not meant to imply that our efforts to help girls remain whole have succeeded. There's a lot going on in girl culture right now that can be interpreted as a backlash, or at least a huge backslide, from their empowerment. One of my chief concerns is the hypersexualization of quite young girls, an apparent return to seeing girls and women as sexual servicers. I'd like us to produce *gender-literate* kids, children who can weigh with some intelligence the pros and cons of staying true to yourself and deal with what that will bring, or choose to let something go in order to conform; kids who can speak with you realistically about the consequences of giving up their individuality in order to fit in, as well as the consequences of choosing not to. Remember, it's rarely your decision; it's theirs. But give them words for the struggles they face—and guidance. As much as possible, make the issue of their health, and of relationship health in general, a normal topic of conversation in the family.

Finally, short of protecting your kids from abusive treatment, you cannot healthfully be at odds with your mate; you cannot undercut each other. If you're having trouble working as a team, deal with it. If you need help on this issue, get it. Parents routinely polarize about how to raise their kids. It's not the end of the world. But don't disengage with this issue unresolved, leaving your child in the middle. You all deserve better than that.

CHERISHING YOUR OWN SUCCESS

It has been my observation that as people develop healthier ways to relate to themselves and to others, there is often significant movement in their public lives, or their avocations. And I think I know why that is. Speaking as someone who has been through this process, and who uses every scrap of technique I've been introducing to you, what I have found, and what my clients report, is a tremendous freeing-up of energy. I've said over and over that relationship practice is demanding. But, to be clearer, what it demands is the exercise of maturity and discipline. The demand comes in that moment when you're flooded with a knee-jerk reaction to do something counterproductive and yet you somehow manage to will yourself to try something brand-new. That's the type of demanding that this work is.

On the other hand, it has become increasingly clear to me that being screwed up and having screwed-up relationships also takes an enormous amount of work! If I could only go back and recapture all the energy I've spent over the years fighting, nursing my sense of injury, feeling like a big victim, scheming, obsessing, doing damage and then doing penance, wow! I could power a rocket to the moon and back and have plenty of energy to spare.

It takes a lot less energy to feel something, even if it's unpleasant, than it takes to keep pressing it down. It takes less energy to tell the truth than it does to swallow it and then stew about it. And while I've said a few times that men and women are more relationally skilled at work than they are at home, that's not the same as saying that they're nearly as skilled as they should be.

RULE: SINCE SUCCESS IN TODAY'S WORLD SO OFTEN DEPENDS ON ONE'S ABILITY TO ESTABLISH AND USE RELATIONSHIPS EFFECTIVELY, INCREASED RELATIONAL SKILL USUALLY CORRESPONDS TO SIGNIFICANT IMPROVEMENT IN ACHIEVING ONE'S LIFE GOALS AND AMBITIONS.

Isn't that great? You get to feel better, have a better family life, and do better in the world. And while we're talking about the link between success and better relationships, let's not forget your important relationship to yourself. Along with freed-up energy and better relationships with those around you, the other big factor linking relationship practice with success is that you *start staying out of your own way.* You're not wracked with shame; you're not arrogant; you feel like you have a right to succeed. These three factors in combination unleash enormous creativity:

- Liberated energy
- Improved relationship skill
- Decreased self-defeating behavior

SUCCESS: CAN YOU STAND IT?

The only thing that you have left to do is to tolerate the discomfort of doing so well.

As your relationship practice grows stronger, as you learn to bring yourself into center more quickly, have healthier boundaries, trade passive immaturity for proactive maturity, your baseline begins to shift. You start spending more and more time feeling untroubled. Not that life doesn't pull you in a hundred directions, or that you never feel hurt, scared, or angry. But, over time, you start feeling more and more clear about how to deal with these challenges. Over time, almost without noticing it, you realize that whole periods have gone by—hours, days, weeks, even months—without feeling knocked out of kilter. Your relationships start feeling less complicated and difficult. You become more forgiving of yourself and consequently less defensive. You begin to experience what in the past would have felt dark, gnarled, and confusing as clear and straightforward. Sure, tough issues will come, but you start to have faith that *you'll be smart about them* and they'll work out. Yes, you'll screw up sometimes, but these mistakes no longer tip you so easily into thinking that there's something fundamentally wrong.

Full-respect living has begun to take hold. You are starting to trust in abundance.

CHERISHING ABUNDANCE

What do I mean by abundance? Here, as you read these words, take a moment to appreciate the pleasure of reading. Wherever you are, take a moment to feel the beauty in it—even if you're in a place that most might find ugly. Breathe. Breathe deeply. Feel your body as it sits or lies down. Feel the great pleasure of a good breath of air. You're alive. Isn't that amazing? In this moment, right now. Tomorrow your fortunes might shift but right now, in this moment, you are blessed. Your life is bountiful, filled with things that have meaning and with people who care about you. Can you feel that at all? Can you remember, when you slow down for a moment and sit, when it all drops away for an instant, how rich your life can feel?

Intimacy is our natural state, our birthright. When you're centered, with nothing to apologize for or hide because you are trying your best, you live with integrity. How that feels, if you just stop for a moment to let it in, is good. It feels good to be healthy, in exactly the way that you begin feeling good physically as you get fit. What does it feel like to get strong physically? Pretty miserable at first if you're seriously out of shape, just as the early stage of relationship practice might feel at the start. But as you exercise regularly, week after week, it will take hold. And one afternoon you'll be sitting somewhere thinking of nothing in particular and you'll notice this really nice feeling suffused throughout your body, a sensation at once relaxed and poised. And you'll suddenly realize that this pleasurable sensation in your body is health; it's just what your body feels like when you start getting in shape.

RULE: AS YOUR RELATIONSHIP PRACTICE GROWS STRONGER, YOU
  WILL BECOME MORE AND MORE AWARE OF THE ABUNDANCE
  INSIDE AND AROUND YOU.

CHERISHING YOUR OWN POWER

As a boy who grew up with a warm, tortured, violent father, as a boy growing up on the Jersey shore end of the American Dream, I spent many years being awfully confused about power. I mostly saw people either misuse power or not have any. As a young adult I was plagued with writer's blocks, self-defeating behaviors, oscillations between feeling gifted and cursed, grand and worthless. I began what turned out to be years of healing work; I became a therapist myself. I was doing all right, but I felt I had more in me to give and no idea how to bring it out into the world. But I was healthy enough to ask for help.

Over the years several wise and wonderful people have mentored me, and every one of them gave me his or her version of the same advice. Call it grace, call it power, intuition, inspiration, the sweet spot, or the flow state—call it anything you like. But whatever it is that flows through you in that wonderful state, don't call it yours. Don't take credit for it. Don't act as if you own it. And don't shrink away from it either, from its scale or its power.

RULE: THE WAY TO STEP INTO THE FULL ABUNDANCE OF YOUR OWN POWER, YOUR UNIQUE GIFTS AND TALENTS, IS BY NEITHER OWNING NOR DISOWNING THEM, BUT BY DOING YOUR WORK AND COOPERATING. INSPIRATION WILL NEVER SERVE YOU. YOU SERVE IT.

Realizing fully the talents, the gifts, that lie at the core of who you are at your best, allowing yourself to be as big as you are, means cherishing the abundance inside you. In order to flourish, stay out of its way and do whatever you need to do to become a worthy vessel. As you grow healthier and more skilled, your relationship to your own unique form of abundance may be among the last, and among the most difficult, of your relationships to straighten out.

The metaphor that works best for me is art. You do your work on your end. You put in hour after hour of practicing your instrument. You repeat the same drills hundreds of times. And then, on a good night, in the middle of a concert somewhere, inspiration appears. You no longer play well; you play brilliantly. Should you be proud? Hell yes. Proud of your part in the collaboration, proud of the skill you've earned, and even proud of the gift that spoke through your fingers. And you must also be grateful.

The most important way to cherish your own talents and gifts is simply to use them. If you've been blessed with a beautiful, powerful voice, then open up your throat and *sing*! Find a voice teacher and develop it. If you have a great sense of humor, make people laugh. If you have an instinct for business, make money. At this point you might be thinking, "I'm not really sure *what* I've got inside that would be much of a gift to anyone." Don't wait until it's all perfectly clear to you. Jump in where you are, choose something close at hand, and begin. It's like writing a first draft. Where you start may not be where you end up. But you'd never have reached the finished piece if you'd lacked the courage to begin.

———

Wherever you are, in whatever form you choose, you must give back to the world. You must use your gifts—including whatever you get from relationship practice—to contribute to something beyond yourself: a cause, a child, a neighborhood. This isn't out of altruism but enlightened self-interest. You won't grow if you don't have the daring to let go and give what you've got to the world. Do it now. Do it badly. But get going.

You won't have to look high and low for ways to contribute. As you get less tangled up in old struggles, old miseries, opportunities will naturally present themselves to you, opportunities to stand up for something, be of help to someone, or bring something beautiful into the world.

Take them.

Resources

The Relationship Empowerment Institute
(www.terryreal.com)

This is my website, and it contains all of the information in this section along with many links to other relevant websites. These resources are periodically updated. Also on the website you will find lists of recommended books and tapes by others, my own books and tapes, free monthly telephone gatherings on topics related to relationship empowerment work, free monthly gatherings for mental health professionals, and listings of workshops, conferences, and other trainings that are available.

Books and Tapes

With a little digging, most books concerning particular conditions, such as alcoholism or depression, are best found in the recommended books section of the websites of the major recognized associations concerning the disorder. For example, if you go to the Attention Deficit Disorder Association's website, click on "store" at the bottom of the page, and then click on "Amazon books," four excellent books on ADHD appear.

What follows is a list of books I have found particularly helpful or moving. It is very much a general and a personal list.

Patricia Evans
The Verbally Abusive Relationship: How to Recognize It and How to Respond

The author does a terrific job of describing verbal abuse and many of the specific maneuvers used by controlling and abusive people.

Carol Gilligan
The Birth of Pleasure

I had the privilege of collaborating with the author in an informal project that she describes here, and that I describe in *How Can I Get Through to You? The Birth of Pleasure,* is a meditation on love that is poetic in its language and far-reaching in its scope.

Elan Golomb
Trapped in the Mirror

An accessible and helpful book on narcissism.

John Gottman
The Seven Principles for Making Marriage Work: A Practical Guide from the Country's Foremost Relationship Expert

The author is one of the few empirical researchers on marital satisfaction.

Harville Hendrix

Getting the Love You Want: A Guide for Couples

This classic has reached millions of readers. The author's ideas about mate selection, based on the works of many psychoanalytic writers of the time, is similar to mine, although his dialogue method differs from my repair process in some respects.

bell hooks

The Will to Change: Men, Masculinity, and Love

A terrific book on men's psychology from a leading feminist thinker.

Pia Mellody

Facing Codependency: What It Is, Where It Comes From, How It Sabotages Our Lives

Facing Love Addiction: Giving Yourself the Power to Change the Way You Love

The Intimacy Factor: The Ground Rules for Overcoming the Obstacles to Truth, Respect, and Lasting Love

In addition to these books, my recommended list of her audiotapes can be found on my website (www.terryreal.com). I cannot recommend them highly enough.

Keith Miller

Compelled to Control

An excellent examination of codependence.

Terrence Real

How Can I Get Through to You?: Reconnecting Men and Women

I Don't Want to Talk About It: Overcoming the Secret Legacy of Male Depression

Relational Parenting: Raising Healthy Boys and Girls on CD-ROM. Only available from www.terryreal.com.

Relationship Turnaround: Empowering Women, Connecting Men on CD-ROM and cassette tape. Only available from www.terryreal.com.

Cheryl Richardson

Stand Up for Your Life: A Practical Step-by-Step Plan to Build Inner Confidence and Personal Power
Take Time for Your Life
The Unmistakable Touch of Grace

The author is a personal coach, whose approach differs from therapy in its directive, action-oriented focus. I find her work both practical and inspirational.

Michele Weiner-Davis

Divorce Busting: A Step-By-Step Approach to Making Your Marriage Loving Again

The author provides clear, practical advice to help stop the degeneration of your marriage.

The Sex-Starved Marriage: A Couple's Guide to Boosting Their Marriage Libido

This book is notable for its practical advice.

Quick Reference Guide

Section One: Four Principles

1. Relationship Empowerment

In contrast to the disempowerment inherent in *acquiescence* and the anti-relational bias inherent in *personal empowerment*, relationship empowerment brings your full assertiveness into your relationship in a manner that cherishes your partner and helps him succeed, thereby empowering both of you. Its golden rule is *What can I give you to help you give me what I want?*

2. Full-Respect Living

The commitment to respect both yourself and others at the same time. You may need to be assertive, to protect yourself, or to rock the boat, but none of these behaviors sinks below the line of respectful treatment.

There is no excuse for abuse—either dishing it out or putting up with it. Full-respect living is the framework for *living a nonviolent life*.

3. Relationship Practice

The deliberate cultivation of *second consciousness*, a mindfulness practice of bringing the *functional adult* part of ourselves into relationship with the childish parts of ourselves over and over again. Relationship practice occurs at the *micro level*, minute by minute, when despite every muscle and nerve screaming to do the same old same old, you will yourself onto a new, learned track.

4. Second Consciousness

The voice of reason, maturity, and relational savvy, which interrupts your initial (first-consciousness) knee-jerk reaction and offers a more constructive—usually learned—alternative. Growing this functional adult part of the self, arming it with tools, and strengthening its power to override automatic reactions is the essence of relationship practice.

Section Two: Twenty Practices

1. Appreciating

A. Appreciate each other at least once a day. At the end of the day, tell your partner *three things you appreciate*, either about something current or something more long-standing. "I really appreciate your listening to me earlier this evening" is one example. But so is "You have always had the most beautiful eyes."

B. Develop "an attitude of gratitude." Throughout the day, notice and shift all victim thinking. If you don't like something, change it, leave it, or embrace it. If you choose to neither change nor leave, then *own your choice* and appreciate the good qualities in the situation.

2. Boundary Practice

Take a moment to visualize setting your boundaries at the beginning of each day. Throughout the day, take a moment to reset them through visualization. Take stock of where you might be at a given moment and correct if necessary, softening walls and strengthening appropriate containment and protection.

Avoid all boundary-violating behaviors by *staying on your side of the line*. Speak from the "I," not the "you" or the "it." Remember, there is nothing that you need to say that cannot be said from the "I" with practice.

3. Cherishing

Cherishing is the deliberate cultivation of your capacity to take pleasure in and celebrate what you have. Cherishing your partner's progress by giving him specific positive feedback is the best way to engender more of the behaviors you'd like.

You cherish your relationship by making time for it, putting energy into it, and by giving your partner gifts in word and deed that demonstrate your care.

You cherish yourself through active self-care.

You cherish your commitment to continued growth and relationship practice by becoming *partners-in-health*, sharing information and inspiration.

And you cherish abundance by stepping into your particular passions and gifts with no attempt to either own or disown them, but rather with joy and respect for your own success and a wish to contribute to the world.

4. CNI-Busting Behaviors

With your partner, draw up a list of CNI-confirming and CNI-busting behaviors—behaviors that are like or very much unlike your partner's negative expectations, or *core negative image*, of you. This list serves as your relationship compass, as specific operating instructions for how best to please your partner. Decrease CNI-confirming behaviors and increase CNI-busting behaviors.

5. Coming to Center
Use the *relationship grid* to provide a snapshot of where you are, and correct for any imbalance by doing self-esteem and boundary work.

6. Contracting
Making explicit contracts protects you, the contractor, in two ways, by:

A. Making it difficult for the other person to take a victim position, since he's agreed to the contract
B. Making each other's expectations and commitments clear

Contracts always concern behaviors, not attitudes or feelings, and are best when they are specific and close-ended.

7. Cultivating a Sense of Abundance
In both ordinary moments and, especially, in moments of upset, stop, either look down or close your eyes for a few seconds, and *breathe*. Feel the sweetness of a good, deep breath. Feel the warmth or coolness of the air on your skin. Feel the beauty of your surroundings, the sun, or the sight of trees outside the window. Remember that your life is abundant, that this moment is abundant, and that a particular disruption in your relationship or your circumstances will not take that abundance away.

8. Daring to Rock the Boat
In even the healthiest of relationships, getting what you want often involves assertively going after it. If something is important to you, and your partner doesn't "get it," you may need to stand up for your wants and needs by fighting for them. This means being willing to behave in ways that your partner will be uncomfortable with — acting as unhappy as you are about the issue, and, while remaining moderate and respectful, not backing down.

9. Dead-Stop Contracts

A dead-stop contract is an agreement to interrupt the vicious cycle of CNI-meets-CNI. The agreement goes like this: "If I feel, rightly or wrongly, that you are behaving in ways that reinforce my CNI of you—if I feel, for instance, that old, horrible feeling of being bossed around by you—I will signal a *dead-stop*. And you promise in advance that if you hear that signal, understanding that your behavior is CNI-triggering, you will come to a dead stop—*whether you agree with my perception or not.*"

When you use a *dead-stop contract*, nothing short of physical safety takes precedence over your goal of stopping your repetitive pattern, no matter what you think of your partner's perception or motivation.

10. Helping Your Partner Succeed

Once your partner has responded by acknowledging and giving, you:

A. Appreciate what you've been offered
B. Ask what you might do to help

If your partner describes something you might do differently, it is now your turn to acknowledge and give what you can.

11. Listening to Understand

Remember, the speaker role and the listener role are two different roles. As the listener, *listen.* Focus on your partner and not on your rebuttals, explanations, or concerns, either spoken or merely thought. Turn points of contention into points of curiosity.

12. Making Requests

Instead of focusing on what your partner has done wrong, discipline yourself to focus on what he could do now or later that would be right. You shift from a *negative/past* focus to a *positive/future* focus.

Don't criticize—ask!

13. Meeting Immaturity with Maturity

On those occasions when your partner is obviously operating from an immoderate, childish part of himself, hunker down and *stay moderate yourself.* Try two or three times to help your partner reseat himself in his *functional adult* self, as in, "Honey, I'm sorry. I really didn't mean to put you down. All I meant was . . ." If, after a few such efforts, it becomes clear that your partner is simply behind a wall and not listening, politely and respectfully disengage. Don't bother getting indignant or hurt, but also stop banging your head against the wall. Don't argue, reason, or cajole. Just let go and give your partner space to figure it out.

14. Remembering Love

Before bringing up a difficult topic, recall that the person you're about to speak to is someone you care about and that your goal in speaking is to make things better. Keep your eyes on the prize!

15. Responding with Generosity

Remember that in the *repair process,* the respondent's only goal is to help his partner move back into harmony. You are "at his service."

Your response is a two-step process. You:

A. Acknowledge all that you can of what your partner has said
B. Give all that you can of what your partner has asked for

When responding, lead with agreement, not argument.

16. Responsible Distance Taking

In contrast to unilateral, or provocative, distance taking, responsible distance taking always includes two elements:

A. An explanation
B. A promise of return or a proposed alternative

You don't simply say, "I don't want to talk," you say, "I don't want to talk right now. Here's why, and here's when I can."

Anytime you say no to someone, you are taking distance, and should do so responsibly.

17. Self-Esteem Practice

Check to see where you are—one-down, one-up, or same-as—and correct if necessary.

In your mind's eye, reach down if you are in a toxic shame state and visualize pulling yourself up into your body so that you look squarely out of your eyes at the other person, from a level, same-as, position.

In your mind's eye, reach up if you are in a grandiose state and visualize pulling yourself down into your body so that you are looking squarely at the other person, from a level, same-as, position.

18. Smart Generosity

Giving your partner more of what he's asking for by asking yourself, "What will giving this cost me?" Things that aren't difficult to give but that mean a lot to your partner, such as remembering an important date, admitting when you're wrong, or agreeing to do something you intended to do anyway, are low-cost, high-yield investments.

19. Time-Outs

When either partner calls a time-out—by saying the word "time-out," by using the "T" hand signal, or by using any agreed-upon sign—the interaction comes to an immediate stop. The spoken or gestured signal is understood by both partners to be an abbreviation of the following words:

> "Dear partner, for whatever reason, right or wrong, I am about to lose it. If I stay here and keep this up with you I am liable to do or say something stupid that I know I'm going to regret. Therefore I am taking a break to get a grip on myself and calm down. I will check back in with you responsibly."

The default interval for a time-out is twenty minutes. Checking in does not necessarily mean getting back together. You can check in— either in person or by telephone—and tell your partner that you need more time. With each extension, the time-out interval gets longer. The recommended length between check-ins is:

- Twenty minutes
- One or two hours
- Half a day
- A whole day
- Overnight

When reconnecting after a time-out, you must take a twenty-four-hour moratorium on the subject that triggered the initial fight.

20. Using the Feedback Wheel

    A. Contract with your partner to do the process; don't just dump.
    B. Remember love.
    C. Use the four steps of the feedback wheel:

    1. What I saw or heard
    2. What I made up about it
    3. How I feel about it
    4. What I'd like

    D. Let go of outcome.

Section Three: Overviews

The Five Losing Strategies

1. Needing to be Right

a. Finding out whose view is more "valid" or "accurate."

b. Leads to endless *objectivity battles*.

c. Fuels the *psychological violence* of self-righteous indignation.

2. Controlling Your Partner

a. Can be *direct* or *indirect* (manipulation).

b. Short of outright coercion, control is an illusion.

c. People don't like being controlled. Payback is inevitable.

3. Unbridled Self-Expression

a. "I have the right and the need to share my feelings with you 'spontaneously.' "

b. The idea that all sharing is authentic and will increase closeness.

c. Rarely engenders generosity in others.

4. Retaliation

a. Perverse justice: "Offending from the victim position."

b. Perverse communication: Trying to "make you feel what I feel."

c. Can be *explicit* or *covert* (passive aggression).

5. Withdrawal

a. Differs from *responsible distance taking*.

b. Stems from either resignation or retaliation.

c. Often masquerades as mature acceptance.

The Five Winning Strategies

1. Shifting from Complaint to Request

a. Move from a *negative/past* to a *positive/future* focus. Don't criticize—ask!

b. Make your requests specific, behavioral, and reasonable.

2. Speaking Out with Love and Savvy

a. Contract with your partner to engage in *the repair process.*

b. *Remember love.*

c. Use the four steps of the *feedback wheel:*

   1. What I saw or heard

   2. What I made up about it

   3. How I feel about it

   4. What I'd like

d. Let go of outcome.

3. Responding with Generosity

a. Listen to understand.

b. Acknowledge whatever you can.

c. Give whatever you can.

4. Empowering Each Other

a. Acknowledge the gifts the responder has offered.

b. Ask what you might do to help the responder deliver.

c. Acknowledge whatever you can and give whatever you can.

5. Cherishing

a. *Remember abundance.*

b. Give your partner specific positive feedback.

c. Nourish yourself and your relationship with time and energy.

d. Practice *smart generosity.*

e. Inhabit your talents and gifts without owning or disowning them.

f. Give back to the world.

The Repair Process Overview

Phase One: Speaking and Listening

1. *Speak out* with love and savvy
   a. *Remember love*
   b. Use the *feedback wheel*

2. Listen with a generous heart
   a. Contention becomes curiosity
      Understand the internal logic of your partner's experience
   b. Questions stop when you can accurately *reflect* and *empathize*

Phase Two: Responding with a Generous Spirit

1. *Clarify* your partner's wishes
2. *Acknowledge* whatever you can
3. *Give* whatever you can

Phase Three: Empowering Each Other

1. Switch roles
   a. Speaker *appreciates* and then asks how he might help his partner
   b. Listener makes a request
   c. Speaker acknowledges and gives

2. Both seal deal and appreciate

A REPAIR PROCESS MINI GUIDE

Speaker:	1) Describe	2) Ask	3) Appreciate	4) Help out
Responder:	1) Listen	2) Clarify	3) Acknowledge	4) Give

Acknowledgments

I want to thank Caroline Sutton at Random House for her belief in this project and for her capacity to seize with gusto the essence of things. The same holds true for my agent, Richard Pine: This could be the beginning of a beautiful friendship. I am ever grateful to Heidi Krupp, publicist, pal, and all-around shaper-upper. An enormous debt is owed to *The Muse*, Marilyn Abraham, who taught me so much every step along the way. I want to acknowledge my wonderful colleagues at the Relational Life Institute, Jan Bergstrom, Lisa Merlo-Booth, John Badalment, and Cara Weed. My assistant, the irreplaceable Lisa Sullivan, worked with me on many aspects of this book. Thanks to Steven Carp, financial wizard and guardian angel. I will always be grateful to Beth Vesel, Gail Winston, and Nan Graham, for trusting in me before there was any particular reason to do so. Heartfelt thanks go out to Cheryl Richardson for her generosity and wisdom over many years; to my fellow traveler, Carol

Gilligan, whom I hold so dearly; to Michele Weiner-Davis, friend and ally; and to Jane Fonda for her encouragement and support. The thoughtful reading and comments offered by Henry Friedman and Gail McGovern were a great help in preparing the manuscript. A warm appreciation goes out to Maryanne Thompson for routinely mixing genius with beneficence, and to Michael Van Volkenberg for going beyond the extra mile. Thanks to that manly ideal, Marvin Ettiene. And to Annette Ben Menachim, Rita Sigura, and Sharon Coyne for keeping me sane.

I am forever indebted to those special mentors who pulled me along for no reason beyond their own impressive generosity: First among equals is Olga Silverstein, along with the incomparable David Treadway. To Charlie Verge, Caroline Marvin, Sally Ann Roth, Rick Lee, Richard Chasin, Gerry Schamess, Connie Zweig, John McCormack, Jean Parrish, and the ever-surprising Mel Bucholtz, I owe you all respect and appreciation.

I am grateful for my treasured friends, and most especially for Jack Sternbach, who, more than anyone else, taught me how to work with men. Jackie-boy, wherever you are, I hope they know what they're in for.

I want to acknowledge the generation of women theorists, researchers, and practitioners who dared to question the conventional model of human development, introducing, instead, a revolutionary new vision of growth-in-relationship. My approach is thoroughly and essentially *relational*, and a direct beneficiary of their contribution.

As is true of all my work, the ideas and techniques described in this book owe a fundamental debt to the genius of Pia Mellody, a pioneer in the field of both addiction and trauma recovery. My close collaboration with Pia began over a decade ago and continues to this day. So many of her concepts have permeated my own thinking, and vice versa, that it would be tedious and perhaps even impossible to accurately ascribe them all. Suffice it to say that my work on relationality rests on top of her work on the restoration of the self, and that my work, and this book, would not exist without it. Pia Mellody's introduction into my life, as healer, colleague, and friend, has been one of my life's great gifts.

Finally, and most important, I want to thank my family—Justin, who is so indomitable; Alexander, who is so elegant; and Belinda, the greatest teacher and the greatest friend a man could ever wish for—thanks for your encouragement, for your patience and pride. I would take one game of Sado-Monopoly with you guys over just about anything in this world.

Blessings to you all.

TERRENCE REAL is the bestselling author of *I Don't Want to Talk About It: Overcoming the Secret Legacy of Male Depression* and *How Can I Get Through to You?: Closing the Intimacy Gap Between Men and Women.* He has been a practicing family therapist for more than twenty years and has lectured and given workshops across the country. In March 2002, Real founded the Relational Life Institute. Real's work has been featured on *NBC Nightly News, Today, Good Morning America,* and *The Oprah Winfrey Show,* as well as in *The New York Times, Psychology Today, Esquire,* and numerous academic publications. He lives with his wife, family therapist Belinda Berman, and their two sons in Newton, Massachusetts.

www.relationallife.com